Discursive Psychology
theory, method and applications

Sally Wiggins

Los Angeles | London | New Delhi
Singapore | Washington DC | Melbourne

Los Angeles | London | New Delhi
Singapore | Washington DC | Melbourne

SAGE Publications Ltd
1 Oliver's Yard
55 City Road
London EC1Y 1SP

SAGE Publications Inc.
2455 Teller Road
Thousand Oaks, California 91320

SAGE Publications India Pvt Ltd
B 1/I 1 Mohan Cooperative Industrial Area
Mathura Road
New Delhi 110 044

SAGE Publications Asia-Pacific Pte Ltd
3 Church Street
#10-04 Samsung Hub
Singapore 049483

Editor: Luke Block
Editorial assistant: Lucy Dang
Production editor: Imogen Roome
Marketing manager: Michael Ainsley
Cover design: Wendy Scott
Typeset by: C&M Digitals (P) Ltd, Chennai, India
Printed and bound by CPI Group (UK) Ltd,
Croydon, CR0 4YY

© Sally Wiggins 2017

First published 2017

Apart from any fair dealing for the purposes of research or private study, or criticism or review, as permitted under the Copyright, Designs and Patents Act, 1988, this publication may be reproduced, stored or transmitted in any form, or by any means, only with the prior permission in writing of the publishers, or in the case of reprographic reproduction, in accordance with the terms of licences issued by the Copyright Licensing Agency. Enquiries concerning reproduction outside those terms should be sent to the publishers.

Library of Congress Control Number: 2016938005

British Library Cataloguing in Publication data

A catalogue record for this book is available from the British Library

ISBN 978-1-4739-0674-7
ISBN 978-1-4739-0675-4 (pbk)

Dedicated to: My parents, Audrey and Stuart Wiggins.

CONTENTS

About the author vi
Preface vii
Acknowledgements x

Part One   Theory **1**

1 Discursive psychology 3

2 DP and other forms of discourse analysis 31

Part Two   Methods **59**

3 Developing a research question 61

4 Data collection and management 73

5 Transcribing and coding data 89

6 Analysing data using DP 113

7 Discursive devices 146

8 Writing up and presenting DP analyses 177

Part Three   Applications **195**

9 DP topics, case studies and project ideas 197

10 Applications and future developments 221

FAQs 232
Glossary 241
References 249
Index 266

ABOUT THE AUTHOR

Sally Wiggins is a senior lecturer in psychology at the Department of Behavioural Sciences and Learning, Linköping University, Sweden. Previously, she was based in the School of Psychological Sciences and Health, University of Strathclyde, Scotland, for 12 years. She has co-edited two books (*Critical Bodies* and *Discursive Research in Practice*) and written numerous book chapters and journal articles featuring discursive psychology as the analytical approach. Her research focuses on the social interactional processes around eating, particularly during family mealtimes. This work has begun to examine the ways in which appetite, food preferences and gustatory pleasure/disgust are enacted and consequential for children and parents in everyday mealtime situations.

PREFACE

The aim of this book is to demystify discursive psychology (DP): from the theoretical principles on which it is based, to the method of how to 'do' DP and use it in different ways. It is designed to be a practical and accessible guide, cutting through difficult theory and providing a clear account of the analytic processes. It offers basic starting points and discusses more advanced issues. It is therefore aimed at students and researchers at all levels, from undergraduate through to postgraduate and beyond. It will provide the scaffolding as you develop your understanding and skills, and allow you to progress at your own speed. There will be activities along the way, to help you practise on your own. DP should not be regarded as difficult or for expert researchers. With a little time and care, anyone can use discursive psychology.

The politics of writing a book

I write this book as someone who has been involved in the field of discursive psychology for some time. I am not so established as to have been there at the very start, nor am I so fresh as to not be aware of the political manoeuvring and pot shots from critics in all directions during the intervening years. I was fortunate enough to undertake my doctoral research under the supervision of Jonathan Potter at Loughborough, with Charles Antaki, Mick Billig, Derek Edwards and many others just an office away. I have also been, and continue to be, inspired and supported by many others in discursive and interactional research across the world. I do not consider myself to be particularly politically motivated. Those who know me would be hard-pushed to define me as radical. And yet this book feels like something of a political argument. I have witnessed the various criticisms from many angles: from cognitive psychologists who do not consider discursive work to be anything more than 'just talk' and subjective interpretation, to phenomenologists who argue that we are missing the very nature of what it means to be human, to other discourse analysts who argue that we are neglecting the big issues and have been hoodwinked by the conversation analysts, and finally to conversation analysts, who wonder why we aren't doing CA when we're almost there anyway.

My stance is that while I have endeavoured to be even-handed in my treatment of various issues, I have also aimed to provide a clear and practical guide to DP research, to enable it to continue to flourish and develop. This means that I am fairly prescriptive in places: I have erred on the side of being specific and detailed to provide the 'scaffolding' which I mention in the book. Some readers may find it too prescriptive. They may be disheartened at the inclusion of the stages of analysis of DP, for example, as set out in Chapter 6. They risk turning DP into a formula, restricting creativity and synthesis across different forms of discourse analysis. They also possibly undermine the skilled way in which established researchers can read a short extract of data and produce a brilliant and eloquent analysis, while the rest of us are still figuring out what all the transcription symbols mean. So yes, there is a risk. But I think it a risk worth taking. We need some scaffolding to support new researchers – whether undergraduate students with one class on discourse analysis or postdoctoral researchers tasked with the discursive analysis of six months' worth of data – to ensure the growth and development of work in this area.

Politics also bubble under the surface of the data examples I use throughout the book. These are infused by my own research interests in eating practices and family mealtimes. It is my book, after all. But it might seem that using examples from family mealtimes are trivial or banal, that they don't really tackle the important things, like inequalities, poverty, conflict, prejudice, death and illness. Or perhaps worse, that these kinds of issues *are* inherent in food and eating, and yet still I ignore or gloss over these and focus instead on the features of mundane interaction. But perhaps food and eating is in some ways more fundamental than any of those; that if we don't eat, nothing else is possible. So yes, family mealtimes are just one small aspect of life, and no, we don't all have children. But we all start out as children and we all need to eat. And for those reasons alone, I think it worth researching.

How to use this book

The book is in three parts: the first deals with the theoretical side of DP and how it stands in relation to four other discourse analytical approaches. This should give you an understanding of what DP is 'about' and when you might use it. The second part deals with the practical aspects of DP: how to actually do it, from the stages of deciding on a research question, to collecting and analysing data, and to presenting your work in different formats. The third part provides some 'what next' issues; inspiration from some of the early and contemporary work in DP, as well as some ways in which we might consider the application of either theory or practice.

Each chapter stands alone as a complete unit, so you can dip in and out, in any order. It may be that you only need guidance on understanding the different forms of discourse analysis, so Chapter 2 will show you how these differ both theoretically and in terms of analysing data. Or you may have been given some data extracts to analyse using DP for an assignment, and so Chapter 6 will help you there. Chapter 1 provides the main theoretical and conceptual structure of DP, so that will help you to make sense of the rest of the book, but it can be challenging in places if you are new to some of these concepts. You might find it useful to skim through Chapter 1, then come back to it again once you've had a chance to work through some of the practical chapters in Part 2 of the book. Remember, becoming confident and competent with DP is a skill and it won't happen overnight. You need to spend a little time working through some of the core principles of

PREFACE

DP and applying these in practice. Then, once you've done that, you might find yourself wanting to dig a little deeper into some of the issues raised by Chapter 1.

Throughout the book, references within the text have been kept to a minimum. This was a deliberate move, to keep the text uncluttered and to avoid overwhelming you with names and dates. In terms of learning, I tend to argue that less is more; I have given a couple of references at the end of each chapter, and a few scattered throughout. You will, however, find a whole heap of references in Chapter 9, where I overview DP research in different areas.

The book contains features to help you apply the theory and methods to your own research, whether you have just one lecture on DP and don't 'get it', a coursework assignment to do by this time last Tuesday, or your dream PhD project. There are boxes throughout each chapter which provide: discussion points on key issues, checklists, brief activities, hints and tips, and student reflections. There is a glossary at the end of the book, covering a range of key concepts and ideas in discursive research to help you to learn the jargon. There is also a FAQ (frequently asked questions) section providing suggested responses to some of the questions that you (or your colleagues) may have about DP.

The book is assisted at various points by a short piece of family mealtime data, which was recorded especially for the purposes of teaching students about DP. The full video clip (around four minutes) can be accessed at: www.youtube.com/watch?v=OtKaXw-6WqYM. It is used in Chapter 2 to demonstrate the difference between five forms of discourse analysis, in Chapter 5 to illustrate the transcription process, and Chapter 6 to provide a worked example of DP analyses. You might use it to practise your own transcription, coding and analysis skills, or practise using the discursive devices in Chapter 7.

Most of all, have fun. There are few approaches that we can so readily apply to our own lives, to practise while we're listening to other people or engaged in social interaction. Let's see how far we can go.

ACKNOWLEDGEMENTS

To those who, like me, always read the acknowledgements page first, here is a glimpse into the machinery behind this book. It is, in many ways, the culmination of around 20 years of being immersed in discursive psychology (DP) research and teaching. I was introduced to DP by Nick Hopkins in my final year as an undergraduate psychology student at the University of Dundee. I still have my set texts for that class (Billig, 1987, and Potter & Wetherell, 1987; bought for £13.95 each in October 1996 at Blackwell's bookshop on campus), with notes scribbled enthusiastically (pencil, of course) in the margins. So those of you who are still studying, keep your mind open and be kind to your tutors. You never know where new ideas will take you. My thanks therefore go first to my main tutors in DP: Nick Hopkins, Jonathan Potter and Derek Edwards. There are many others who helped along the way.

Thanks to those who helped to make this book happen:

To Michael Carmichael for getting me started on this adventure and to Luke Block and Lucy Dang for seeing me through to the end. Your encouragement, unwavering confidence and patience were like good coffee; they kept me focused and made me want to write. You also have three of the coolest names in publishing.

To those who provided guidance, FAQ suggestions or support: Adrian Coyle, Stephen Gibson, Gillian Hendry, Emily Hofstetter, Judith Horne, Bogdana Humă, Ryan Kelly, Eric Laurier, Jessica Lester, Abi Locke, Clare MacMartin, Robert McQuade, Jane Montague, Jonathan Potter, Sarah Riley, Sarah Seymour-Smith, Liz Stokoe, Margie Wetherell and Sue Widdicombe. Stephen Gibson, Clare MacMartin and Sarah Riley deserve particularly fond thanks for their detailed and critical comments on some of the draft chapters. You improved the book in many ways, though any remaining flaws are, of course, my own.

To the Scottish family who so kindly offered to record their meal and let me use the video as 'data' for the book, may your food always fire your rockets.

To all the undergraduate and postgraduate students who I have tutored over the years, I hope I made some sense. To those who really 'got' DP and, even better, were as excited about it as I am: you made it all worthwhile.

And so to home. I wrote most of this book into the night at my beloved writing bureau. Thanks to Kate Bush, First Aid Kit, Florence & the Machine and London Grammar for the soundtrack, and to Lucy for sleeping by my feet and taking me for walks. To Mum and Dad, for providing an unexpected writing retreat in my old bedroom and for the many, many times that you cared for me when I needed to rest, and cared for the boys and dog when I needed to write. To Phil and my extended family, for all your support and for coping very well despite having an academic in the family. To Beth and Rach, for showing me that every obstacle can seem daunting at first, but that we can do amazing

ACKNOWLEDGEMENTS

things when we help each other. To Angus and Callum, for filling my days with love and laughter, the comfort of daily routines and a good excuse to always bake. You're both still the most enjoyable projects I've ever undertaken, and the best reasons I have for doing anything. Sorry for hogging ~~the~~ my laptop and working so often. This book is proof that I wasn't watching Minecraft videos on YouTube, as you may have suspected. To H, for all and everything. Thank you for always believing in me. It is time for new adventures now.

PART ONE

Theory

1

DISCURSIVE PSYCHOLOGY

Chapter contents

What is discursive psychology?	4
What discursive psychology is *not*	6
Core principles of discursive psychology	8
What inspired discursive psychology? (The backstory)	16
From there to here: how discursive psychology emerged and developed	23
The 'difficult relationship' between discursive and cognitivist psychology	28

Discursive psychology (DP) is one of the most vibrant and exciting approaches to emerge within the social sciences in the past thirty years. It provides a lens through which we can examine the social world, to render visible the social practices through which people and their practices are made accountable and factual. It enables us to make sense of talk and text, of the activities that we are engaged in whenever we are interacting with other people. It captures the moments in which psychology is produced and made consequential in the social world. As such, not only does it offer a radical re-working of psychological concepts, it also holds enormous potential for applied research (indeed, it has been argued that it is, by its nature, already applied; see Chapter 10). This chapter will introduce you to the basic underlying principles of DP: what it is, what it isn't, what inspired it, how it developed, and how it contrasts with cognitivist approaches within psychology. It will distil the core arguments of DP to provide you with a clear, practical way to get to grips with DP whether you are completely new to this field or building your analytical skills.

There are, however, two things that you need to know before you proceed. First, the theoretical arguments and principles that underpin DP are intellectually challenging; they require us to think and reflect on what we are studying, and why we are studying it. There will be ideas that challenge what we know about talk, about cognition, and indeed about reality. So yes, you will need to work hard. And yes, it might change you. You might never consider talk and interaction in the same way again. Second, there will be arguments, critiques and political rhetoric. This is a feisty and dynamic area of research to be in. Like any approach that challenges the mainstream, there are vehement critics of DP, and this is before you even consider the academic wrangling that goes on within the field of discourse analysis. As my Dad always says, it would be a dull world if we were all the same. So all this debate makes for a rather exciting and interesting place to be.

What is discursive psychology?

Let us begin, then, with the basics, and start with a definition:

> Discursive psychology is a theoretical and analytical approach to discourse which treats talk and text as an object of study in itself, and psychological concepts as socially managed and consequential in interaction.

The version of DP that is the focus of this book was developed by Derek Edwards and Jonathan Potter, at Loughborough University in the UK, following from earlier work developed with Margaret Wetherell. It treats talk and text as, first and foremost, part of social practices rather than as a reflection of inner cognitive processes. It treats discourse as *doing things* in interaction and examines the ways in which psychological concepts are produced and made consequential in interaction.

DP is a form of discourse analysis, and as such is part of a much broader framework of approaches for understanding discourse (see Chapter 2). It is interdisciplinary, cutting across disciplinary boundaries (such as between psychology and linguistics) and within subject boundaries (such as between the topics of memory and attributions in psychological research). As such, it is predominantly a qualitative approach, in that it analyses words, but is not against quantification. It does, however, challenge the notion that psychological practices can be reduced to numbers. In this sense, it is more akin to a methodology than a method: a programme of work (Edwards, 2012) or a meta-theory (Edwards & Potter, 1992; see also Potter, 2003). There are a set of core principles that underpin the approach DP takes to research and analysis, and when we use DP we need to embrace both the theoretical assumptions and the methods of doing research. This means that it cannot be taken 'off the shelf' as just another way of analysing discursive data, but it also means that it is a coherent, theoretically grounded, and rigorous approach to research.

DP is concerned with psychological issues, but psychology *as it is lived* by people in everyday life – for example, how people make the minds, identities or emotions of others relevant in interaction – by their practices and social interactions rather than their individual thoughts or experiences. It therefore starts with social practices rather than psychological states. Psychological concepts become the object of study, not the framework that determines theory and analysis. So a psychological concept such as 'attitudes' or 'food preference' is not treated a priori as a fact; instead, the focus is on how this concept is described, invoked and consequential for social interaction. DP does not try to 'get inside' people's minds or attempt to understand their motivations or attitudes. This is a subtle but important difference. Like other psychological concepts, the issue of cognition is treated as an analytical object (something we study without first making assumptions about what it is) rather than an analytical framework (something we make assumptions about and which then directs what we study).

Let us consider an example to illustrate what DP is and why we might use it. The short extract below represents a brief section of conversation between a boy (Joseph) and his Mum at the family dinner table. Some of the family members have finished eating, but Joseph still has quite a lot of food on his plate. The transcript here is presented in turn-by-turn order (as you will see later in the book) but is simplified to make it easier to read:

Mum: could you eat a bit more Joseph please, instead of staring into space

Joseph: no, I don't like it

Mum: a little bit more if you don't mind

Joseph: no *((shakes head))*

There are many ways in which we might approach this piece of interaction, to understand what is going on between the mother and her son. We might try to figure out why Mum is asking her son to eat more; perhaps she is concerned that he is not eating enough or she may be trying to avoid wasting food. We might also approach it from Joseph's point of view: why does he not like it? Is there another reason that he does not feel like eating it? Alternatively, we might look more broadly at the cultural conventions that determine how food is eaten in a particular way, with family members sitting round a dinner table, and with it being normative that a mother (or parent) is in part responsible for how much, and what, a child eats.

In each of these possible interpretations, we would be making assumptions about what people are thinking or feeling, or about the existence of cultural norms that shape how we eat. These interpretations are potentially limitless, and hard to evidence from the basis of a single piece of conversation. In contrast, DP focuses attention on the social interaction at just this point in time: on what actions are being performed (requests to eat more food, refusals) as well as the psychological business that is being managed (Joseph's appetite and his food preferences, as well as Mum's authority to ask him to eat more food). For example, what is being accomplished when Joseph says 'I don't like it', as an addition to the 'no'? We do not have to look 'behind' the words to find out what is going on here. We can examine the interaction *as a piece of interaction*, in a specific context, and as consequential for the people therein. In this case, it is what gets eaten, and who is held accountable for not eating food. As we will see later, there are problems in treating words as simply a reflection of people's thoughts and experiences. Instead, we can examine how realities are produced through the ways in which people live their lives and through the discursive practices that make up these lives.

> ### Box 1.1: A comment about names
>
> As we will see in Chapter 2 (see also Box 1.5) there is more than one version of discursive psychology, just as there are many forms of discourse analysis. One of the ways in which we can distinguish between these forms is through reference to the names of researchers who have developed, or who use, those approaches. For example, we might refer to the form of DP advocated in this book as 'Edwards and Potter DP'. When reading discourse analytic research, it can be helpful to check which names are referred to, to help you identify which form of DA they are using, if this is not specified. The problem with this, however, is that it risks promoting some researchers at the expense of others, and associating an approach with individuals rather than as a collective body of work. Yet DP was the culmination of a number of different inter-disciplinary ideas and research findings. It is not owned by anyone; it is not a 'thing'. Instead, it is a theoretical and analytical approach, a way of examining the world in a particular way; a type of camera lens through which we can investigate life. So use names to help familiarise yourself with DP, but remember that researchers can move between approaches, and approaches themselves will grow and evolve.

What discursive psychology is *not*

While discursive psychology provides a unique and powerful means of understanding discourse, interaction and psychology, as with any approach there are limits to what it can do. Being aware of these limitations – as well as the possible misconceptions of DP that have emerged over the years (see also the FAQ section) – will better equip you to develop your own competence in this area.

Discursive psychology is *not:*

A critique of psychology. DP does challenge a body of psychological research – and particularly, that which relies on a cognitivist interpretation of language in social settings – but psychology as a discipline is much broader than this. DP is not a threat to psychology, and should instead be regarded as a different way of doing psychology.

The application of discourse analysis to psychology. Psychology is a very broad discipline, and there are numerous theoretical and analytical approaches within the discipline; so there is no single notion of 'psychology' for discourse analysis to be applied to. Instead, we can understand DP as a re-working of the very objects of psychology itself, of the concepts used by psychologists to define individuals and their behaviours. So it begins with people's practices in everyday life, and in how psychological concepts (e.g., attitude) or processes (e.g., appetite) are enacted and contested in social interaction.

A causal account. DP does not provide evidence for *why things occur* in terms of underlying causal factors. This is because it is argued that discourse constructs rather than reflects reality, so what people say is not a reflection of what has happened or what their intentions are (see 'core principles' section). What it can do, instead, is to identify patterns, norms and regular features of interaction that might be produced in different settings. In that way, it can account for what happens (i.e., provide an explanation for) but not predict or determine what *will* happen (i.e., suggest a causal relationship).

A research method. DP is a methodology, not a method, in that it provides a theoretical framework for understanding discourse and interaction, and that in turn provides for a particular way of doing research. But it is not a research method that can be combined simply with other methods or theories. It requires an understanding and application of specific theoretical principles. In the same way, other research methodologies also make assumptions about the world and what we can know about it, but they may not make these explicit. DP does; it is very clear about how we can understand discourse and how this plays out in practice.

A psychology of language. Many textbooks on psychological research on language focus on issues such as how we develop language (as babies and infants), how we mentally process and understand meaning, language and communication, and how we produce speech. There is often very little content about how we use language in everyday social settings; much of psycholinguistic work is based on laboratory studies or situations that are set up to limit variables and prescribe what can be said or understood. The use of the term 'discourse', by contrast, highlights the focus on *language in use*, and to capture both talk (spoken) and text (written) language, in its many forms.

Behaviourism. DP focuses on talk and text as social practices, and examines interaction between people rather than individual 'behaviours' as separate events. Unlike behaviourism, DP does not reduce discourse and interaction to an individualistic level and it works with participants' own categories and sense-making practices (not with analysts' categories about inputs and outputs). Unlike behaviourism, DP does not treat psychological concerns as analytically unavailable. Quite the contrary; these are analysed in terms of how they are invoked, constructed and made consequential in social interaction.

Impression management. Goffman's theories of the presentation of self and impression management assumed a 'real' self behind the mask and performance in social settings, and that our behaviours are motivated by maintaining a particular role or 'face'. By contrast, DP argues that there is no single real self that is being maintained (it is a relativist approach; see 'core principles') and that our identities are multiple and produced in interaction. It also argues that there is no way of getting 'behind' the discourse; that motivations are analysable in interaction, not hidden somewhere internally.

Linguistic relativity. This is the argument that language shapes thought. It is sometimes referred to as the Sapir-Whorf hypothesis. By contrast, DP is concerned with discourse in social interaction and how it is constructed to accomplish particular actions in specific contexts. It makes no claims about 'thought' as an internal object, and there are theoretical issues around assuming that thought can be shaped in particular ways. It treats talk-in-interaction as a flexible resource, not one variable that can be tracked for its impact on another.

Core principles of discursive psychology

This section outlines the core principles that make up the meta-theory of DP, and from which all other features of DP follow. So take your time working through these, and ensure that you are clear about what they mean and their implications for examining discourse before you move on to the other sections. In Chapter 6, you will be able to see how these principles work in practice in the analysis of data, but for now we will use the following piece of interaction to help work through some of these issues. This interaction takes place between three women (Kate, Lucy and Martha) – all friends since school – now in their early 20s and spending the evening at Kate's house. They have just finished drinking one bottle of wine, and Kate offers to go to the local shop to buy another bottle. The transcript has been simplified here for ease of reading, but overlapping talk (noted here by square brackets [ ]) and pauses of one second (1.0) or less than one second (.) are indicated here. Question marks (?) indicate a slight rising, questioning intonation. We will refer to Extract 1 at various points throughout the discussion below.

Extract 1

```
1. Kate:      what do you want (.) white or red
2. Martha:    either
3.            (1.0)
5. Martha:    whatever's [cheapest (.) hehh
6. Lucy:                 [red?
7.            (1.0)
```

```
 8. Kate:    heh heh [heh that's-
 9. Lucy:            [I prefer red (.)
10.          I like white [but I prefer red
11. Kate:                 [that alright?
12. Lucy:    [yeah
13. Martha:  [mmm
14. Kate:    okay
```

The three core principles of DP are:

Discourse is both constructed and constructive

Discourse is situated within a social context

Discourse is action-orientated

1. Discourse is both constructed and constructive

The first principle of DP requires some philosophical considerations about how we understand the relationship between things in the world and our knowledge of those things. In many disciplines, research assumes that things (e.g., gravity, oxygen, attitudes) are real and exist, and that by applying the correct methods (e.g., experiments, observation, questionnaires) we can accurately examine these things. That is, that we can represent these objects and report on them – through writing, thoughts, illustrations, and so on – and that our representations are independent of the things we are investigating. This is what is known as a realist stance. An alternative argument is that the things in the world (our objects of study) cannot be separated from our representations of them. That is, that we cannot identify an independent (and single) reality. This is what is known as relativism, and this is the argument that DP embraces. Relativism, then, is agnostic about the existence of a single reality; even if one exists, we would not be able to determine which was the correct version of reality.

These two arguments (realism and relativism) are part of a broader set of approaches that are often referred to as *social constructionism*. Collectively, they treat our knowledge about the world as created by social practices, as being historically and culturally situated, and which questions the taken-for-granted knowledge that we have about the world (see Burr, 2015 for an excellent book on social constructionism). In other words, the things we take to be common sense or 'normal' are challenged and examined for *how* they become common sense. Discursive practices – how we talk and write about the world – are then argued to be one of the main ways in which the world is socially constructed. So a relativist stance is always questioning what and how we know about things in the world. What counts as knowledge (or 'truth' or 'reality') is then argued to be the product of social and cultural practices – such as the ways we talk and behave, and how these differ in different cultural contexts, and across time – and that knowledge has different consequences for different people. For example, depression is currently defined as a mental illness in western cultures, as being associated with particular individual, behavioural, hormonal and experiential symptoms. It may be diagnosed by a medical professional, and treated via anti-depressant drugs and talking therapies. Yet this particular truth about depression – and who can diagnose it – is only recent and limited to western cultures. It relies on theorising the separation of mind and body, and of the identification of neuro-biological causes of depression that then make relevant medical intervention. Relativism argues that there are many different truths about the world, and so we need to be clear about our role in the construction of a particular truth.

Social constructionism, then, is a powerful way of addressing some big questions in research: what is knowledge, how does knowledge change, and who has ownership of this knowledge? While social constructionism as a broad set of approaches offers a radical critique of mainstream psychology, it is a feisty area of discussion in itself. There is much debate, for instance, between those who argue for a realist or critical realist stance and those, like DP researchers, who argue for a relativist stance (see Edwards et al., 1995). The philosophical debates around social constructionism, realism and relativism are complex and exciting areas, and what is presented here is a simplification of the issues. It should be enough, however, to give you a foothold into DP and begin to grasp why we do not take discourse at face value.

Returning to our first principle of DP, then, taking a relativist stance, discourse is argued to be both construct*ed* and construct*ive* of the world. It is construct*ed* through a range of cultural resources: words, intonation, gesture, and culturally available phrases and expressions. These are the building blocks, as it were, of talk and text. DP can then examine how different discursive practices are constructed: like a mechanic, taking apart the machine of interaction and finding out what the component parts are and how they fit together. Discourse is also construct*ive* of different versions of the world, through the way in which we talk about people, events, actions and organisations. It brings particular versions of reality, particular 'truths', into being. DP can then examine how these different versions have implications for the context within which the discourse is produced. If we apply this principle to our example in Extract 1, we can examine how the discussion about the choice of wine is constructed out of particular words (*white, red, prefer, cheapest*) that are themselves culturally situated. Other terms might have referred to the region where the wine was produced, or the variety of grape from which it was produced; cost may or may not be relevant, nor what someone 'prefers'. So these terms are also constructive of the world in a particular way: they create a version of reality in which people have preferences (for what wine they consume), and that choices might be dependent on other people's preferences (see line 11: 'that alright?') and that wine can be distinguished in terms of two broad categories (red or white).

Box 1.2: Gender and age as socially constructed

Social constructionism claims that the social world, and our knowledge of it, is constructed through social practices, and that these are built up over time, to the point at which they become common sense. For example, in many western cultures, it is normative to categorise people in terms of their gender (male or female) and age (young/old, child/adult, and so on). These categories often overlap, so we can get age- and gender-specific labels such as girl, boy, man and woman. These labels have become so normative that we tend not to question them on a daily basis. With age categories, we have more labels to distinguish between finer gradings of ages of children (e.g., baby, infant, toddler, child, adolescent, teenager) than we do of adults, where categories often refer to much broader age-range periods, such as 'middle aged' and 'elderly'. But even the categories of 'male' and 'female' are socially constructed: while there may be physical or physiological differences between people (e.g., genitals, reproductive systems, breast tissue, hair growth), these might be considered more of a continuum than an either/or, mutually exclusive category. Some people have larger or smaller breasts, finer or thicker hair growth, or have had reproductive systems removed or altered in some way (e.g., hysterectomies, vasectomies), and yet many people would still claim to be *either* male *or* female. We might also take into consideration other features, such as hormonal levels (and changes in these over time), which are not so easily seen. It is only when someone tries to move between categories, such as through gender reassignment, or identifies as transgender that we begin to question what it means to be that category. So even something as apparently 'obvious' as gender can be questioned for how our social practices have made it appear obvious. If you want to explore this area a little further, start out with Speer and Stokoe (2011) then move onto Butler's *Gender trouble* (1990).

Box 1.3: Activity

To help you become more familiar with the idea of social constructionism, consider one food that you eat (or drink) on a regular basis. This might be something you eat as part of a 'main meal', such as potatoes or rice, or eat as a snack on its own, such as fruit or chocolate, or hot drinks such as tea or coffee. Think about how and when you eat this

(Continued)

> *(Continued)*
>
> food (or drink), and whether you would eat it if you were on holiday or away from home: Do you take supplies with you? Do you miss it if you don't eat/drink it? Do other people eat this food, and in the same form that you do? When we start to consider the foods and drinks that we consume *from a different perspective*, we can become more aware of what we treat as 'normal' and how there are other versions of 'normal'. We can take this even further. Consider, for example, what you think constitutes a typical meal at particular times of the day (e.g., breakfast). What kinds of foods does it include? When would you eat it? Or consider what foods you think are inedible or disgusting. What kinds of plants or animals are classified as 'food' and which are not? Before long you should see how much of what we take for granted about the foods that we eat is dependent to a large extent on our social context.

2. Discourse is situated

The second core principle of DP is that discourse is situated in a particular context. While it is constructed/ive of the world, it also does so in a specific place and time, and as such we need to analyse it within this context. Discourse is situated in three ways:

- Within a specific *interactional context*: for example, chatting with friends, talking to a doctor in hospital, discussing issues in a classroom or online forum.
- Within a *rhetorical* framework: there are always alternative versions of reality that discourse counters, even if these are usually not made explicit.
- Within the *turn-taking sequence* of interaction: it is situated in relation to what precedes and what follows the talk or text.

Let us refer back to Extract 1 to show how each of these aspects of 'situatedness' apply to a specific example. The interactional context is of friends talking together in Kate's home, so we might treat it as informal talk in that there are no official 'roles' of any of the people present; they are talking as friends, not as, say, a fire-fighter, a postgraduate student and a project manager. So when we analyse this piece of interaction we need to analyse it *in situ*, and as part of the social practices that are being undertaken within that setting (in this case, making a choice about what kind of wine to buy). It is important to note that DP understands context from an 'emic' perspective (this is an anthropological term broadly meaning 'insider' or participants' perspective; the opposite term is 'etic', meaning the outsider/analyst's perspective). While I might gloss this interaction as informal and 'friends talking together', for example, it is only that: an analyst's gloss.

To identify the interactional context of the talk, we need to examine how the speakers *themselves* orientate to it; in other words, how the context is *shaped* by the talk. This is what DP researchers refer to as the context-shaping or context-dependent nature of discourse: that when we talk (or write) something, what we say shapes the context as much as it is dependent on, or produced by, the context. We can examine this in the way that all three speakers have the same opportunities to talk (and ask questions or make suggestions), and that apart from a one-second pause (line 6), the conversation is not stilted and there are many overlapping turns. Both Martha and Lucy make tentative statements about the choice of wine and the decision to choose red wine is apparently achieved through mutual agreement. In that sense, the interaction at this point is defined on the basis of fairly equal status of each speaker.

The second aspect of situatedness is the rhetorical framework: how the discourse constructs one version of events and how this undermines alternative versions. This understanding of situatedness follows most closely from the first core principle of DP, that discourse constructs reality. So there will always be different constructions, different versions of reality, that might have been used. We can use the analogy of news reporting – whether in newspapers or on national news programmes on television or radio – to show this more clearly. Each news report might cover the same content (such as a crisis situation, where people are fleeing their homes as a result of war or natural disaster) but construct different versions of events. For instance, they might refer to the people as 'refugees' or 'migrants', but even that single word can create a different set of assumptions and solutions for the crisis situation (including whether other countries offer aid or allow those people to seek refuge and new homes). In Extract 1 above – while seemingly mundane and trivial in comparison – we can still examine the rhetorical context for this interaction. For instance, in line 1, Kate's 'what do you want, white or red' constructs the choice as between one kind of wine over another, rather than wine in contrast to beer, fruit juice or water. That Lucy or Martha might like a different beverage is not enabled by this construction, so the rhetorical framework of this piece of interaction produces a version of events in which drinking more wine is normative and individual choice or preference is an expected way in which to make a decision about which colour of wine should be purchased.

Finally, we can examine the situatedness of the talk in terms of the turn-by-turn interaction. This is sometimes referred to as the indexicality of utterances (what is said): that in order to understand how an utterance should be interpreted, we should always examine *what comes before* and *what comes after* the utterance. Take line 11 in Extract 1, where Kate says 'that alright?'. How are we to make sense of this? First, we can note how Martha first states 'either' (line 2), then 'whatever's cheapest' (line 4) in response to Kate's initial question. This doesn't directly answer the 'red or white' issue, but instead leaves open the possibility for Lucy to make the decision. Rather than do this directly, however, Lucy suggests 'red' (line 6, with a questioning intonation), then supports this further by contrasting her preference (red) with what she also likes (white) on lines

9 and 10. So Kate's 'that alright?' (line 11) is then placed in overlap with Lucy's turn and seems to suggest a request for a confirmation that *red wine* be the wine of choice. We can then examine the turns immediately following this – both Lucy (line 12) and Martha (line 13) make affirmations – and this is receipted by Kate on line 14 by 'okay'. In summary, then, Kate opens up the decision to Lucy and Martha, Martha is non-committal while Lucy makes a suggestion, Kate then seeks confirmation of this suggestion and finally confirms her own acknowledgement of this confirmation. During the course of this brief discussion, the speakers have also made relevant taste preferences as not only individual qualities (e.g. 'I prefer red', 'I like white') and therefore unique to them, but also as having an obligation to take other people's taste preferences into account. Psychological issues (taste preferences, attending to the needs of others) are as much a part of this interaction as making a decision about wine.

To summarise this second principle, then, discourse is understood not as a passive means by which we tell people what we are thinking and feeling, or report on events, but a social action and always contextually-bound. When we talk or write, we always do so within a specific context. Therefore, to make sense of discourse we need to understand it *in context*: where, when and how it is produced and organised. DP therefore shifts the focus of discourse from individual cognition to social practices. It is from this principle (and in relation to the first, based on a relativist, social constructionist position) that the anti-cognitivist stance of DP becomes clear. If discourse is situated within a specific context, it is as much socially produced as cognitively produced. That is, while there are undoubtedly mental processes going on which enable us to talk, *what we say is not a direct route to what we think*. When we talk (or write), we do so within a particular interactional context, a specific rhetorical framework and within a temporal sequence of interaction. Our discourse will therefore vary all the time, according to contextual variation.

3. Action orientation of talk and accountability

The final core principle of DP follows almost automatically from the first two: that if discourse constructs particular versions of reality, and these constructions are situated in particular social contexts, then there will be particular functions or actions that are accomplished by the discourse. In other words, that discourse (talk and text) *acts on and in* the context in different ways. In the next section of this chapter we will see the history of this theoretical assumption about language, but for now let us focus on how this works in practice.

If we look once more at Extract 1, we can start to break down the talk into different kinds of actions, different things that are going on in the interaction. So first, Kate begins by asking a question ('what do you want (.) white or red', line 1). Even without having any video to accompany this (so we cannot check eye gaze, for example), we can identify from the talk alone that both Martha and Lucy treat this question as relevant to them both. This is even though the word 'you' in English does not specify on its own a singular or a plural 'you'; compare with other languages, such as in French, Italian and Swedish. Note, however, that the term 'yous' or 'youse' is often used in North-East England, Ireland and Scotland to refer to more than one person, the equivalent of 'y'all' in the USA, but this is informal usage. Very simply, then, the first 'social action' occurring in this piece of interaction is to ask a question and to reply to a question. But note how Lucy's turn – 'red?' (line 6) – itself appears in questioning intonation. So she answers a question with another (possible) question. What this does, then, is to provide an answer to Kate while treating this answer as conditional on what Martha (or Kate) might themselves choose. We have a further social action, then: attending to the needs or wishes of others, a kind of democratic move. Similarly, Lucy's 'I prefer red, I like white but I prefer red' (lines 9–10) does something quite unique. Note how this doesn't actually answer Kate's question directly. Lucy doesn't – at that point – say what she wants, but instead states a preference and a liking for different kinds of wine. And yet this is treated by Kate as answering the question, and the decision is confirmed soon after. So we can also begin to see how, through particular situated constructions (just this word, said in this way, at this precise point), people can accomplish a whole range of social actions without having to 'signpost' or label these in a deliberate or obvious way (this is referred to as indirection, which we'll discuss in the next section).

The focus on the action orientation of discourse therefore also means that we do not just identify the types of words used in a piece of talk (such as verbs or detailed descriptions), but also where they are sequentially located in the talk, how they are responded to by other people, and what social action they are involved in. This is one of the ways in which DP differs from other forms of discourse analysis, which also examine verbs or linguistic format but without examining the organisation of the talk. If we had taken Lucy's 'I prefer red. I like white but I prefer red' turn out of context, it would appear that she was just telling us about what kind of wine she likes to drink. Seen in its specific interactional, rhetorical and turn-by-turn context, however, it works as a 'request for red wine while also accommodating any potential disagreement from the other people present' type of social action.

So, do not be fooled into thinking that DP is 'just about talk'; there is much more to it than this (and one could analyse such descriptions that minimise the role of discourse – 'just about talk' – as exactly the kind of rhetorical and consequential construction that we need to look out for, as discursive psychologists). As Edwards and Potter (1992: 2) note: 'We are concerned with the nature of knowledge, cognition and reality: with how events are described and explained, how factual reports are constructed, how cognitive states are attributed.' By now, it should also be apparent that DP is not simply a theory or method, but rather a whole approach to research. We will pick up the implications of this in the various chapters in Part 2 of the book, where the theoretical assumptions help to guide us in our choice of research question, data choices, and analytical tools.

What inspired discursive psychology? (The backstory)

Now that we have a basic understanding of DP and its core principles we can explore some of the history behind DP to provide a clearer understanding of how it has been influenced by a range of disciplines and theoretical perspectives. This should also help you to see where the core principles emerged from, and how they fit in relation to a broader theoretical context. The historical roots of DP are an exciting mix of radicalism, politics and social philosophy. Do not expect dusty old books and boring theories. Here lies passion and debate on the meaning of reality itself. Understanding something of the history of DP can also, therefore, provide us with a clearer understanding of *why DP does the things it does*, and how it differs from other approaches that study language. Like the backstory for a film's central character, delving into its history helps us to understand why DP is the way it is. If you had any need to appreciate DP's interdisciplinary potential, you only have to look at the main areas of research that influenced its development. Indeed, DP can be used to argue that discipline boundaries are themselves a rhetorical device, used to separate scholars and create university departments. For each area, we will highlight the features of that approach that are particularly relevant for DP. The influence of these areas is not as simple as ingredients for a recipe (in that by adding them together, in the right amounts, we might produce DP); but rather, they provided theories and ideas that stimulated and continue to enable cross-fertilisation of ideas into DP and back again. These can be distilled into the following six main areas (in no particular order).

Wittgenstein's philosophy

Ludwig Wittgenstein was a philosopher whose own life was as interesting and convoluted as his theories on language, mind and reality (read Monk, 1990, for instance). His work, and specifically his later book, *Philosophical investigations* (1953), deals with fundamental questions about what we can know and with the logical relationship between words and the objects they speak of. This is powerful stuff, and while many have already been inspired by Wittgenstein, there is still much here to stimulate psychological, linguistic and communication research. Like Austin's speech act theory (see below), Wittgenstein emphasised the social nature of language; that words *do* things. His work challenged much of contemporary linguistics at the time, and rather than treating language as a system of symbols to represent events and objects in the world, Wittgenstein argued that language was more like a toolkit. Like tools, words have many different functions, not just the ones they were designed to do (a knife, for example, can cut but also scrape, pick up and carve things). So it is with words and language: when we look at language *in use*, we can understand the multiple functions and uses of words more clearly. Extract 1 and the phrase 'I prefer red' is a good example of this. Similarly, Wittgenstein used the metaphor of language games to emphasise the practical, context-bound nature of language; that there are different games we play with language, each with their own rules and aims. An important part of this work is therefore to emphasise the flexibility of words and language, and to focus on the uses of language in everyday social settings.

Another important element of Wittgenstein's work that is of particular relevance to DP is the focus on language in relation to mind, knowing and reality. In many ways, his work tackles core psychological topics, such as the nature of self and mind. Much of psychology is concerned with trying to understand people's private, inner worlds: their thoughts, opinions, feelings and sensations, for example. Yet we cannot really get inside other people's minds or bodies. Even if we use the same words (e.g., I love you), we cannot know if what the person is feeling (love) is the same as what we are feeling. As soon as they begin to describe what they are feeling, they are using language, which only works if there are public, socially-shared understandings of that language. So while this argument does not deny that we have feelings, thoughts, and so on, it argues instead that these 'inner worlds' are inaccessible through language. When we talk to each other, we are not communicating our thoughts. As soon as we utter something it is separate from what is in our heads (the thought) and uses a language (words, grammar, etc.) that does not exist in the private realms of our minds and bodies. This challenges work which assumes that language has primarily a communication function, to transfer ideas from one individual to another. The implications of this for psychology, in particular, are huge. Most psychological research is based on the premise that by talking to people we can find out what they think and feel about a topic.

In the same way, Wittgenstein argued that we cannot get outside language; that there is no distinction between 'language' and 'the world/reality'. While things exist (ontology), the form and meaning of their existence is entirely dependent on the language we use to name them and orientate to them. For instance, a wooden and metal object might be called a 'chair', and if I call it a chair I might use it to sit on; its shape and presence in my home might also then structure how often, when and how I sit. There is no way to then get around or behind language. These issues are related to Wittgenstein's private language argument and 'beetle in a box' arguments. In summary, then, Wittgenstein's influence on the development of DP was to provide the basis for some radical re-working of how we understand language, mind and reality. In summary, some of the elements of Wittgenstein's philosophy that are particularly relevant for DP are:

- A focus on language *in use*: that we should study the practicalities of language and its functions in different settings (language as a toolkit).

- The argument that we cannot get 'outside' language, and that language is not separate from reality.

- The argument that people's inner worlds (thoughts, feelings, etc.) are public events: that we can only make sense of them through public language.

Speech act theory

Another philosopher who was also concerned with the social uses of language was John Austin. While Wittgenstein provided an understanding of the various language games that can be used, and of the inseparability of language and reality, Austin (1962) provided a more global characterisation that put language *function* in centre-stage. His theory of speech acts stated that all forms of talk have a function, that they do things in social interaction. For example, whether we are describing something, making a claim or a request, our utterances have a particular 'illocutionary force' (i.e., they act on the world in a particular way) and that force is dependent on the particular circumstances and context within which the utterance is made. Austin's theory developed out of his distinction between two types of utterance: constatives (utterances that state something, e.g., 'you are married') and performatives (utterances that do something such as ask a question, e.g., 'are you married?'). While he first noted that these types of utterance might appear different, in that constatives might be considered true or false whereas performatives either worked or didn't work, he then went on to argue that they both act upon the world (and therefore it is a false dichotomy to distinguish between constatives and performatives). For performatives to work, they need to satisfy certain 'felicity conditions' or rules. These conditions include the appropriate context or persons present. For example, to be married you need to say the right words at the right time, in a setting that has been approved and performed by a legally appointed registrar. Just saying 'I do' (or 'I will') and putting a ring on someone's finger would not constitute a marriage in legal terms – probably just as well for all those children who may do something similar in the school playground.

Austin's work therefore offered a radical point of departure from much of the linguistic work at the time – much of which was inspired by Noam Chomsky – arguing against the idea that language was a referential system. He was also one of the inspirations behind the broader 'turn to language' (see Box 1.4) that sent ripples of discontent across the social sciences. His work emphasised the practical uses of language, its flexibility and functions in social interaction, rather than with grammatical correctness or cognitive understandings of language (see also Levinson, 1983; Searle, 1969). This meant that speech act theory could address the issue of how statements can do actions (something other linguistic theories cannot do). For example, by saying 'I prefer red' in Extract 1 above, Lucy makes a statement about her taste preferences but in doing so also makes a request for red wine. This is what is referred to in speech act theory as 'indirection', and it is something that conversation analysis also focuses on, albeit with real-life examples. This is where Austin's work parts company with DP: like Chomsky, he also used idealised (made-up) language examples and as such could not really account for the many different *types* of action that can be achieved by the same statement. In other words, once we begin to look at discourse in use – in everyday settings – the flexibility and variability of social actions becomes much more evident. In summary, the features of speech act theory that are particularly relevant for DP therefore are:

- A focus on language in use (as with Wittgenstein): to understand the meaning of words, we need to examine them in their social context.
- The functional approach to language: words *do things*, they act upon the world in very concrete ways.
- The argument that *all* talk has a function, and that words can be used with different 'forces' (or functions) depending on the context and the conditions within which they are uttered.

Ethnomethodology

In an entirely separate area of research – with its roots in sociology – ethnomethodology was being developed and also emphasised the importance of using empirical research. The very name of ethnomethodology gives a hint as to its main concerns: literally, the study (ology) of people's (ethno) methods. So ethnomethodology focuses on understanding how people make sense of each other in everyday settings: what methods they use, how they arrive at mutual understandings, and so on. The important thing, then, is to get close to the action: to see (and record) people living their lives. Its founders – Harold Garfinkel and Erving Goffman – both conducted research in a range of different everyday situations. Garfinkel's work (e.g., Garfinkel, 1967) often involved what he termed 'breaching experiments', where he sent students out to disrupt everyday normative practices in order to reveal the common-sense (but often unnoticed) practices that we treat as normal and unexceptional. For example, students might be told to behave in their own home as if they were lodgers or strangers or to stand in a busy public place and 'do nothing' for 10 minutes (see Stanley et al., 2015, for an example of how this can be done as part of a class assignment).

Goffman's work (e.g., Goffman, 1959) similarly challenged what we know about everyday life and institutional practices (such as his work on asylums: Goffman, 1961). He examined the ritualistic nature of social interaction, of the way in which people continually engage in 'face work': the maintenance of an individual's positive social identity or presence. Like Garfinkel's work, then, Goffman sheds light on the everyday practices that constitute cultural norms, and how these have impact at an individual level. For example, when we turn down an offer by a friend, we can 'save' their 'face' by providing a legitimate excuse rather than giving a blunt refusal. Goffman also likened interaction in social settings as being like a performance – this was his dramaturgical model – and as such we play different roles, have back-stage and front-stage behaviours, and can shift our roles according to the context. From this comes the notion of footing: the conversational shifts we make to present ourselves in relationship to the source of the account that we are providing (see Chapter 7 for more detail on footing shifts).

Another crucial argument that has arisen out of ethnomethodological research – not just that of Garfinkel and Goffman – is that context is understood as being a product or outcome, rather than a precursor to, interaction. This means that the things that are relevant to making sense of the interaction – the contextual factors, as it were – such as who the people are, what roles or identities they have, what the purpose of the interaction is, are not predetermined. They are produced *within* the interaction. This relates to the context-shaping and context-dependent assumptions about discourse, as seen in the previous section. The features of ethnomethodological work that are particularly relevant to DP are:

- The 'emic' focus: analysis works with speaker's categories, not the researcher's preconceived categories.
- Focusing on life as it happens: much of DP research is concerned with how psychological concepts and social actions are accomplished as people are living their lives, in various mundane and institutional settings.
- Context as being produced within, not prior to, interaction: this is the context-shaping and context-dependent nature of discourse.

Conversation analysis

Conversation analysis (CA) developed from the work of Harvey Sacks, Emmanuel Schegloff and Gail Jefferson (see, for example, Sacks et al., 1974). Given that both Sacks and Schegloff were students of Goffman, ethnomethodology was undoubtedly an influence (as was Austin's speech act theory), and the focus for CA remains squarely on understanding everyday social interaction. One of the main tenets of CA is that talk-in-interaction is systematically organised at a detailed level. Unlike the invented examples of other work (such as speech act theory and Chomsky's linguistics), conversation analysis was perhaps the first approach to analyse talk in real-life settings empirically and systematically. As such, it has been influenced by technologies as these have developed over time (from tape-recorders, to video-recorders and, more recently, to mobile and digital devices), and this means that more recent work in the field has been able to capture more details of interaction as people are moving around in a space. Conversation analysis has two broad strands of research, both of which developed from Sacks' work, though one has received far less attention than the other (see, for example, Stokoe, 2012). One is concerned with the use of categories in talk – such as how we refer to someone as a 'refugee' or a 'migrant'. This is known as membership categorisation analysis (MCA) (see Fitzgerald & Housley, 2015). The other strand is concerned with the structure and organisation of talk, at the level of turn-taking, gesture and prosody. This is just known as conversation analysis or CA, and is the more prevalent form.

The emphasis in CA on the rigorous, turn-by-turn approach to analysis has been a particular influence on the methodological development of DP. In some sense this provided the method that early work in discourse analysis was looking for; some way of identifying the social actions that were being performed and working with everyday examples. Combined with a focus on casual talk – what might also be termed mundane, everyday or informal talk – the attention to the detail of talk-in-interaction has allowed CA to illustrate that even the apparently messiest and most random of conversations are structured and organised. Here we see the influence of ethnomethodology: that social interaction is made normative through people's practices; the job of the analyst, then, is to make those practices visible. In summary, the features of conversation analysis that are particularly relevant to DP are:

- The importance of using empirical data – talk in mundane and institutional settings – rather than invented examples.
- The focus on the sequential organisation of talk, examining interaction turn by turn and using this to privilege participants' orientations.
- The Jefferson transcription system, to capture the details of intonation, pitch variation, pauses and overlapping speech.

Sociology of scientific knowledge

Within sociology, a series of studies emerged in the 1970s that became known as the sociology of scientific knowledge (SSK). SSK takes a fairly radical approach to science, being based on social constructionist principles and arguing that scientific knowledge is also a social enterprise, that it is not separate from the social and interactional processes through which common-sense and reality are produced. Even scientific 'facts' about objects and laws of physics, for example, are argued to be the product of human study and intervention, and as such can be analysed for how they are produced. Latour and Woolgar (1979) argued, for instance, that scientists themselves play a key role in the process through which scientific facts *become* facts, and as objectively separate from observations about the world, through a series of externalisation processes. These include laboratory reports and documents, which rely on specific measurements and the noting down of some, but not all, features of the experiments, as well as published documents (such as journal articles), which use third-person pronouns and effectively remove the scientist as agent and producer of the experiment. All of these processes – while branded as scientific method – are a way of establishing scientific knowledge as 'out there' in the world and as separate from all human subjectivity or intervention.

The arguments of SSK were understandably resisted by scientists since they might be treated as undermining the credibility of scientific research. They do not necessarily do this, of course, in that we could argue that it is impossible to be neutral in any domain, and scientists are no less socially orientated than anyone else. One of the powerful and lingering claims of SSK research, however, noted that scientists themselves orientate to the constructive nature of scientific knowledge through the use of different kinds of repertoires. The work of Nigel Gilbert and Michael Mulkay (1984) used discourse analysis and identified two competing forms of explanation used by scientists in their verbal and written accounts (such as in interviews, as well as laboratory notes and technical reports): the empiricist repertoire and the contingent repertoire. The empiricist repertoire was a way of explaining scientific knowledge or facts through reference to data, methods, laws of nature, and so on. This is the 'objective' account, that which claims to simply report on 'what is happening', and this was seen in scientists' official reports and documents. The contingent repertoire, on the other hand, was a way of explaining scientific findings in terms of personal motives, individual biases or flaws, and rivalries between competing scientists. This repertoire was found in scientists' interview responses, their informal discussions with peers and personal reflections. What Gilbert and Mulkay argued, however, was that these two ways of understanding the production of scientific knowledge were not just their (analyst's) categories; these were also used by scientists to undermine their competitors and to drive forward their own scientific research areas. Both repertoires, while providing contrasting versions of what scientific knowledge 'is', are essential to the production of scientific knowledge as we know it.

In summary, then, the field of SSK provided not only a way of understanding science and research as *itself* constructed and analysable – that is, as not immune to the epistemological relativism seen in the last section – but also a method through which this might be achieved: the use of discourse analysis to analyse repertoires in talk. The elements of SSK that are particularly relevant to the development of DP are:

- Interpretative repertoires: coherent regularities and ways of talking about a specific issue that are culturally specific.

- The idea of a participant's resource: this is similar to the emic perspective noted within ethnomethodological studies.

- Reflexivity: a concern to examine the practices through which researchers themselves produce knowledge in scientific reports.

Semiology and post-structuralism

The final area that influenced the development of DP was post-structuralism. The background to this involves the work of Ferdinand de Saussure, who was a linguist working in semiology, or the science of signs. Part of his work argued that we can make a distinction between a concept (the signified) and its word or sound (the signifier). For example, the word 'cake' might be used to signify a particular type of baked food (concept) that includes some variations on flour, sugar, eggs and fats. There are different kinds of cake – and many cultural variations on what constitutes 'cake' – and so different ways of organising and categorising the world. Most importantly, however, is the *process of signification* that connects the word and the concept together. So here again, we see a focus on language in use (rather than a focus on grammar or abstract notions of language), and of the means through which the signified are created through the signifiers: this is not a simple case of words reflecting what exists, but of words and sounds *creating* that which they signify.

While Saussure's work provided some interesting ideas about sign systems, it was the work that developed from this – termed post-structuralism (compared with the structuralist approach of Saussure) – that was important for DP. Post-structuralism is a movement that rejects the idea that there are absolute truths and hidden structures in the world. It emerged in around the 1960s and 1970s as a shift away from the structuralist movement. It includes a rejection of the theorisation of language as a structured system, hence its relevance for work on discourse and interaction (e.g., Barthes, 1964; Derrida, 1976; Foucault, 1970, 1972). It is also an anti-reductionist approach in that it does not reduce social practices to the mental processes of individuals, and therefore we cannot study social interaction through studying individual cognitions and behaviours.

The following aspects of poststructuralism and semiology have a particular resonance with DP research:

- The focus on the processes that give meaning to words: i.e., that words in themselves do not 'carry' meaning but become meaningful through being used in different ways.

- The importance of oppositions and absences: that what something is *not* is as important as what it *is*.

- The idea of deconstructing texts: of disrupting the authority of some discourses over others and of undermining the idea of a single truth.

From there to here: how discursive psychology emerged and developed

In this section, we will walk through the development of DP as we now know it, from the academic context that preceded the landmark books in 1987 up to the present time (mid-2010s). This is, as you might have guessed from the earlier section on social construction, just one version of this historical development; like any text, it is rhetorically organised, regardless of any efforts to be 'neutral'. But it provides *an* account that should help to illustrate how DP has developed and the arguments and debates that have shaped this development.

First, though, we need to step back in time to the 1950s and 1960s. Behaviourist research in America (e.g., John B. Watson and B. F. Skinner) and Russia (e.g., Ivan Pavlov) had become rather popular in psychology departments but was beginning to be threatened by the emergence of cognitive approaches by researchers such as Noam Chomsky, George A. Miller and Ulric Neisser. Like many times of turmoil in academic departments, much was at stake, including the nature of psychology itself. Part of the argument was about the role played by mental processes in behaviour, and whether or not we can directly examine and theorise about such mental processes. To some extent, these sorts of debates are still going on in psychology today: we know a little more about some aspects of the mind and behaviour, but there is still disagreement about how these concepts should be theorised and researched.

Chomsky's work, in particular, played an important part in critiquing the behaviourist approach in psychology, and this turned the intellectual focus in psychology more closely onto language. Not only did Chomsky's language acquisition device (1965) offer a neat method of categorising and bracketing off the messy, ungrammatical 'performance' side of language in use from 'competence' (people's knowledge of the language), but it also provided a theoretical attack on behaviourism. Like much other experimental work in psychology, it tidied up the rather complex relationship between cognition and reality. The move to study Chomskian linguistics was itself then a political move; it marked a radical shift away from the separation of cognition from experimental study. Since then, linguistics and psycholinguistics (and the psychology of language more broadly) have developed enormously, but the pervasive focus on tying cognitive processes directly with language has remained fairly constant. The field was defined in many ways by what it was fighting against, and some have even argued (Hamlyn, 1990) that cognitivist approaches retained an element of behaviourism, with the input-output approach to understanding models of behaviour and cognition. What is still noticeably lacking in psychology of language studies, however, is a focus on the language as a social practice, and this is where discursive research fits in.

The cognitivist approach had filtered through to social psychology by the 1970s, and at this point was dominated by an experimental, individualistic paradigm. The promise of being able to measure behaviour, control variables and be like 'proper science' – in the safe confines of the laboratory – was alluring for many social psychologists. This did not go unchallenged, and indeed there was a growing area of research, including the work of Rom Harré, Ken Gergen and John Shotter, which became known as the 'crisis in social psychology'. Some of the main concerns were that social psychology was removing people from their social contexts, putting them metaphorically into boxes and categories, removing their agency and rendering social psychology a sterile and de-contextual vacuum. These were hard-hitting and feisty debates, and once again the very nature of psychology (of what it means to be human, and how we should study humans) was being questioned. This is where the work of researchers such as Austin, Foucault, Garfinkel, Goffman and Wittgenstein came in, alongside post-structuralist ideas, as we saw in the previous section. These were immensely useful in terms of challenging theory, and they provided radical and coherent arguments against cognitivist, experimental approaches in social psychology. There were, however, limitations to applying these theories in practice. What was needed was a method, a way of doing research that could put these theories to use.

> ## Box 1.4: What is the 'turn to language'?
>
> In your reading you may come across references to the 'turn to language'. This refers to a movement in the social sciences involving a shift from treating language as *representation* (i.e., that when we use words, they represent other concepts, objects or people and reflect what already exists in the world) to treating language as *performance or constructive* (i.e., that when we use words, these construct versions of the world or perform different functions). For example, when a judge in a baking competition says that he 'loves' the cake, this does not just make a statement about his taste experiences (if we can even assume that it does that); it also functions to validate the baker as having achieved a particular standard of baking and possibly deserving of a prize. This turn to language began around the 1950s, developed by the work of Austin, Foucault, Wittgenstein and others, but it was only picked up in psychology in the 1970s with the work of Gergen (1973), Harré and Secord (1972) and in the 1980s with the work of Henriques et al. (1984) and Potter and Wetherell (1987). It was seen as a radical, challenging move away from established understandings at the time, and marked a turning point for many researchers. The focus of language has far-reaching consequences, for many studies that claim to examine cognitive states do so by making interpretations of language. Here we can begin to see, then, the ways in which cognitivist approaches are slowly unravelled when we start to provide a different perspective on language. So the turn to language was the accumulation of a number of studies, theories, papers and discussion on a central issue for the social sciences: how are we to interpret language? In many ways, this turn is still developing, with the growth of qualitative approaches and the various forms of discourse analysis, grounded theory, phenomenological approaches, thematic analysis, narrative analysis, and so on.

And so we arrive in the 1980s. Despite rumbling theoretical debates and radical critiques, published research in social psychology was still dominated by questionnaire studies and experiments, and most of the participants of such studies were undergraduate psychology students (and mostly white, middle-class and male, at that). Things came to a head when two particular publications helped to prepare the intellectual climate for a more critical approach within social psychology. In 1984, Henriques et al.'s *Changing the subject* was published, urging psychologists to move beyond essentialist and individualist theories of the self and to re-think the relationship between identities, bodies and societies. This was a political as well as a theoretical move, with emancipatory goals and the need to shake-up the establishment and move forward. In the same year, Nigel Gilbert and Michael Mulkay published *Opening Pandora's box*, which shined the SSK spotlight onto researchers' own discursive practices and the fragility of knowledge production. The combination of these two books left no doubt that social psychology was itself under scrutiny and that change was needed. The tipping point came in 1987, with the publication of three important texts: Jonathan Potter and Margaret Wetherell's *Discourse and social psychology: Beyond attitudes and behaviour*, Derek Edwards and Neil Mercer's *Common knowledge* and Michael Billig's *Arguing and thinking*. These texts brought together related ideas that not only wove together some of the earlier critical theory, but they also provided a method of analysis – discourse analysis – that could then be used in practice. In the same year, the Discourse and Rhetoric Group (DARG) also held its first meeting at Loughborough University, and so the academic journey of DP began in earnest.

Looking back, then, we can begin to see how DP emerged within a particular context, with a certain mix of academic tension and confrontation to fuel the development of new ways of working. Like teenagers rebelling against the older generation, researchers within particular disciplines develop and adapt to contemporary society. It is more complicated than that, of course, but the analogy can help us to put things into perspective. Theories, methods and research *must* change and develop; what are important are how these change and the implications of these changes. Now we can return to our account, and consider how DP itself has developed since those early years in the 1980s (see also Edwards, 2005b; Potter, 2010a; Wetherell, 2007, for more discussion on this) up to the present time.

In the late 1980s, as discourse analysis was emerging as an empirical enterprise in psychology, research in this area was heavily influenced by work on interpretative repertoires (as characterised in Potter and Wetherell, 1987; Wetherell and Potter, 1992), rhetoric and ideological dilemmas (Billig, 1987; Billig et al., 1988). One could argue that this strand of DP morphed into critical discursive psychology (CDP; see Chapter 2), as seen in the work of Reynolds and Wetherell (2003) and Edley and Wetherell (1995), for example. It is still a vibrant area of research, often focusing on topics such as gender and identities. Much of this work is based on the analysis of interview data, due to a concern with which repertoires are used, and how people discursively manage particular topics. The point of using interviews, then, is to be able to ask people directly about such issues without having to wait for them to arise 'naturally' in everyday settings. The reliance on interview data became a contentious issue, however, and remains an area of tension. While some researchers argue that it provides the means through which we can access particular discursive practices that are not available elsewhere and that there is a false dichotomy between interviews and 'natural' data (Griffin, 2007), others argue that interview data is only analysable as an artefact of the interview context, that it tells us nothing about everyday life (Potter & Hepburn, 2007; Speer, 2008; see also discussion of this issue in Chapter 4, especially Box 4.2). Alongside concerns that repertoires were not capturing the sequential organisation of interaction, by the mid-1990s the field had already fractured: DP emerged in one direction (with publications by Edwards and Potter, 1992, Potter, 1996 and Edwards, 1997) and CDP in the other (with publications by Edley and Wetherell, 1995, 1997, 1999).

By the late 1990s and into the turn of the century, DP was evolving alongside qualitative research methodologies, and while this provided allies, it also created more opportunities for further debate. DP not only had to define itself clearly in relation to cognitivist and quantitative paradigms, it also had to mark out its distinctiveness from other discursive and phenomenological approaches. So we can see in this period the publication of papers on theoretical issues (Edwards et al., 1995; Hammersley, 2003; Potter, 1998, 2003), on establishing DP as a credible approach (Edwards, 1997; Potter, 1996; Potter & Edwards, 2001) and of collections which demarcated the range of discursive approaches (Jaworski & Coupland, 1999; Wetherell et al., 2001). This was also a period during which some classic psychological topics were examined discursively, *in situ*, and which often directly engaged with cognitivist approaches, such as attitudes and opinions (Puchta & Potter, 2002; Wiggins & Potter, 2003), racism (Augoustinos et al., 1999), identities (Antaki & Widdicombe, 1998) and cognition (Antaki, 2006; te Molder & Potter, 2005). On top of that, it was also engaging more closely with conversation analytic work in epistemics, gesture, prosody and institutional talk. From around 1995 to 2005, it was a rather busy time in DP research, both theoretically and analytically.

Finally, then, we can consider the last decade, from around 2005 to 2015, of DP research. Theoretically, this period has thrown up some interesting discussions about the role of epistemology (e.g., Corcoran, 2009; Potter, 2010a, b) and the limitations or potential of DP research (Wetherell, 2007, 2015). This was also a time during which the Discourse and Rhetoric Group (DARG) at Loughborough celebrated its 25-year anniversary, so reflections and a reaffirmation of DP's core values were appropriate (see articles in the *British Journal of Social Psychology*, Vol. 51, 2012; Tileagă & Stokoe, 2015). Research during this period may be characterised by an increasing interest in issues of embodiment and multimodality: with the ways in which talk and body movements collaboratively produce psychological frames of reference. Technological developments in smartphones and tablets – particularly with the improvement in video capabilities in such devices – have meant that it has almost become normative to video oneself – anytime, anywhere. Combined with websites such as YouTube, this norm includes sharing videos with people around the world. What was once restricted to special occasions and seen only by a small group of people, video has now become the medium for interacting with people, at any time, in any place.

> **Box 1.5: The politics of discourse: the case of 'discursive psychology'**
>
> You might be forgiven for thinking that, while DP might be considered a radical approach to psychology, it is not necessarily political (in that it doesn't focus specifically on tackling inequality or overthrowing oppressive regimes, for example). This is not entirely true. As the section on 'core principles' noted, we can argue that any discursive construction is rhetorically organised to undermine alternative versions. So any text or talk plays some part in silencing other versions. This book is one such example, and so far I have presented a particular version of discursive psychology, referring to certain publications and authors, and using the label 'DP' to reify one understanding of what this approach might be. There are, of course, other researchers who use the term 'discursive psychology' in rather different ways. The most notable use of this term is by Rom Harré, who has described it as the 'new cognitivism', and takes a critical realist stance on the nature of discourse and cognition (see Harré & Gillett, 1994; and Davies & Harré's positioning theory, 1990). That version of discursive psychology is concerned with understanding the logical relationship between discourses and selves, and the conditions under which certain grammatical structures will make relevant certain mental concepts. As such, it works with idealised (invented) examples of discourse, and follows Wittgenstein's and Austin's ideas about the logical functions of discourses and the relevance of these for mental structures. Other researchers also use the term 'discursive psychology' – such as Nigel Edley and Margaret Wetherell (e.g., Wetherell & Edley, 2014) and Ian Parker (1992) – though some of this work is characterised as critical or Foucauldian discourse analysis (see Chapter 2).

The 'difficult relationship' between discursive and cognitivist psychology

It should now be clear that while DP was developed within psychology, its theoretical and methodological approach are quite different from the cognitivist approaches in psychology that seek to theorise, examine and measure mental processes. It is probably fair to say that this has resulted in what might be described as a 'difficult relationship' between DP and cognitivist psychology, and the cause of some tension between researchers and their colleagues, universities and funding bodies. It is therefore worth focusing specifically on this issue to be clear about what these points of difference are and what they mean for research.

DP takes a very different stance on cognition from much of mainstream psychological research (see te Molder & Potter, 2005, for detailed discussion on this topic). This is what is meant when we refer to DP as rejecting cognitivist approaches or as being anti-cognitivist: this is *not* the same as rejecting cognition (which would be 'anti-cognition'). In other words, this does not mean that DP assumes that there is no cognition, and that we do not think, feel or experience things. It does not make ontological claims (i.e., about what exists in the world), but does make epistemological claims (i.e., about what we can know about things in the world). DP does not deny, for example, that cognitive processes exist. Instead, it argues that these should not be the primary focus for studying, and making claims about, discourse and social interaction. In that sense, DP prioritises discourse as action (what talk and text actually does) rather than discourse as representation (whether and how discourse might relate to thought processes). Given that, it focuses on *language in use*, on the analysis of talk and text *in social settings* – hence the use of the term 'discourse'. There are areas of research therefore, such as the neural processes that co-ordinate sounds coming into the ear with comprehension of words, that do not involve social settings (though, of course, it is possible to imagine how this example might involve medical consultations and accounts of those with comprehension difficulties, which would themselves involve social interaction) and for which DP is not appropriate.

Cognitive approaches to language are often based on a referential, representational or structural theory of language, with an emphasis on grammatical knowledge or cognitive understandings of language. This means that they tend to treat language as, at least for the most part, referring to or representing 'inner' states, whether those are thoughts, emotions, attitudes, stereotypes, and so on. Even where such research concedes that people might vary their talk depending on the context, there is still the assumption that there is a reality *behind* the talk. By contrast, DP approaches discourse (that is, language in use, as talk and text) as social action, and primarily as a product of the interactional and sequential environment. In other words, DP argues that there are no mental states that we can access *without language*, that as soon as we might try to represent or identify thoughts, feelings and so on, they become produced (or interpreted) through language. Even bodily gestures, dance or artwork – those things that apparently are separate from language – require some form of language to interpret their meaning. But more importantly, DP is concerned with interaction and social settings, and with how we are to understand the construction and relevance of psychological issues within the social world.

This brings me to the final point, which is that while DP is anti-cognitivist about the analysis of discourse, this is only one small area of the much broader discipline of psychology. DP has its roots in ethnomethodology, sociology and post-structuralism, and so has a much broader sphere of relevance. Psychology is also an extremely broad and vibrant discipline in itself and thrives on debate and competing paradigms. So DP is just one of a range of approaches, and part of the way in which disciplines develop interdisciplinary connections. Even in the 25 or so years since DP emerged, there has been considerable change within psychology. Qualitative research more broadly has grown from being the footnote at the bottom of a questionnaire to a diverse and vibrant field in itself. The computational model that lurks among the theories of many cognitivist approaches might itself need an upgrade, given increasing developments in social technology.

The main point here is that when seeking to understand and examine people and psychological concepts, DP starts with people's practices in interaction: it begins with the observable and the analytical, not because thoughts, feelings or bodily sensations are not considered to be important, but because humans are primarily social beings, and that discourse is the primary means through which, it is argued, we create our social worlds.

KEY POINTS

- DP is an approach to analysing discourse that treats talk and text as social action, and psychology as an object to be analysed for how it is made consequential in social interaction.
- DP takes a relativist, social constructionist stance to knowledge.
- DP was developed within psychology but is influenced by linguistics, philosophy, sociology, post-structuralism, ethnomethodology and conversation analysis.
- DP is anti-cognitivist but not anti-cognition; it does not deny that mental processes take place, but does argue against the prioritisation of these when analysing discourse.
- Discourse is treated as social action rather than representation; talk and text are argued to accomplish actions in the social world.
- Discourse is treated as constructed and constructive, as situated in a particular context, and as action-orientated.

Recommended reading

Edwards, D. & Potter, J. (1992). *Discursive psychology.* London: Sage.

Potter, J. & Wetherell, M. (1987). *Discourse and social psychology: Beyond attitudes and behaviour.* London: Sage.

2

DP AND OTHER FORMS OF DISCOURSE ANALYSIS

Chapter contents

Seeing life through a lens: the world of discourse analysis	32
Comparing the five forms: theoretical and analytical differences in discourse analysis	35
Conversation analysis	36
Discursive psychology	40
Critical discursive psychology	44
Foucauldian discourse analysis	49
Critical discourse analysis	54

The term 'discourse analysis' (DA) is used to cover a range of approaches across the social sciences and the different ways in which it is used can be confusing and overwhelming. It is not always easy to know which form of DA you are reading about and which one is suitable for your own project or data analysis. For example, some of the terms that you might find when searching for DA are: computer-mediated discourse analysis, conversation analysis, corpus-based discourse analysis, critical discourse analysis, critical discursive psychology, dialogical analysis, discursive psychology, ethnography of communication, feminist post-structuralist discourse analysis, Foucauldian discourse analysis, functional grammar, linguistics, pragmatics, rhetorical analysis, sociolinguistics and textual analysis. No wonder it is a confusing field. The aim of this chapter, therefore, is to provide a brief and simple introduction to *five* of the main forms of DA that are commonly used in research across the social sciences: conversation analysis (CA), critical discourse analysis (CDA), critical discursive psychology (CDP), discursive psychology (DP) and Foucauldian discourse analysis (FDA). In addition to DP – which is the focus of this book – the other four have been chosen because they are most closely related to, and sometimes confused with, DP. The chapter will begin with a brief discussion of how we might approach this field before considering each of these five forms of DA in terms of what makes them theoretically and analytically distinct.

Seeing life through a lens: the world of discourse analysis

Discourse analysis, in all its forms, seeks to understand the role of discourse in the construction of our social world. It works a little like a video camera: a mechanism to examine discursive practices and social interaction. We might, then, be documentary makers, eager to record some aspect of the social world and thus render it observable and analysable. Using this analogy, we can consider each form of discourse analysis to be like a different camera lens that enables us to take a broader or narrower view of the setting in front of us. For example, we might use a fish-eye lens (panoramic, ultra-wide angle: like critical discourse analysis and Foucauldian discourse analysis), a pancake lens (moderately wide-angle: like critical discursive psychology), or a zoom lens (narrow focus: like discursive psychology and conversation analysis), depending on what features or discourses we are interested in. Each lens renders visible a different perspective, whether that is a panoramic view to provide a broad overview of a scene without focusing on one specific area in particular, or a zoomed-in image, capturing the detail of one aspect, but, potentially, missing the bigger picture. The camera lens analogy also means that we cannot use more than one form of DA at a time. We must make a choice as to what we want to focus on and then choose the appropriate form of DA to perform that analysis. There are also problems with each lens; they cannot alone perform every function, and inevitably we are accountable for the choices we make. Table 2.1 provides an overview of some of the differences between these five forms of DA.

Before we begin this journey into DA territory, however, three caveats are in order. First, although this book is focused on discursive psychology, it is important to be aware of what questions it *cannot* answer and how it relates to other forms of DA. There is no hierarchy in discourse analysis; each has its own advantages and challenges. While there may be tensions between the different forms (and, indeed, between researchers themselves), these tensions should be used to stimulate academic debate and to enable each form of DA to evolve and adapt to new research insights. No form of DA is perfect, nor should it be.

Second, it will become apparent that each of these five forms of DA has its own subtle variations. Each form is a vast world in itself, and it is hard to do justice here to the range and depth of research carried out by researchers in each of these fields. Since the early 2000s, for example, the differences between the forms of DA have become more emphasised, as each strand developed empirically and theoretically with new research and writing. In that sense, you may come across earlier writings (i.e., from the late 1980s or 1990s) that position these forms of DA slightly differently. So the distinction between the five forms of DA provided here is historically bound and these distinctions will shift again in the future.

Table 2.1 A comparison of five forms of discourse analysis

Form of discourse analysis	Key aim	Example data	Example analytical tools	Classic study
Conversation analysis (CA)	To identify the organisational structure of talk that underpins social actions in mundane and institutional settings, and the categories invoked by speakers to perform interactional business.	• Naturalistic interaction (talk) • Asynchronous or synchronous online interaction (text)	• Turn-taking organisation • Sequential organisation • Paired actions • Repair organisation • Deviant cases	Sacks, H., Schegloff, E. & Jefferson, G. (1974) A simplest systematics for the organization of turn-taking for conversation. *Language*, 50(4): 696–735.
Discursive psychology (DP)	To examine how psychological concepts are used and managed in discourse, and the implications of these for our understanding of both social interaction and psychology.	• Naturalistic interaction (talk) • Asynchronous or synchronous online interaction (text) • Interviews • Focus groups	• Category entitlements • Disclaimers • Extreme case formulations • Scripting • Footing shifts	Edwards, D. (1991) Categories are for talking: On the cognitive and discursive bases for categorization. *Theory & Psychology*, 1(4), 515–542.
Critical discursive psychology (CDP)	To identify the culturally available repertoires that shape our understanding of a particular topic and which define the subject positions available within that topic.	• Interviews • Focus groups • News media text	• Interpretative repertoires • Ideological dilemmas • Subject positions	Wetherell, M. & Edley, N. (1999). Negotiating hegemonic masculinity: Imaginary positions and psycho-discursive practices. *Feminism & Psychology*, 9(3), 335–356.
Foucauldian discourse analysis (FDA)	To examine how discourses make available particular truths about the world and how these influence people's subjectivities and practices (ways of being in and experiencing the world).	• Interviews • Focus groups • Written texts, e.g., government documents, advertisements, historical documents • Visual images	• Discourses • Subject positions and positioning • Subjectivity • Genealogical analysis	Foucault, M. (1979).*The history of sexuality*. London: Allen Lane.
Critical discourse analysis (CDA)	To reveal the hidden ideologies that marginalise or oppress individuals or groups in society and to undermine these ideologies.	• Media text and images e.g., advertisements, policy documents, webpages • Political speeches and debates	• Lexical choice • Absences • Over-lexicalisation • Ideological opposites	Fairclough, N. (1993). Critical discourse analysis and the marketization of public discourse: The universities. *Discourse & Society*, 4(2), 133–168.

Finally, and true to a social constructionist book, it should also be noted that the distinction between these five forms of DA – and my description of each – is itself a construction. Those working in discourse research may well find some descriptions inadequate or misleading. Some researchers have argued that we should not try to distinguish between different forms of discourse analysis, and that this might be divisive between researchers and be unhelpful analytically (see Box 2.1). Others argue that conversation analysis is not a form of discourse analysis, although I include it in my list here. There are also likely to be a range of research areas that I have overlooked or neglected to cover. It is, as they say, impossible to please everyone. What I hope to have done, however, is to provide a brief and illustrative introduction to the field of DA and to show how DP, specifically, can be distinguished from other forms of DA.

Box 2.1: Bottom-up or top-down: do we need to choose one or the other?

There are other ways of representing forms of DA in addition to the camera lens analogy used in this chapter, such as a distinction between 'micro' and 'macro' DA, and bottom-up (data-driven) or top-down (theory-driven) analyses. The first (micro/bottom-up) typically defines those forms of DA which are focused on the turn-by-turn organisation of talk and which situate the analytical context within the conversation itself (i.e., CA and DP). These might also be referred to as 'fine-grained' approaches to discourse analysis. The second (macro/top-down) tends to be associated with forms of DA that engage with ideological aspects of discourses, that define discourse as more than talking or writing, including issues such as subjectivity (ways of being in the world) and the socio-historical context of discourse (i.e., FDA and CDA). Somewhere in the middle – combining the micro and macro elements – is CDP. These ways of categorising DA may help us to recognise and distinguish between different approaches, but they are also limiting in the way that they put forms of DA into boxes with apparently clear boundaries. They can also be divisive, setting researchers against each other in a bid to defend their own territory. There have been persuasive arguments, therefore, for the use of synthesised or multi-level DA, which draws across these classifications and aims to engage in a theoretical and analytical dialogue. While this book focuses on one form of DA (discursive psychology) and as such attempts to demarcate its theoretical and analytical principles, it is important to remember that this is just one approach, one way of analysing the discursive and social world. For examples of papers arguing for, or using, synthesised forms of DA, see Korobov (2001), Riley et al. (2010), and Wetherell (1998, 2007).

Comparing the five forms: theoretical and analytical differences in discourse analysis

The following five sections of this chapter will discuss each of these forms of DA in the following order: conversation analysis, discursive psychology, critical discursive psychology, Foucauldian discourse analysis and critical discourse analysis. The order proceeds from the narrow zoom-lens to the wider panoramic approaches. Each section will cover: (1) theory, (2) history, (3) how we can use it, (4) how it compares with DP (note that the DP section will obviously miss this out), (5) research questions, (6) transcripts and (7) analytical tools. To exemplify the differences for the last three of these points, each has been applied to a single piece of transcribed data, which is detailed below. This is not intended to provide a detailed analysis of the data, nor a methods-guide to using these forms of DA. The descriptions provided here are necessarily limited and are used to highlight the comparisons with DP.

The piece of transcribed data that will be used for this section is taken from a video-recorded family meal, involving a married couple (Bob, aged 54 years, and Linda, aged 55 years), their 26-year-old daughter (Lesley), and Bob's mother, Edith (aged 84 years); see Figure 2.1 below for a still image from the video. Pseudonyms have been used here to protect the individuals' real names. The four-minute video can be accessed directly on YouTube (www.youtube.com/watch?v=OtKaXw6WqYM).

The full length of the meal was just over one hour long, and it was recorded in early 2015 in Bob and Linda's home in the west of Scotland. Full written permission was granted to use the anonymised transcript and still images from this video for this book,

Figure 2.1

and for the section of video to be published on the internet for teaching and learning purposes (see Chapter 8 for more discussion on using images, videos and transcripts in written work). The family talked about a range of issues during the mealtime, but the section that we will focus on here involves the family members talking about the steak that they are eating, as well as shopping for, and eating, different kinds of fish.

Conversation analysis

Theory

Conversation analysis (CA) is one of the zoom-lens approaches discussed in this book, being the most detailed and narrow of the five forms of DA in its focus on discourse. CA argues that talk is primarily about actions; that when we talk we are accomplishing different activities, such as complaining, giving advice or accounting for our behaviour. It focuses on the structure and organisation of talk and on how actions are achieved through the careful arrangement of talk, gesture, eye gaze and objects. CA, then, is primarily used to analyse talk-in-interaction rather than written texts, though recently it has been applied to asynchronous and synchronous interaction in online environments. This form of DA is the one that captures the most detail in transcripts because it is argued that all aspects of talk (even our audible breaths, hesitations, 'mms' and 'ohs') are organised and consequential for interaction. For CA, then, the aim is to understand the mechanics of interaction, such as how we start a conversation, how we make assessments, and how refusals or offers are made. By addressing these 'building blocks' of interaction, CA can then be used to understand how social order and social norms – regular and normative ways of behaving – are accomplished by people in everyday social interaction.

History

CA has its roots in ethnomethodology and was developed by Harvey Sacks, Emmanuel Schegloff and Gail Jefferson in the 1960s and 1970s. Sacks was perhaps one of the few academics whose lectures have been turned into a bestselling book (Sacks, 1992), and Jefferson developed the transcription system used by CA and DP (see Chapter 5). Sacks and Schegloff were students of Erving Goffman, and later also worked with Harold Garfinkel, the latter two being founding figures in the world of ethnomethodology (see Chapter 1). One of the pioneering aspects of Garfinkel's and Goffman's work was to demonstrate the taken-for-granted practices that make up everyday common sense. For instance, Garfinkel's (1967) breaching experiments demonstrated that by small changes in everyday social practices we can expose the norms and rules that underpin social structures. Just try queue-jumping in the UK, for instance, to see what happens when norms are transgressed. CA emerged, then, from an intellectual environment that focused on mundane, everyday interaction and highlighted the normative aspects of our behaviour.

Alongside the technological development of the tape-recorder at the time, these influences provided the stimulus for Sacks to develop an approach that would enable him to analyse people's sense-making practices in careful detail: he could tape-record conversations and play them back repeatedly (see Silverman, 1998, for a very accessible book on Sacks). Since the early work of CA, there has been extensive debate about interpretations of Sacks' work, with some areas of CA highlighting the importance of categories and identity work in the form of Membership Categorisation Analysis (Fitzgerald & Housley, 2015; Stokoe, 2012), others advocating 'applied' CA (Antaki, 2011; Richards & Seedhouse, 2004) and the inclusion of more linguistically-orientated work such as that on prosody (Szczepek Reed, 2010).

How we can use CA

We can use CA when we are interested in how particular activities are accomplished in interaction, and how talk, eye gaze, gestures and objects are co-ordinated in order to carry out these actions. This is sometimes referred to as multimodality: the analysis of different aspects of interaction alongside speech (see later how this compares to multimodal critical discourse analysis). CA can be used within everyday or institutional interaction, such as medical settings (Heritage & Maynard, 2006) or in the workplace (Drew & Heritage, 1992). Some of the areas of research that have been developed using CA are issues around embodiment and gesture (e.g., Goodwin, 2000; Heath et al., 2010; Streeck et al., 2011), interaction with objects (Haddington et al., 2014; Nevile et al., 2014), communication issues in training (Stokoe, 2014) or where individuals have specific communication difficulties (Finlay et al., 2008; Goodwin, 1995; Wilkinson, 2015).

How it differs from DP

While there are extensive overlaps between CA and DP (see Chapter 1), there are also two important differences. First, whereas CA is primarily focused on the social organisation of talk and of how people make sense of each other in interaction, DP has an explicitly constructionist focus. That is, DP is concerned with the way in which categories are produced and performed in discourse; with the versions of reality that are invoked and made available for psychological and social actions. So while CA might examine how talk is socially organised, DP would examine how *this particular version* of talk is socially organised. A second difference is DP's anti-cognitivist stance, in which there is an explicit rejection of the theory that cognitions can be 'revealed' in talk and that the organisation of discursive practices can be reduced to intra-individual states of mind. CA is less directly concerned with cognition and, while most CA work does not make any assumptions about cognitive structures underlying talk, there is some work that does imply particular cognitive underpinnings of interaction. See Wooffitt (2005) for a detailed comparison of CA and DP.

Research question

The main aims of CA are to examine social actions and the sequential and organisational features of talk that accomplish these actions. As such, working with video-recorded family mealtimes (as an example of naturally occurring interaction) is familiar territory for CA because it enables researchers to examine a range of issues, from when food assessments occur during a family meal (Mondada, 2009) to how parents use directives (such as 'eat that up!') towards children at mealtimes (Kent, 2011) or when children report bodily expressions at mealtimes (Jenkins, 2015). For CA, the food and eating practices during the meal do not need to be the focus of analysis, however; the interaction during the meal in itself provides a rich source of data of everyday (i.e., mundane, rather than institutional) talk-in-interaction. So we could examine how assessments (of food or other objects) are produced in the interaction and how these are structured, what follows them, and how, in making an assessment, speakers are also demonstrating an entitlement to assess the object (Pomerantz, 1984). We might also examine how membership of particular categories is used to invoke identities during a meal, such as those that distinguish between family member statuses (Butler & Fitzgerald, 2010). In the transcript opposite, for example, we could focus on how and when family members draw on category entitlements, and how these might be challenged or resisted by others, to make decisions about what food will be eaten in the family home.

Transcript

It was noted earlier that CA provides us with a tool to examine the messiness of ordinary interaction, with all the sighs, hesitations, in-breaths and pauses that litter our everyday talk. As such, a transcript produced for CA would need to include as much detail as possible, because it is argued that each and every aspect of interaction is organisationally important. Line numbers are used to help identify the sequentiality of talk, clearly showing what happens in the order in which it occurs in the interaction. Speakers (and they are typically referred to as speakers in CA, rather than participants) are often denoted by a pseudonym; this can be as a first name (e.g., 'Bob') or title (e.g., 'Dr Larsson'), depending on whether the interaction is mundane or institutional. The transcript opposite shows 21 seconds of talk from this clip, marking out as many details in the delivery of the talk as possible, including rising or falling pitch, loudness, extended or emphasised speech, and length of pauses between speakers. For example, CA distinguishes between gaps and pauses. A gap is a silence that occurs between 'turn completion units' (TCUs: a point at which the speaker completes a turn at talk) and these are placed on a new line. A pause is a silence *within* a TCU and these are placed within the same line as the talk (Hepburn & Bolden, 2013). There are also ways to transcribe eye gaze and gesture that can capture additional and important aspects of interaction and include these in the written transcript. We can also make greater use of 'screen grabs' or single frames from a video, or cartoon sketches of gestures to highlight particular visual aspects of the interaction (see Streeck et al., 2014). The transcript below presents a form that is consistent with CA research, though does not include eye gaze or visual detail.

Extract 2.1: Example CA transcript (see Box 5.4 for a transcription key)

```
1.  Bob:     mine's is >qui- a lot of<
2.           (1.0)
3.  Bob:     I don't like steak.
4.           (0.4)
5.  Lesley:  no: [don't do either
6.  Bob:        [.pt >d'sna< (.) d'sna fire >ma rockets it
7.           just disnae<
8.  Lesley:  I like fish::=we >niver have enough< fish:
9.  Bob:     w- we:ll. see that fish you bu::y, (0.4)
10.          <don't buy that> see that thing that gets like-
11.          (.) incarcerated in some kin'a-
12.          (0.8)
13. Bob:     <chemic'ly:> (0.2) compound (.) >th'ng<
14.          (.)
15. Edith:   mm
16.          (0.2)
17. Bob:     THA- (.) you get it like- >it doesn't look like a
18.          fish< that thing we had the other night
```

Analytic tools

CA typically works by identifying a particular phenomenon – a social action of some kind – in the data corpus, and then assembling a collection of instances that contain this phenomenon. This stage of building up a data set is often iterative; sometimes in those early stages it is not always obvious what it is that you are searching for (e.g., at what point does a raised hand become a pointed finger or a move to scratch one's nose?). We noted above that one of the research questions might be to focus on the use of assessments during the meal. One of the analytic tools of CA is to examine sequence organisation and turn-taking; to identify the turn that precedes or initiates the action and then to identify what action follows it. We can see how Bob's assessment 'I don't like steak' (line 3) is followed immediately by Lesley's 'no don't do either' (line 5) as a second assessment. This has already been found in previous research to be a common pattern where an assessment is typically followed by another from a different speaker (Pomerantz, 1984). While Bob continues with further details about his assessment (lines 6–7), Lesley then offers another assessment ('I like fish', line 8) which then serves to shift the topic to a different food, and to potentially making a complaint about not having enough fish. So we would begin CA by identifying the different actions (first and second assessments, making a complaint, and so on) in this particular sequence, and unpacking those further to examine how they actually work. For instance, Lesley's 'I like fish' is used as a preface to the complaint; it works to make relevant the complaint at just this point in the conversation (given that this is a considerable jump from the discussion about steak) as well as Lesley's entitlement to make the complaint as a family member (note the shift from 'I' to 'we') within this turn. We could also then add in more details about multimodal features of the interaction – how eye gaze and facial expressions are co-ordinated with the assessments, and the footing shifts from 'I' to 'we' to 'you' – alongside the business of eating food at the same time.

Box 2.2: Exploring CA further

One book chapter

Ten Have, P. (2007). *Doing conversation analysis: A practical guide.* London: Sage. Chapter 1 for an introduction to CA.

One journal article

Raymond, G. & Heritage, J. (2006). The epistemics of social relations: Owning grandchildren. *Language in Society, 35*(5), 677–705.

Discursive psychology

Theory

Discursive psychology (DP) is the second zoom-lens approach to DA. As noted in Chapter 1, and elsewhere throughout this book, DP is focused on the construction of psychological issues within discursive practices, and the consequences of these constructions for both theory and practice in psychology. For instance, DP might examine how emotion terms are used not as evidence of physiological or cognitive states, but in particular interactional settings to undermine or bolster accounts of people's activities (Edwards, 1999). Rather than treating psychology as an individual issue, therefore, DP treats psychology as first and foremost an interactional concern. Like CA, DP also treats social interaction as the primary focus for research, and there is a concern with both the structure and the content of interaction (how, when and what is said). So DP will examine how people and their identities, responsibilities and behaviours are produced in particular ways in talk, and the implications of these constructions for that specific context. A classic focus of DP has been to consider how attitudes are formulated in talk: their format and rhetorical impact, rather than their status as a cognitive concept (Potter, 1998; Wiggins, 2015). So DP treats psychological concepts (attitudes, emotions, identities, for instance) as public and practical, rather than private, concerns.

History

DP emerged from within psychology in the 1980s and was inspired by research and theory within CA, ethnomethodology and post-structuralism, the work of Wittgenstein (1953) and Austin (1962) and the sociology of scientific knowledge (e.g., Gilbert & Mulkay, 1984). It was developed partly out of a critique of cognitivist approaches to psychology which were dominant at the time, in terms of how behaviour was being reduced to cognitive states, how people's psychologies and subjectivities were regulated by mainstream psychology (Henriques et al., 1984) and by the 'turn to discourse' more broadly in the social sciences (Parker, 1989). The form of DP advocated in this book is that developed by Derek Edwards and Jonathan Potter in the late 1980s and 1990s. As with the other forms of discourse analysis, DP also has its tensions and variations, such as in the work of Rom Harré (Harré & Gillett, 1994) and Ian Parker (1992). Harré's work, for instance, advocates what he calls a 'new cognitivism'. Rather than eschewing cognitive theory, this work locates discursive psychology alongside processes of perception and intention (e.g., Davies & Harré, 1990) and deals with illustrated examples of discourse rather than empirical data. Parker's work defies simple categorisation in one area or another, for his theories draw on psychoanalysis, the work of Lacan, and some aspects of political theory. While he has used the term 'discursive psychology', he has also characterised his work as critical discursive psychology and one might even see his work fitting in with Foucauldian DA. These different strands of DP research often revolve around the status of cognition and subjectivity in discursive practices, and highlight the contested nature of these concepts.

How we can use DP

We can use DP when we want to focus on psychological issues in terms of when and how these emerge as part of everyday social interaction. So we stay focused on the detail of talk and text (how words are said, the organisation and sequential nature of talk) as well as how psychological concepts are produced and made relevant in particular ways. DP has been used to examine classic psychological topics such as attitudes and assessments (Potter, 1998; Puchta & Potter, 2002), cognitions (Antaki, 2006; Auburn, 2005; MacMartin & LeBaron, 2007), emotions (Edwards, 1999), identity (Eriksson & Aronsson, 2005; Lamerichs & te Molder, 2003), memory (Edwards & Potter, 1992), and racism and prejudice (Augoustinos & Every, 2007; Tileagă, 2005). Due to its inclusion of a broader range of discursive practices, DP has also been applied to interaction in focus groups (Goodman & Burke, 2010; Puchta & Potter, 2004), online interaction (Burke & Goodman, 2012; Horne & Wiggins, 2009; Lamerichs & te Molder, 2003), media texts (MacMillan & Edwards, 1999), interviews (Locke, 2004), and everyday face-to-face interaction (Wiggins, 2013). Note that the use of different kinds of 'researcher generated' data is not without its criticisms (see Box 4.2 for further discussion on this matter).

Research question

The main aim of DP is to examine how psychological constructs are enacted and made relevant in interaction and the implications of these for social practices. Like CA, DP is predominantly used with video or audio recordings of everyday or institutional life. Using the meal example here, DP could be used to examine how the constructs of food preference (e.g., liking or not liking foods) or disgust (e.g., the facial expressions alongside 'chemically incarcerated') are produced in particular ways and for particular purposes in the interaction (Wiggins, 2013, 2014). So the topic of eating and food practices within the mealtime could be a particular focus. Alternatively, we could examine other psychological issues, such as those around identity and responsibility: how choices are made (in choosing food), who has entitlement to say what gets eaten, and whose responsibility it is to ensure that those choices are carried out. These issues could be tackled from a DP perspective, specifically in relation to accountability and fact construction: how are people held accountable for food choices or food preferences? How do speakers orientate to food preferences as being 'real' and relevant at particular moments in the mealtime?

Transcript

As the form of discourse analysis that is most closely aligned with conversation analysis, the type of transcript that is typically used in DP research can look very similar, if not identical. What may differ is the way in which words are written. In CA, words are typically transcribed phonetically (as they sound) rather than using standard spelling. By contrast, DP transcripts use either phonetic or standard spelling. Line numbers are used to highlight the focus on sequence and organisation, and to enable us to readily point to specific parts of the data in the written analysis. The participants (sometimes referred to as speakers, as in CA) are denoted by pseudonyms, and again there is variation in terms of whether informal or formal names are used. One of the issues around labelling participants even at the stage of transcription is that if we refer to someone as 'Mum' rather than 'Linda' then the implication might be that all their talk should be interpreted in terms of their identity as the mother in this context. Given DP's social constructionist assumptions, this can be problematic, so in many cases, DP transcripts use a pseudonym that does not infer a particular role. Like CA transcripts, DP transcripts also aim to capture as much detail about the delivery of the talk as possible, though details relating to eye gaze or gesture may be characterised by labels rather than with particular transcription symbols.

Extract 2.2: Example DP transcript

```
1.   Bob:      mine's is >qui- a lot of< ((looks down at his plate))
2.             (1.0)
3.   Bob:      I don't like steak.
4.             (0.4)
5.   Lesley:   no: [don't do either
6.   Bob:         [.pt >doesna< (.) doesna fire >ma rockets it
7.             just disnae<
8.   Lesley:   I like fish::=we >never have enough< fish:
9.   Bob:      w- we:ll. see that fish you bu::y, (0.4)
10.            <don't buy that> see that thing that gets like-
11.            (.) incarcerated in some kin'a-
12.            (0.8)
13.  Bob:      <chemically:> (0.2) compound (.) >thing<
14.  Edith:    mm
15.            (0.2)
16.  Bob:      THA- (.) you get it like- >it doesn't look like a
17.            fish< that thing we had the other night
```

Analytic tools

As will be detailed in Chapter 6, DP typically focuses on how and when psychological concepts are produced in interaction, and the consequences of these constructions for social practices. DP draws on many of the tools of CA, including focusing on turn-taking and sequential organisation, but rather than starting with social actions, DP focuses first on a specific psychological issue or the production of categories in talk. We noted earlier that food preference might be a relevant topic for this mealtime example, so we could focus on lines 3, 5 and 8, where Bob and Lesley both make claims about their food preferences. Here, we could examine how they are formulated, as 'I like/I don't like', rather than a more extreme form (e.g., I love, I hate) or a softened version (e.g., I prefer, I'm not so keen on) of similar assessments. So we could examine the specific way in which they have been stated, and also how this 'locates' the preference in the individual. For instance, if we look at lines 9 to 17, we see how Bob is describing the fish in a particular way; this constructs the food as having particular characteristics ('incarcerated', 'doesn't look like a fish') that are separate from, and apparently independent of, Bob's own food preferences or taste experiences. We could then continue to examine how assessments of food are enacted differently throughout the mealtime – as individual preference, as a claim about the food as an object – and how these not only have consequences for how we understand food preference (that if an adult makes a claim about an individual food preference, that it cannot be challenged, for instance), but also for the current interaction (that food preferences can be used to make claims about what foods should or should not be eaten during family meals).

Box 2.3: Exploring DP further

One book chapter

Edwards, C. (2005b). Discursive psychology. In K. L. Fitch & R. E. Sanders (Eds.), *Handbook of language and social interaction*. Mahwah, NJ: Lawrence Erlbaum Associates, pp. 257–273.

One journal article

Stokoe, E. & Hepburn, A. (2005). 'You can hear a lot through the walls': Noise formulations in neighbour complaints. *Discourse & Society, 16*(5), 647–674.

Critical discursive psychology

Theory

As we move from the zoom-lens to the wide-angle forms of DA, critical discursive psychology (CDP) is the one which sits most readily in the intervening space, capturing some of the detail of discourse while also addressing broader cultural issues. Crucially, it is argued that these issues – such as gender, class, sexuality – cannot be reduced to a sequential analysis of talk (as would be argued by CA and DP). While CDP might analyse everyday interaction, for instance, it would also examine this in light of how that interaction is located within a particular social, cultural and historical setting. So for CDP, discourse is understood as the intersection between the everyday and the cultural; that one can see cultural influences in the way we talk and write, and that these *are influences* in that they shape our discourses. It does this through the concepts of ideological dilemmas, interpretative repertoires and subject positions. Ideological dilemmas (Billig et al., 1988) are contradictory or oppositional ways of understanding the same concept, but unlike the hidden ideologies of critical discourse analysis (see later), CDP argues that people can actively use these dilemmas to argue for different positions. Similarly, interpretative repertoires (Potter & Wetherell, 1987, inspired by Gilbert & Mulkay, 1984) are coherent sets of ways of talking or writing about an issue – patterns in discourse, as it were. They are flexible discursive resources in that they can be used to argue for or against a particular issue, and there can be opposing repertoires used for the same issue. For example, you might draw on a romantic repertoire to justify a marriage that lasts for a lifetime or a realist repertoire to justify marriage that ends in divorce after a few years (Lawes, 1999). CDP argues, then, that we can draw on a range of repertoires at any time, but that some repertoires are more culturally dominant than others. These dominant repertoires are established over time, and can become so normative and established in a culture that they become naturalised and understood to be common sense or 'fact'. Interpretative repertoires can include bodily practices (e.g., ways of eating) and ways of dressing, walking or behaving (see Edley, 2001 for some useful examples in relation to masculinity and normative practices) and they make available different subject positions. So discourses not only impact on how we talk, but also how we behave in particular ways. For instance, repertoires around eating can shape the types of food we treat as 'normal' or 'traditional' food, as well as how often and when we eat, and what we talk about when we're eating.

History

CDP developed within psychology primarily through the work of Margaret Wetherell with Jonathan Potter, and later with Nigel Edley – out of a concern that the zoom-lens approaches to discourse (CA and DP) were missing historical context, and that the wide-angle lens approaches (Foucauldian DA (FDA) and critical DA) were missing an empirical rigour (Wetherell, 1998). So it can be understood as a synthesis between DP and FDA, and the concept of subject positions used in CDP is very similar to the subjectivities referred to in FDA. CDP draws on many of the same influences as DP, then, because it has the same intellectual roots. Where it differs is a movement away from CA and ethnomethodology towards a stronger post-structuralist focus. There are other strands of CDP, most notably that referred to by Ian Parker (see also DP section above), which adopts a more political (and therefore, arguably, a more critical) approach to CDP.

How we can use CDP

We can use CDP when we want to understand how a particular issue, such as gender or sexuality, is understood in a cultural context and how this translates into people's discourses about that issue. So we can begin to see some of the 'critical' side of discourse analysis here – hence the 'C' in CDP – in that it seeks to identify the ways in which people are positioned in particular ways and how repertoires are reproduced and held to be common sense. CDP has been used to examine issues of parenting (Edley & Wetherell, 1999, 2001; Locke, 2015), gender (Reynolds, 2013; Seymour-Smith et al., 2002; Seymour-Smith & Wetherell, 2006), emotions and gender (Walton, Coyle & Lyons, 2004), racism (Wetherell & Potter, 1988) and citizenship (Gibson, 2009).

How it differs from DP

The overlap between DP and CDP should therefore be apparent from the similar roots of both forms of discourse analysis and the collaborative work of Margaret Wetherell and Jonathan Potter, which was the foundation of these two approaches. The main point of tension between DP and CDP is, however, what has become known as the context debate: should we focus only on which topics are raised within a conversation explicitly by participants (what has been termed *participants' orientations*: Schegloff, 1997) or which topics are thought to be relevant from a broader cultural or social perspective (Billig, 1999). CDP is argued to bridge this theoretical and analytical gap, bringing to bear both a broader understanding as well as the empirical focus of *what is actually said* (Wetherell, 1998). CDP is less concerned with the sequential aspects of talk (as DP is) and more concerned with the broader patterns of talk across a particular data set. What is more important is how these words draw on wider social meanings and make them relevant in the here and now. CDP also assumes that discourses have an action orientation; that when we talk or write, these discourses have specific functions that are grounded in particular contexts. This means that a phrase such as 'I love broccoli' can do different things depending on when it is spoken (or written). So the *meanings* of words are not abstract and universal, nor are they formed through the speaker's intentions (cf. critical discourse analysis), but they derive meaning in interaction itself.

Research question

The main aim of CDP is to examine the repertoires, dilemmas and subject positions that shape our discourses in particular ways. As such, CDP can make use of data from naturally occurring interaction (such as a family meal), but might also draw on interviews and focus groups, where there can be greater opportunity to access the repertoires that people use (i.e., one can ask direct questions in an interview or focus group, and so we can ensure that the topics we want to explore are covered in sufficient detail). A research question for CDP might then be to examine the dilemmas around choice of food for the family: how individual versus collective preferences are organised, how issues of gender, age or family status are used to negotiate meal choices in family settings. Like DP, CDP research might be interested in how choices are negotiated in the family home, but would examine how these relate to culturally available repertoires about choice (e.g., choice as an individual right) rather than focusing on how choices are formulated in a specific conversation in one family meal.

Transcript

As CDP is concerned with the patterns in the way in which we talk or write, there is less of a concern with capturing the detail of intonations and the sequential features of the talk; what is more important is that the transcript captures *what is said*. So a transcript typically features the words spoken, any noticeable but un-timed pauses (depicted as (.) in the transcript), and any emphasised words (noted by underlining in the transcript). As with DP and CA, CDP does not typically use punctuation in its grammatical use. Line numbers can be included but are not necessary because the analysis often pulls across broader stretches of text. We are less focused on specific lines of data and more focused on words and phrases that feature across a conversation. As a consequence of including fewer phonetic details, a transcript can cover a greater length of the interaction in the number of lines of transcript. The transcript in Extract 2.3, for example, captures 31 seconds (compared with 21 seconds) of this mealtime in about the same number of lines as the transcript shown for DP above.

Extract 2.3: Example CDP transcript

```
Bob:      mine's is quite a lot of- (.) I don't like steak
Lesley:   no don't do either
Bob:      it doesn't fire my rockets it just doesn't
Lesley:   I like fish we never have enough fish
Bob:      well see that fish you buy (.) don't buy that
          see that thing that gets like incarcerated in some
          kinda (.) chemically compound thing you get it like
          it doesn't look like a fish that thing we had
          the other night
Lesley:   that battered thing no I don't like battered fish
          I mean proper fish
Linda:    plaice
Bob:      it wasn't
```

```
Linda:    it was plaice (.) it was plaice out of Moors
          and Shawlands

Bob:      it was horrendous
```

Analytic tools

There are three core analytic concepts within CDP – interpretative repertoires, ideological dilemmas and subject positions – each one draws on the others, making a link between broader social or cultural concepts and situated discourses. A CDP analysis would therefore begin by searching through the data corpus for ways of talking about a particular issue. In the meal example here, that might be food preferences, food quality, or choice in food purchasing. For instance, in the first part of Extract 2.3, Bob qualifies his statement about not liking the steak by also stating that 'it doesn't fire my rockets'. This frames it as if it were a biological or chemical reaction, and perhaps also that food can (and should) provide pleasure from eating, and that food tastes are important when considering choice of food (rather than, for example, nutritional requirements or cost-efficiency). So we might begin to search for other ways of talking about food preference to see if there is a pattern here and a possible interpretative repertoire. Alternatively, we might focus on the latter part of this extract where the quality of the fish is being disputed. Here, we see Bob describing it in chemical terms and as being 'horrendous', Lesley also talks about 'proper fish', and Linda draws on a particular high street shop (Moors and Shawlands) that suggests that this is superior to fish from other shops. There may be, then, an interpretative repertoire about what counts as 'proper' food and better quality; this may also relate to the subject positions of the speakers. Linda, for example, appears to be criticised for buying the 'wrong' kind of fish, and thus is positioned as unable to judge the quality of food. In response, she defends her subject position through reference to not only the particular type of fish (plaice) but also the associations of a particular brand of shop, and, by corollary, her subject position as a good judge of food through her shopping choices.

Box 2.4: Exploring CDP further

One book chapter

Edley, N. (2001). Analysing masculinity: Interpretative repertoires, ideological dilemmas and subject positions. In M. Wetherell, S. Taylor & S. J. Yates (Eds.), *Discourse as data: A guide for analysis*. London: Sage. Chapter 5.

> One journal article
>
> Reynolds, J. & Wetherell, M. (2003). The discursive climate of singleness: The consequences for women's negotiation of a single identity. *Feminism & Psychology, 13*(4), 489–510.

Foucauldian discourse analysis

Theory

The first of our wide-angle lens approaches to DA is Foucauldian discourse analysis (FDA). The core focus for FDA is to examine the relationship between discourse and subjectivity. Discourses are understood not only as constructing a particular version of the social world, but also as having an impact on subjectivities and practices; that discourses shape how we think and feel (our subjectivities) and how we can talk and behave (our practices). For example, discourses construct 'objects' in the social world, such as intelligence, and these objects have real consequences for people: our intelligence can be measured and we can be separated in education or workplaces on the basis of such measurements. Discourses therefore produce truths about the world (which have real effects on people), and in turn these truths influence what we can say, think and do. This is where power comes into play, in that discourses privilege some ways of being over others. Some discourses have become so embedded within a culture that they are considered to be common sense, and they can be resistant to change. Within FDA, however, power is understood as being a productive or circular (rather than linear, top-down) force, in that it produces 'truths', but it is also maintained by the ways in which discourses are used by people. For example, discourses produce certain social structures (such as intelligence and educational institutions), and these structures in turn validate the discourses (the grading of student work, for instance, supports the discourse of intelligence). Discourses can also change over time. Truths about sexualities and genders, for example, have changed considerably over the last century. People can also draw on different discourses at different times – even over the course of a day – and so subjectivity is understood to be a fluid and dynamic process of the subject positions that are available to us.

History

FDA has its roots in the work of French philosopher Michel Foucault and post-structuralism, which challenged assumptions about a simple structural relationship between language and culture. Developed in the late 1970s, it draws heavily on Foucault's classic works, such as those on sexuality (Foucault, 1979), and the historical changes within discourses; that what we understand to be truth here-and-now is very different from what was truth twenty years ago, or in a different society. FDA was also influenced by Henriques et al.'s *Changing the subject* (1984), as was DP and CDP, and with how people are positioned or constrained by particular social practices. FDA works across the social sciences, due to the influence of Foucault in these areas, and perhaps because of this there are variations and tensions in how FDA is understood (see, for example, Hook, 2001). Some variations emphasise the historical analysis of discourse (e.g., Carabine, 2001), others draw on psychoanalysis (e.g., Hollway, 1989), for example.

How we can use FDA

We can use FDA to examine how discourses make available different ways of being and speaking in the world. This focus on discourses and their impact on subjectivities makes it ideal to examine issues where people's own bodies are regulated in some way, such as gender and sexuality (Bernasconi, 2010), child-bearing (Barcelos, 2014), children and health (Gibson & Dempsey, 2015; Walters et al., 2015) and fashion (Jackson et al., 2012). FDA has also been developed in slightly different ways across the globe, such as in gender studies in the USA (Butler, 1990, 1993), sociology of knowledge work in Germany (Keller, 2007), and the related work of Laclau and Mouffe (1985) in what has become known as the Essex School of discourse analysis.

How it differs from DP

There are a few main differences between DP and FDA (see also Willig, 2013). First, FDA is interested in the influences that discourses have on people's subjectivities and practices; on how they shape our ways of experiencing the world. So while DP would analyse subjectivity in terms of how people account for their experiences, or construct sensations, feelings or emotions in particular ways in interaction, FDA would treat subjectivity as more than just a discursive construction. Second, FDA takes a different approach to agency. Whereas DP mostly treats people as active users of discourse, FDA theorises people as being both shaped by discourse and having the ability to make choices over which discourses are used. The process of data analysis and illustrating the consequences of discourses can thus help to enable people to make different choices about the discourses that they use. Finally, FDA situates discourse within a wider context than DP: it examines the discourse not only in terms of what is said, but how it relates to social, cultural or historical issues. Discourses are understood, then, like a bridge between social structures and subjectivity; that our words have meaning beyond the local context of the conversation or interaction.

Research question

FDA would typically collect samples of discourse that focus around a particular 'discursive object', so it would not necessarily use a video-recorded family mealtime for the same reasons as CDP: if we are interested in a particular topic this may not readily occur in everyday or institutional talk. Using our meal example, instead of recording family meals, what might be more appropriate would be semi-structured interviews with adults about the process of buying and choosing food, for instance, or government policy documents about recommendations for healthy eating. In contrast to CDP, therefore, the emphasis with FDA would be on how discourse constructs particular knowledge about 'recommended' or 'correct' foods to eat, and about typical (or 'normal') family arrangements; so not just identifying ways of talking about the topic, but how subject positions and possibilities for agency and choice are limited through the construction of the topic in a particular way. In the example data, we can see the discussion at the family meal beginning to cover issues around what the family members (Lesley and Bob) like or don't like about the food. As we will see in the transcript below, the conversation soon moves onto issues of choice and money: who buys the food, whose money is used, and who gets to choose the type of food eaten by the family.

Transcript

In order to identify subject positions and the construction of the discursive 'object' (in this case, food choice), we will need to include a little more transcript than those shown above. This is consistent with the wide-angle lens analogy; we need to look more broadly across the text to understand how discourses weave through at different points, rather than to focus on just one section of the interaction. We pick up the interaction just as the discussion about the choice of fish begins. Note that the transcript here does not have line numbers because the focus is more on discourses across a corpus rather than with the sequentiality of the interaction, though line numbers can be used in FDA research. In fact, due to the overlaps between CDP and FDA, there is considerable variability in how transcripts from these two DA forms are presented, and the transcript shown below is just one example of how this might be represented. In practice, an FDA transcript can look very similar to a CDP transcript because they are interested in similar issues (just as DP and CA transcripts are often very similar). Speaker names have also been replaced with family status labels (i.e., Mum, Dad) to highlight their position with respect to a family structure; given that FDA is focused on social structures (such as the family as an institution), it is relevant and important for FDA to know which family member is speaking.

Extract 2.4: Example FDA transcript

```
Dad:        well see that fish you buy? (.) don't buy that.
            see that thing that gets like incarcerated in
            some kinda (.) chemically compound thing
```

Gran:	mm
Dad:	you get it like it doesn't look like a fish that thing we had the other night
Daughter:	that battered thing (.) no- I don't like battered fish I mean proper fish
Mum:	plaice
Dad:	it wasn't-
Mum:	it was plaice (.)
Dad:	listen- (.) plaice is-
Mum:	it was plaice out of Moors and Shawlands
Dad:	it was <u>horrendous</u>
Daughter:	yeah but I'm not talking about battered fish I'm talking about fresh fish
Dad:	fresh, fresh, fresh-
Daughter:	why do we never have some sea bream or sea bass or some tuna steak?
	(.)
Mum:	there's some in the fridge
Dad:	listen, everything's out of a tin in this house (laughs)
Daughter:	when I contribute I'll be inputting in my demands for my food
Dad:	oh!
Gran:	oh my (.) oh my
Dad:	listen-
Mum:	she was trying to put demands in the other day, because I had gone to Mindletons and bought prawns
Daughter:	they were bowfin! ((*disgusting*))
Mum:	and she went 'these are dry (.) I've told you, don't buy Mindletons' and I said 'see when you contribute (.) you say to me where I can go to buy'

Dad: no don't bother (.) listen, you'll just contribute and get no choice same as I contribute and get no choice. Unless you get the messages ((food shopping)) then you can go and buy

Analytic tools

FDA is concerned with the ways in which discourses produce particular ways of seeing and ways of being in the world; how subject positions and subjectivities are produced in discourse. Instead of focusing on the interaction between the family members during the mealtime, therefore, we could use FDA to examine the subject positions that revolve around the complex issues of money, choice and food. We have already seen with the CDP analysis that the mention of particular shops ('Moors and Shawlands') can be interpreted as invoking the status of both the food and the person doing the shopping. With FDA, we might also interpret the different claims about foods here – plaice from Moors and Shawlands versus prawns from Mindletons – as setting up a dichotomy between 'good' and 'bad' foods. The family members could therefore be interpreted as drawing on discourses around quality of foods through reference to particular shops. The daughter also mentions particular types of fish that are likely to be less common in the average household in the UK, so there is a status of food being invoked here; it is not just 'fresh' or 'proper' fish that is requested, but a less common and possibly more expensive type of fish. The daughter then raises the issue of contributing money to the family income as a means of justifying her 'demands', and both Mum and Dad take this further: stating that contributing money does not necessarily give you choice in what the family eats. So there are culturally relevant topics here about who pays into the family income, whether or not this entitles that person to make food choices, and expectations about the standard of food that the family should be eating. This in turn might lead to analyses around the family as an institution, and how different ways of being a family are made relevant and available through different discourses.

Box 2.5: Taking FDA further

One book chapter

Willig, C. (2013). *Introducing qualitative research in psychology: Adventures in theory and method.* Maidenhead: McGraw-Hill Education (UK). Chapter 11.

(Continued)

> *(Continued)*
>
> One journal article
>
> Riley, S., Thompson, J. & Griffin, C. (2010). Turn on, tune in, but don't drop out: The impact of neo-liberalism on magic mushroom users' (in)ability to imagine collectivist social worlds. *International Journal of Drug Policy, 21*(6), 445–451.

Critical discourse analysis

Theory

Critical discourse analysis (hereafter, CDA) is perhaps the most critical of the five forms of DA discussed in this chapter as it takes an explicitly political stance and argues first and foremost for the emancipation of marginalised groups and individuals in society. The aim of CDA research is to reveal the ideologies that underpin oppressive discourses, and to highlight subversive or resistant discourses that can be used to liberate people from oppression. The starting point is typically a social problem or issue relating to power or political inequality. CDA aims to reveal the underlying ideologies behind discourses, what kind of power is being used, and how this is achieved through text and images. Discourses are not, therefore, separate to issues of power: they are the means through which power is exerted in society. For example, language choice is regarded as a political act because it has implications for people and their actions. Discourses are also understood in terms of their broader context – hence the wide-angle lens – not just the immediate context of what is said, and to whom, but how the discourses draw on the socio-political context and cultural context and have implications for a broad spectrum of people in society. For example, if a newspaper reports on immigration as being problematic and makes a distinction between the 'we' who are being 'invaded' and the 'they' who are coming into our country, then this has consequences for anyone who comes to live in that country from a different place. It doesn't just effect whoever is reading the newspaper report; it has wider implications, like water ripples when a pebble is dropped into a lake.

History

The roots of CDA are embedded within critical linguistics, sociolinguistics and semiotics – and, to some extent, build on FDA – and so CDA is often focused on the 'meanings' underlying language. Whereas other forms of DA might argue that meaning is constructed *in* interaction, as people are talking for example, CDA research often argues that meanings are hidden within the text or talk. That is, that meanings pre-exist in the words or images used. What unites researchers within the CDA approach is a focus on language, ideology and power, and here we see the main difference from FDA: critical discourse analysts are more concerned with the *ideas or ideology* that underpin discursive practices than with *knowledge*, which can in practice be 'owned' or used by anyone in society. An ideology is the domain of the dominant group or groups in society, and therefore there is a political and motivated edge to CDA research. Various strands of CDA research exist, from the socio-cognitive model of Teun van Dijk (1993, 2001), the discourse-historical model of Ruth Wodak (1996), the dialectical-relational modal of Norman Fairclough (1989, 1995) to multimodal CDA (Kress, 2009).

How we can use CDA

We can use CDA when we want to address a social issue or problem, where individuals or groups of people are being marginalised or oppressed. The 'critical' element of CDA is that it aims not only to illuminate how discourse creates certain types of reality, but also to highlight power inequalities in order that these might be subverted or removed. This can be particularly important for those researchers who want to make an impact: to analyse discourse in a way that can potentially have wide-reaching implications. CDA works for the oppressed and the dominated, and thus it is not sufficient merely to highlight dominant discourses; one must also use the research to make a political statement. CDA is therefore ideally suited to research on racism (e.g., Van Dijk, 1993; Wodak & Matouschek, 1993), political speeches and documents (Bhatia, 2006; Fairclough, 2001), and national identity and immigration (e.g., Banda & Mawadza, 2015; Paltridge et al., 2014).

How it differs from DP

The main differences between CDA and DP are similar to those between FDA and DP; both CDA and FDA treat issues such as power, agency and society as existing at a broader level than DP. That is, that they cannot – and should not – be reduced to a sequential analysis in a specific interactional context. While both FDA and CDA are concerned with power, however, CDA argues that power is controlled by dominant groups and organisations in society through the use of discourse. With FDA, power is a more flexible and bi-directional concept; power can come from using discourses in particular ways as well as *being used by* discourses. Another defining feature of CDA is that it treats language use as a matter of individual choice: that people deliberately make use of particular word choices in order to express an argument or communicate an idea. By contrast, DP is agnostic about word choice and does not make claims about whether people intentionally use particular discursive practices, focusing on the social actions performed in talk rather than cognitive processes of word selection.

Research question

The main aim of CDA is to begin with a social problem, and with our meal example this might be to consider the rising costs of food and the need for 'food banks' to help support those families who are not able to buy enough food to eat. Like FDA, CDA would preferably work with texts that have an impact at a cultural or societal level, rather than focusing on what might be considered an idiosyncratic family situation. With a focus on revealing the oppressive discourses that underlie everyday texts, then, media advertisements about 'typical' family meals or political speeches about the causes of food poverty might be more appropriate. While CDA might typically examine media texts, it can also be applied to everyday interaction because it is argued that individuals are as much a part of semiotics (making meaning) as public texts or images (Machin & Mayr, 2012). It can also be argued that this is one of the ways in which oppressive discourses can impact on individuals: through the way in which we use or re-make meanings to frame the world around us. If we were to use CDA to examine this family meal, we might therefore focus on how different family members use different frameworks of talking to justify their positions. For example, Dad talks about contributing to the family budget, and makes inferences about his own lack of agency and the importance of traditional working values.

Transcript

Rather than focusing on the interaction between people at this family mealtime, CDA might consider instead the language used by one of the people present. To remain consistent with the earlier transcripts above, the extract here presents Dad's (Bob's) part of the discussion as a series of statements, to collect together the discourses he used and present them in a way that is easy to read and to search for key terms and word choices. Note how there are no line numbers here, and punctuation is used grammatically rather than to represent intonation. Again, there is variation in the transcripts used within CDA research and the example given here is just one possible representation of the data.

Extract 2.5: Example CDA transcript

```
"Well see that fish you buy? Don't buy that. See that thing
that gets like incarcerated in some kind of chemically
compound thing. You get it, like it doesn't look like
a fish, that thing we had the other night. It was
horrendous. Everything's out of a tin in this house.
You'll just contribute and get no choice same as I
contribute and get no choice. Unless you get the messages
((food shopping)) then you can go and buy."
```

Analytical tools

The starting point for CDA would be to focus on lexical choice, that is, what kinds of words have been chosen, what vocabulary has been used? The use of language in this way has been likened to marking out the territory on a map (Fowler, 1991). Certain features may be highlighted, boundaries may be established and other features made absent (or suppressed). A common type of lexical choice that a CDA analysis might focus on would be verb choice. Verbs are particularly useful because they can imply responsibility, authority, agency and formality (Caldas-Coulthard, 1994). In the extract above, then, we might examine how Dad uses the directive statement 'don't buy that' as a way of asserting an authoritative voice; someone who has control or expertise in this situation (as claiming greater knowledge about the chemical-compound covered fish; again, the use of more technical terms presents Dad in an authoritative position). The 'chemically incarcerated' term may also be considered a type of 'ideological squaring' (Van Dijk, 1998), where meanings (in this case, 'natural' or 'free from additives') are invoked through opposites. Note how Dad then presents his position as lacking agency despite having contributed to the family income, and asserts power over his daughter to be treated in the same way. It is also interesting to note that CDA makes use of some terms or concepts that appear in other DA forms (e.g., directives, CA; hyperbole, cf. Extreme case formulations, DP/CA; modal verbs, DP). The main point of difference here is that CDA would interpret their use as a deliberate choice; that they are being used by speakers to achieve a particular social goal, one that exerts power over others. CDA would also be more prepared to argue that issues that are not explicitly said can still be present in texts; that absences are not just analysable but necessary for understanding the discourse.

Box 2.6: Taking CDA further

One book chapter

Machin, D. & Mayr, A. (2012). *How to do critical discourse analysis*. London: Sage. Chapter 1.

One journal article

McGannon, K.R., Berry, T.R., Rodgers, W.M. & Spence, J.C. (2016). Breast cancer representations in Canadian news media: a critical discourse analysis of meanings and implications for identity. *Qualitative Research in Psychology, 13*(2), 188–207.

KEY POINTS

- There are many different forms of discourse analysis, though they all share the assumption that discourse constructs, rather than reflects, reality.
- The analogy of camera lenses can be used to help distinguish between those which focus on the detail of talk or pan out to incorporate a wider social context.
- Conversation analysis and discursive psychology are two of the 'zoom lens' or fine-grained approaches to analyses of talk and interaction and focus on turn-taking and the immediate interactional context.
- Critical discursive psychology examines the detail of what was said in the broader context of social and cultural issues.
- Foucauldian discourse analysis and critical discourse analysis are like 'wide-angle' lenses and study the ideological aspects of discourse and the influence of these on subjectivities or power relations.
- There is no hierarchy of discourse analysis approaches; each has its own advantages and should be chosen on the basis of the research questions that you want to address.

Recommended reading

Wetherell, M., Taylor, S. & Yates, S. J. (2001). *Discourse as data: A guide for analysis.* London: Sage.

Wooffitt, R. (2005). *Conversation analysis and discourse analysis: A comparative and critical introduction.* London: Sage.

PART TWO

Methods

3

DEVELOPING A RESEARCH QUESTION

Chapter contents

Getting started with a DP project	62
Selecting a topic	64
Turning your topic into a research question	65
Ethical and practical considerations	67
Examples of research questions from student projects	70

The starting point of any research project or data analysis is with a question. Not all questions are relevant or appropriate for a DP approach, so you will need to ensure that your question fits with the epistemological, theoretical and analytical approach of DP, or else choose a different approach to fit your question. While you may be eager to start collecting your data and diving into the analysis, you first need to plan out your research project and define your research question. This is essentially the process of clarifying exactly what it is that you want to study. This chapter therefore presents a dilemma. Ideally, you should choose a research question and then an appropriate analytical approach that is compatible with this question. In this case, a chapter on developing a research question might not really be necessary in a book that focuses on a specific methodology, because it assumes that you have already gone through the process of refining your research question and have chosen DP as the appropriate approach. On the other hand, you may have decided *before you designed your research question* that you wanted to use DP for your research, in which case this chapter could help you to develop your research question and ensure that it is compatible with a DP perspective. There is a risk here, however, that this can lead to 'methodolatry', where the methodology is given priority over other concerns, so we need to be careful here.

Our research question should be driven by the issues that you want to address as much as by the approach.

The aim of this chapter, therefore, is to guide you through the process of developing your research question: that is, a specific type of question that can be answered with a DP approach. This is an important stage and can ensure the success (or failure) of your DP project; planning, therefore, is essential. When developing your research question, you will need to consider issues such as: What do I want to know? Why is this important? How am I going to do this? When will I tackle each stage? Where will the research take place? What, why, how, when and where questions. Developing your research question, therefore, is also the stage at which you'll move from possibly idealistic, abstract questions (such as *How do infants learn about tastes?*) to focused, concrete questions (such as *How do parents manage and orientate to their infant's responses to 'first foods' during the early weeks of weaning?*). You might want to read this chapter in combination with Chapter 9, where you'll find examples of DP research across different topic areas.

Getting started with a DP project

The first step in undertaking a DP project is in beginning to approach the world from a DP perspective; to use our DP 'camera lens' (see Chapter 2) as a way of observing and examining social interaction. Developing your research question is the bridge between theory and practice, between the assumptions DP makes about the world and how these translate into research projects. For example, DP offers a radically different re-working of psychological concepts and topics, and as such requires us to take a different stance on how we approach empirical work. We cannot simply take an existing psychological theory or topic and 'apply discursive psychology', because DP starts from a different place: it starts with people's practices rather than theory. For instance, instead of examining 'how people's attitudes might be changed by others in interaction' or 'how people are persuaded to change their attitudes', we would focus instead on how assessments are produced in interaction, and in different kinds of social situations. Table 3.1 provides a comparison between the kinds of questions that would, or would not, be appropriate for DP research.

Before we think about a topic area, then, we need to align our research gaze with DP and to begin to identify the kinds of questions that it can answer. DP research examines discursive practices and the psychological issues that are enacted within these practices. Our analytical gaze is on people and interaction, not individuals or their mental processes. If you are not already familiar with DP research, take some time now to read through Chapter 1 (for DP theory) or Chapter 9 (for DP research ideas), and then consider the activity in Box 3.1 to test out your understanding of how DP might approach different topics.

Table 3.1 Comparison of example research questions

Suitable for DP	Not suitable for DP
To examine how different versions of reality are constructed in talk and text	To find out which constructed version of reality is the correct one
To examine how and when people are held accountable for different behaviours or events	To establish the cause of an event or behaviour and who is to blame
To examine how people's reported thoughts or beliefs are used to perform different social actions	To find out what people think, or why they think or believe something
To examine how the meaning of an utterance is collaboratively constructed in social interaction	To identify what people intend, or intended to say (i.e., what do they 'mean' when they say something)
To analyse how psychological states are invoked in social interaction for different institutional or everyday functions	To find out people's emotions, attitudes or personality (i.e., what they feel about something, what kind of person they are)
To examine how and when identities shift discursively in face-to-face or online interaction	To find out someone's core identity, and who someone 'really is' in online interaction

Box 3.1: Activity

Using your understanding of DP so far, consider how we might use the DP lens to examine the following issues:

- Military conflict and war
- Children's emotional development
- Tackling climate change

What areas of focus might DP enable us to examine? What would it miss out? Each of these issues is deliberately very broad but it should encourage you to think about the possible relevance of DP for issues such as these and to consider *how* DP might be used. To get you started on the first issue, think about where conflict might be reported (e.g., news media, political speeches, government documents) or where we might see conflict in action (e.g., confrontation between political leaders or military personnel, interaction between military troops and civilians in war zones, soldiers' messages and video footage from the front line). Focusing on *psychology in interaction* should help you to work through the kinds of issues that DP can examine.

Selecting a topic

The topic you select will be partly dependent on the purpose of your research project, whether this is for undergraduate coursework or a large research grant. Time and resources are important considerations, so you will need to be practically, as well as theoretically, grounded. Some topics may be of interest to you but would require access to the kind of interaction that you may not be able to gain easily. For example, the decisions made within advertising companies about tobacco marketing or the lunch-time conversations in a secure prison might be rather difficult to access, so some topics may require ingenuity in identifying alternative sources of data.

Ideas for DP research topics can come from many sources. For instance, you may have read research that you were particularly curious about, or which identified key areas of new research that might be developed further. Reading is also essential to the process of developing your own ideas for topics and research questions, as you will need to know – if not now, then when you are at the stage of writing up your research – how your work fits in with existing research developments. Better to find out early on if your amazing idea for a project has already been done, to save you the time and heartache of finding out once you have collected and analysed your data. Do not worry about coming up with a completely original idea either; sometimes all you need is to think of a slightly different angle for an existing study. For instance, you might use a different cultural context, participant sample or choose a different analytical focus for the same kind of data. This is true of most kinds of research – not just DP research – but the beauty of discursive research is that conversations and social interactions are unique and hard to replicate exactly. In that sense, there is always something new to analyse and a different interpretation to be made.

Since DP is focused on psychological business in social interaction, we can also get ideas for topics in the social world around us: with how people make accusations of blame, how our identities are often implied in particular settings, and with how some people appear to be more knowledgeable than others. Being engaged in the social world – listening and watching others around us, reading the news and social media – can thus often inspire great research projects. That is another benefit of discursive research: it studies people in real-time interactions, and so our research is already applied in the sense that it is based within an empirical context.

One of the most important things about choosing a topic for your study is that it should be something that motivates you, even if the reason for using DP is for a particular course requirement that has been assigned by a tutor. DP research takes time and effort, and cannot be accomplished by pressing buttons or ticking boxes. You need to work through it carefully and rigorously, and spend time thinking through and reflecting on the analysis. For this reason, you should ensure that you plan in as much time for the analysis stage as possible, as it can lead to unexpected interpretations and sometimes requires you to return to the transcription and coding stages to refine your analyses further. Choosing something that you are interested in will make it much easier to stay focused on your project at each stage.

Turning your topic into a research question

Once you have chosen a topic, you now need to refine this to develop a research question: a question that will drive the project in a particular direction. The research question needs to be specific enough so that it can be answered by DP, but not so specific that you constrain or limit the analytical work that can be done (i.e., it should not be a question that can be answered with 'yes' or 'no'). Unlike a hypothesis, which is designed to make a very clear prediction about the effect of one variable on another variable, a research question is designed to guide both the design of the project and the analysis itself. It should state clearly *what it is you want to know* about a specific topic. The proof of the research question is whether or not you can answer it once you have conducted your analysis. This is vital: your research question should not be too ambitious or too unstructured. Keep it focused on a specific interactional context (e.g., a veganism online discussion forum rather than any online discussion forum) and don't try to do everything. No matter how large your research project, you can't answer everything. The best research projects are those that are clearly defined and carefully conducted. That is, do something simple and do it well.

What also distinguishes a research question from a hypothesis is that it is okay to refine and adapt your research question once you have begun your data collection and analysis (see Box 3.2). This is because our understanding of the research context and our data develops as our analysis develops and we may need to slightly shift our focus to better capture the phenomena we are examining. Before you get too excited (or worried) about how 'flexible' a research question can be, bear in mind that you can only go so far. Any refinements to the research question will have to remain compatible with the type of data you have, and with the topic area within which you have based your study. For example, my own research on family mealtimes was initially interested in how people discussed weight issues while eating; when they made reference to their own body size or processes while making choices about how much or little to eat, for example. Once I had collected some data, I soon realised that these issues were very rarely discussed in my data corpus, so I shifted the focus onto what people actually talked about much more often: food assessments.

Box 3.2: A student's perspective on changing research questions after data collection

'The research question in my proposal for my PhD funding was great. It was an important issue to investigate, and tied in with the ethos of my external funders, so I was excited to get started once I had collected my data. However, once I started viewing my recordings

(Continued)

> *(Continued)*
>
> and typing up the transcripts I had a sinking feeling that my original question was simply far too broad and impossible to cover coherently in the three years of my PhD. Tentatively, I broached the subject with my supervisors, who almost laughed and told me this was totally normal, and ultimately my research focus went from being this massive topic to one tiny aspect of it which, even still, involves a huge amount of work. The advice I would give to a student undertaking a discursive PhD is be prepared for your research question to change. Yes, it's important to have a focus, but be guided by the data and analyse what is there, not what you thought was going to be there.'
>
> Gillian Hendry, PhD student (2012–2016), University of Strathclyde

Although there are variations in how a research question might appear, a rule-of-thumb for a suitable DP research question would:

- Be a single sentence if possible: this forces you to keep it simple and focused
- Use specific psychological concepts (e.g., accountability, blame, identities)
- Use terms that capture DP issues (e.g., manage, construct, negotiate)
- Specify the participants (e.g., older men) or discourse type (e.g., ice hockey matches)
- Specify the cultural context (e.g., urban areas in south-east Canada)

Given that the aims of DP are to examine the action orientations of talk and text, the management of psychological business in interaction, and the functions that these serve (i.e., the consequences that these have for theory and everyday practices), research questions tend to be focused on 'how', 'what' and 'when' questions. For example, how is accountability managed in marriage counselling? What identities are produced in an online food blog? When are food assessments used in mealtimes and what functions do these serve? There is one kind of question that you will not see in DP research, and that is the 'why' question: *Why do people say that? Why does that occur then?* This is because DP does not claim to identify or measure causality.

Box 3.3: Top tips for DP research questions

- Use open, not closed, questions (e.g., *How does...* not *Does...*).
- Focus on actions in discourse, not meaning (e.g., *When are assessments used...?* not *Why do people use assessments?*).

- Common terms used in DP research questions are: *examine, explicate, identify*, as these focus on the interactional context within which discourse features, rather than the people 'behind' the discourse.

- Avoid terms such as: *effect, impact, cause, relate, influence*, as these suggest a causal relationship between different factors.

- Stay focused on a specific research context (e.g., gender identities in sports news reporting on television).

- Ensure that your research question matches the data format (i.e., online discussions, face-to-face interaction) as well as the epistemological stance.

With larger projects, or when you have a large data set, you might find that you need more than one research question or one main question and a series of sub-questions. This can help you to tackle a number of issues within the same project, though do be careful to keep these focused and limited. There is a risk, if you add more research questions, that your project will 'grow arms and legs'; it will try to do more than is feasible within the limited period you have for your research.

Finally, when developing your research question, you need to know when your question is good enough to get started; how do you know when you have a 'good' research question? First, consider how you are going to collect and analyse your data. You may not have planned this yet, but if you cannot anticipate your data then it will be very difficult to proceed with your research question. In some ways, your question should specify the kind of data that you will be analysing either in terms of data collection method, participants or interactional context. If it does not do this, then consider how you might refine your question a little further or be more specific on these issues. Second, in most cases it is possible to refine your research question after data collection, coding or analysis. Your research question will become 'fixed' during the writing up process (see Chapter 8), and up until that point it can be changed slightly to reflect a more specific, or slightly different focus on the context that you are analysing. As long as you have planned out the practical and ethical aspects of your research, you can proceed with a research question that might not yet be perfect, but which is good enough to get you started and to focus your analysis. And so it is to the practical and ethical aspects of research questions that we turn next.

Ethical and practical considerations

All research involving people should engage with ethical considerations. With DP research, we are analysing the words and interactions of people in everyday or institutional settings, and so it is important that we are sensitive to the data as, first and foremost, people's practices. While ethics are particularly important at the data collection stage, we also need to be aware of this during the design and planning of our project. Ethical considerations can also be considered from a social constructionist stance, in terms of how we produce knowledge through our own discursive practices. For example, our status as researcher brings with it rights to construct our own version of reality in research papers and textbooks (mitigated, of course, by reviewers and editors), as well as issues around privacy and anonymity of those whose discursive practices we are examining. These rights should not be treated lightly; we are in a position of power in being able to produce 'knowledge' in published form, and as such ethical issues involve not only protecting our participants in terms of anonymity and respect, but also doing justice to the data we have and to ensuring that our research is rigorous and sensitive.

When considering your research question, then, you should also think through the implications of this question in terms of ethical considerations. Which participants are we hoping to collect data from and what format of data will we use (audio or video recordings? Written documents? Online discussions?). Will our research involve people who are more vulnerable, such as young children or those who have a limited ability to make decisions or understand the implications of our research aims? Are we considering doing research on sensitive issues?

The range of ethical issues to consider while developing your research question might therefore involve the following considerations:

- *Participants*: are they likely to be able to give informed consent? Are there alternative participants that you might be able to recruit to your research in the case that consent is not given by your preferred participants?
- *Topic*: is it a particularly personal or sensitive issue? How will you handle this? Does it require seeking audio or video data directly from participants? If it is online or textual data, will the participants be aware that you are using their words?
- *Data collection method*: are you using audio, video or collecting textual data? Will you need to acquire an extra layer of consent for this? Who will be operating the recording devices, and will consent be required for those people to access the research setting?

In addition to these considerations, you should also become familiar with the process of gaining ethical approval from your own institution. This is likely to differ depending not only on your departmental or institutional requirements, but also the discipline and the country you are based within. Becoming familiar with the procedures for gaining ethical approval will help to ease you through this process, and also to be aware of the limitations of the kinds of data you are likely to get. Doing this *before* you set your heart on a particular project would be wise; we can change our research ideas much easier than we can change the policies of a particular institution or discipline-governing organisation. Alongside ethical considerations there are also practical ones, and these can be no less complicated. We will deal with equipment and recruiting participants in Chapter 4, but for now it is worthwhile thinking through your research question in terms of the practical implications. You might find the checklist in Box 3.4 useful as a way of pre-empting any potential issues at this early stage.

Box 3.4: Checklist for practical considerations

- Project timetable
    - How long will you have to conduct the research?
    - What happens if there are delays at any stage?
    - What other commitments will you have to maintain alongside the research?
- Resources
    - Does the research need specific equipment or software?
    - Can you make use of available equipment (e.g., your own, or your participants' smartphone or tablet devices may have recording functions that are easy to use)
    - Is anyone else going to help with the research?
- Participants
    - Do you need specific access to a certain participant group, and can you gain this yourself, or will you need help with this?
    - How many participants will you need? What happens if you have difficulties recruiting them? Do you have an alternative option for recruitment (i.e., other participants)?
    - Will you need to reimburse the participants for their time or efforts, with money or vouchers, for example? Who will pay for this?

There may well be other practical and ethical concerns that are unique to your research project, and so it is important to talk through your ideas – while you are still at the ideas stage – with peers, tutors or colleagues for advice or to act as a sounding board. It can be very easy to become attached to an idea or research question that you think will be a fabulous research project and which you feel perfectly suited to, but which has serious flaws or unforeseen problems ahead. Seek feedback at an early stage in the development of your research, to save yourself time and effort in the long run.

Examples of research questions from student projects

The final section of this chapter provides examples of some of my own students' projects that made use of different types of data, to illustrate the kinds of research question that can be produced with DP research. Even in the same interactional context – such as a family mealtime – many different research questions can be asked. In this way, multiple projects can develop from the same data source. This might be a way in which student projects could be combined, or build on an existing project and use the data for secondary analysis later on. The student examples shown here are drawn from undergraduate, Masters and PhD levels, so the research question can be adapted according to how much time is available and your research skills and knowledge.

Everyday family mealtime interaction

My own research interests focus around family mealtimes and so it is probably no surprise that some students of mine have conducted projects in this area, focusing on issues such as: parents weaning their infants onto solid foods, families with younger children negotiating food preferences, and adolescents with Type 1 diabetes dealing with carbohydrate counting around mealtimes. Research questions for everyday mealtimes might include:

- How and when are food preferences claimed by parents and/or children during family mealtimes? What kinds of activities are these involved in?
- What strategies are used by parents to negotiate children's consumption of food at different ages? What strategies are used by children, and how do these relate to parental strategies?
- How are specific eating requirements (such as diabetes, food allergy, vegan or gluten-free diets) managed within a social eating context (e.g., family mealtime, dinner with friends, work canteen)?

Institutional interaction

Institutional interaction is not as formal or serious as you might expect; it is any interaction where there are constraints on what different participants can contribute, where there are specific goals for the interaction, and where the interaction is interpreted in terms of institution-specific frameworks (e.g., Drew & Heritage, 1992). This could include, for example, interaction between tutors and students, doctors and patients, in courtrooms and police stations, and in shops or cafés. The physical location is not important; what matters is that the participants orientate to the interaction as being institutional. Using data from such settings therefore provides another important way in which we can examine how people manage psychological business and the functions this serves. We can also consider interaction in an interview or focus group setting as being institutional, with a specific agenda and conversational structure. Examples of student work that I have supervised in institutional interaction include: examining identity management in weight loss support groups, dealing with accountability for children's behaviour by parents in a parenting support group, examining student interaction in a problem-based learning tutorial. There are many examples of institutional interaction that do not require a lengthy process of gaining access and consent, and you might belong to an organisation or do voluntary work in a setting where institutional work might be examined. Examples of research questions for institutional settings might include:

- How do students make decisions in group tutorial settings? How are their identities or accountabilities for 'knowing things' managed in such settings?

- How is 'good parenting' defined in a parenting group? How are praise or rewards used to construct particular understandings of good practice?

- How do young men account for alcohol consumption in an interview setting? What strategies do they use to normalise or attribute responsibility for their drinking behaviour?

Online discussion forums

While everyday and institutional interaction provide examples of face-to-face interaction, the expansion of the internet and social media provide an alternative landscape where we can examine discursive practices and psychologies in interaction. The internet now provides multiple and various forms of potential data sources: YouTube videos (and comments), blogs and vlogs, access to radio and TV programmes, and online discussion forums. The data on the internet are interactive in ways that are not possible in face-to-face interaction; people can interact across time and space, and using multiple modalities (i.e., text, talk, images). As a starting point, online discussion forums can provide a large amount of data that can be collected fairly quickly and easily. My own students have examined online interaction, including forums for discussion about eating disorders and for discussions about suicide. The benefits of using online interaction are the ease and speed with which data can be collected, without needing to transcribe any audio or video footage. While it might not provide the variety of analyses that can be developed using face-to-face interaction, it does lend itself very well to student projects. Examples of research questions for online data could include:

- How do people manage their identities in online forums as new members, returning members or 'experts' on particular issues? How are these orientated to by other forum members?
- What discursive strategies do people use to challenge other people in online forums or discussion boards? What psychological notions are used to support or refute their accounts?
- How do websites on mental health issues construct particular understandings of 'illness' in relation to people's accountabilities for 'being ill' or seeking support?

KEY POINTS

- All research begins with a question, so find a question that you want to answer.
- Research questions can be refined as the research develops.
- DP research questions often begin with 'how' or 'when' rather than 'what' or 'why'.
- Think practically: a research question won't work if you can't get the data or find the participants.
- Think creatively: DP works with most forms of talk or text, so consider approaching your research question or topic area from other angles.
- Ethical considerations need to be addressed throughout the research process and you need to be prepared to adapt your plans if concerns arise.

Recommended reading

Braun, V. & Clarke, V. (2013). *Successful qualitative research: A practical guide for beginners.* London: Sage. Particularly Chapter 3.

Read as many research articles as you can – in any field, using any approach – and use these to get ideas for your own research questions. See also Chapter 9 for past DP research in different topic areas.

4

DATA COLLECTION AND MANAGEMENT

Chapter contents

Types of data for DP research	74
How much data do I need?	77
Gaining access: ethics, consent and trust	79
Recording data: video and audio equipment	82
Storing and archiving digital data	85

At the heart of a discursive psychology (DP) project is the data set: the collection of words and interaction that you will analyse. This is the reason many of us became interested in DP in the first place, because we were curious about how people talk about things and how different kinds of interaction have consequences for people as they live their lives. This is where we can examine all the complexity and messiness of social interaction: whether chatting with friends, discussing responsibilities at work or making decisions on immigration policies. So this is the exciting part, where your research questions and interests are translated into practice. There are, however, a few issues that you will need to work through first. You will need to consider what type of data to use, how you will gain access to this data source, how you will record the data, and how you will store and/or archive the data. The process of data collection and management is thus one of the most practical phases of your research project. Due to the reliance on technology and other people for data collection, this is also the part where things are most likely to go wrong. Prepare yourself for this: allow for extra time, have alternative options that you can use if your first choice does not work out, and most of all, stay calm. No research project is perfect and we can often learn unexpected things when something goes wrong or if we make a mistake. There is usually something that can be analysed: even small sections of discourse and interaction can show important features of psychological business being performed. While you might have ideas and research questions about what you think you will find or analyse, once you begin to collect data you may be surprised. Like Forrest Gump and the box of chocolates, you never know what you're going to get.

Types of data for DP research

Before we can identify what types of data are appropriate for DP research, we first need to be clear about what *data* actually are. In DP research, data consists of the ways in which people produce words in social settings and interact with other people. These can include: the things people say, the words people write (i.e., different forms of talk and text), and the gestures, eye gaze and physical movements they make while talking and interacting with other people. So data for DP is as much about social practices as it is about discourse; someone talking to themselves in a room, or writing in a diary is not primarily a social setting and, in that sense, solitary acts of talking or writing are not of interest to DP. What is important is that the discourse is part of *social actions*.

In a similar way, while DP is primarily considered a 'qualitative' approach, this does not mean that numbers are not relevant or used in DP research. Indeed, sometimes it is through counting the number of times a particular word is used in interaction, or the proportion of one type of phrase compared with another, can alert us to some interesting analytical points. My own research on family mealtime interaction, for example, has benefitted from identifying how frequently a particular kind of phrase (e.g., 'I like' or 'mmm') occurs in interaction, and how often it is used by different kinds of people. This can alert us to emerging trends in the data, rather than any statistically significant calculations. So the distinction between qualitative and quantitative methodologies is less helpful here; what is important is the approach that is taken towards discourse and interaction.

Our guiding principles, then, to determine the types of data that are suitable for DP are those that feature both of the following elements:

- Social interaction or a social setting, e.g., spoken with or for other people, or where the textual data are visible and responded to in a social setting. Social interaction can be broadly defined as: face-to-face, on the telephone, or online. In this way, we can also examine the ways in which interaction is mediated through different tools and technologies (such as computers and telephones).
- Discursive practices, e.g., some form of talking and/or writing. DP research typically focuses on discourse that occurs in everyday life, rather than within interviews or focus groups, because the concern is how psychological business is implicated in social actions (for a detailed discussion on this, see Box 4.2).

The type of data (and how much) you collect will be dependent on a range of issues, such as the purpose of the research (e.g., as a practical exercise for an undergraduate class or a large grant proposal), your level of experience with DP research, your access to different social groups or institutions and the ethical issues that arise from your particular research focus (see Box 4.1 for some suggestions on data collection when you are short on time). You may well have been given some data to work with for a class assignment, or be using data that were previously collected for a different project (i.e., secondary data analysis). Practicalities are paramount, and it is better to undertake a small and modest piece of data collection and to analyse this thoroughly than to tackle something ambitious that will leave you no time for analysis. So in all decisions you make, work through the time and resource constraints that you have as well as the likelihood that your ideal choice may not work out as planned (see the section on 'gaining access').

Box 4.1: When you need some data, like, yesterday

There may be occasions when you need to find a small piece of data quickly, such as for a classroom assignment or when you want to practise your analytical skills before you move onto your main data collection. In this case, the internet is a valuable source of video and audio clips (as well as huge volumes of written text) that can be accessed relatively quickly and easily. Take care, however, to ensure that the data you are using is publicly accessible, and that you are not breaching ethical considerations in using these data. To give you some ideas, some of my own students have used the following kinds of material as data for short class assignments: television documentaries, sitcoms, stand-up comedy routines, radio phone-in shows and televised political debates. Using data that appears very familiar (such as your favourite comedy show) can be illuminating as well as fun; it may leave you with a totally different perspective on what is going on in the talk (see Stokoe, 2008, for an analysis of breaching social norms in the American sitcom *Friends*, for example). While some of this material might be scripted or edited – and therefore not naturalistic or researcher-generated – they can still be used as examples of talk and interaction to practise your analytical skills before you move onto a more formal data collection procedure.

In summary, the following list provides examples of the types of data that are suitable for DP research, and examples of how these might be used (see also Table 9.1 in Chapter 9 for examples of DP research by data type):

- Face-to-face interaction: any form of interaction between people in a face-to-face setting.
    - Everyday settings (e.g., in family homes, cafés and public places)
    - Institutional settings (e.g., in schools, workplaces or medical establishments)
    - Researcher-generated settings (e.g., in interviews, focus groups or experimental situations)
- Mediated interaction (talk): these can be most forms of interaction between people that are mediated by a physical object or piece of technology.
    - Telephone conversations (e.g., with family or friends, or with organisations)
    - Radio programmes where discussion is the primary form of activity (e.g., chat shows, discussion panels, news interviews)
    - Televised discussion programmes, particularly those which are broadcast live or are less-heavily edited or scripted (e.g., talk shows, audience-participation debates, documentaries, political speeches and debates)
    - Video chat online (e.g., Skype, FaceTime, Adobe Connect)
- Mediated interaction (text)
    - Online discussion forums
    - Text-based helplines on the internet
    - Facebook chat
    - Twitter messages
    - Texting on mobile phones (cell phones)

Similarly, it can be helpful to know what data are *not suitable* for DP research, and why this is so. These can include the following:

- Solitary acts of speaking or writing (e.g., talking to oneself, writing a diary) because although they involve discourse of some kind, there is no *social action* being performed here; these are primarily individual actions.
- Purely visual data, such as photographs, silent videos or images, because there is no discourse to analyse. These *could* be included, however, if people are talking about them (such as friends talking about photographs on social media sites).
- Social interaction where people are not speaking (this does not include people who are using sign language, which is a form of discourse in itself). While in practice there may be social actions being enacted in such settings, if there is no discourse to analyse, then it will be difficult – particularly for new DP researchers – to identify what psychological constructs are being used in this setting.

Box 4.2: The naturalistic data debate

There has been considerable debate within discursive research about the relative status of different kinds of data and of the privileging of 'naturalistic' interaction over more structured means of data collection, such as interviews and focus groups (e.g., Edwards & Stokoe, 2004; Griffin, 2007; Potter & Hepburn, 2005; Rapley, 2015; Speer, 2002; see also Chapter 1). The debate centres around whether or not we should use data that have been 'researcher-generated' or 'contrived', or what Potter (2004) referred to as the 'dead researcher test' (i.e., would the interaction have taken place if the researcher was killed on the way to work that morning? If it wouldn't, then it is considered researcher-generated). Those who are cautious about using interview or focus group data argue that it tells us more about 'how people behave in interviews' than it does about the topic being studied; that people's discursive practices will only ever be a product of the question-answer framework of the research setting. On the other hand, others argue that we should not set up a dichotomy between natural and contrived data, and that all research settings are in some way researcher-generated. Even so-called 'naturalistic' data involve the actions of the researcher – we have requested permission and either provided video/audio cameras or set these up ourselves – to acquire recordings we have had to intervene in some way. So it is a question of *how much involvement* the researcher has had in the unfolding of the interaction being studied. This is a live and contentious issue, and one which has implications not only for what kind of social interactions are studied, but also for how such research is published and responded to by other researchers. As discussed in Chapter 1, the status of different kinds of data often lies at the core of theoretical distinctions between different kinds of discourse analysis. Whatever stance you take on this, there are often very practical and ethical limitations that might restrict your choices or which might lead you to one form of data collection over another. For instance, those conducting an undergraduate project may have only limited time, resources and access to participants which precludes more adventurous research ideas. For those developing more advanced research in DP, however, this is an issue that you will need to be aware of and address at some point in the analysis and dissemination stages if you are using more structured means of data collection.

How much data do I need?

This might possibly be the most common question for those embarking on a DP project when they begin to consider data collection: how much data do I need? In fact, it is exactly the kind of thing that other researchers – whatever their analytical approach – need to consider, as the sample size can determine whether or not your research is valid. The quick answer, though probably the one you don't want to hear, is that there are no rigid rules about how much (or how little) you need. It all depends on what kind of project you are undertaking: how much time and equipment you have, what your research questions are, and the purpose of the project. The following can be used as guidelines, however, to help you plan ahead and to give a sense of what you should be aiming for when collecting data.

The first rule-of-thumb is to collect enough data that will enable you to make robust claims about your data. If you choose too small a sample, you will not have enough data to be able to identify sufficient patterns in the data; too large a sample and you will not be able to manage and realistically work with the data. In the case of DP research, more data is not necessarily better. What you are aiming for are analyses that are coherent, consistent with the context, and add insight or a new approach to the data. It also depends on your research question: you may need lots of instances of one type of interaction (such as telephone helpline calls) or one type of psychological concept (such as gender identity). Working with naturalistic data will often mean that you cannot predict when the discursive practice that you are interested in (such as gender identity in telephone helpline calls) is made relevant in the recorded data. This can mean that you might have to estimate how much data you will need, then review the corpus as you are collecting it. You may have to collect more, or less, data than initially anticipated.

It can often be more appropriate to consider *hours* of data needed as a guide to the amount that will be sufficient for your project. This could then cover different forms of data that have been audio- or video-recorded. For textual data, we can consider *pages* of data as an alternative indicator: i.e., how many sheets of paper, using a standard font (around 10 to 12 point size) and single-spaced lines. The following can be used as suggested amounts of data for different types of project, though you should also be guided by your own institutional or tutor recommendations:

- For a small project – such as a classroom activity taking place over one to two weeks – around 1–2 hours of video/audio data (or 15–20 pages of paper) should be sufficient. Not all of this will need to be fully analysed, but it should provide a searchable corpus for a specific, narrow example.

- For a medium project – such as an undergraduate dissertation level (circa 6–9 months) or coursework at undergraduate or Master's level – around 5–10 hours of video/audio data (or 40–80 pages of paper).

- For a long project – over a few months, such as a Master's project (circa 6–9 months) or doctoral research (circa 3–5 years) – then anywhere between 20 and 40 hours of video/audio data (or around 100 pages of paper) should be sufficient. This is obviously dependent on the specifics of the project and the quality of the data.

Gaining access: ethics, consent and trust

Once you have decided what type of data you might use for your DP project, the next step will be working through the issues of gaining access to this data, including securing ethical approval from your institution, identifying your participants and obtaining consent from them (if the data involves direct contact with participants). Remember that we are going to be analysing people's discursive practices, even if we never meet our participants directly, or seek to analyse them as individuals. We are going to be analysing their words in more detail than they might ever have imagined. So we need to be respectful of the fact that discourse is produced by people, and that we may be delving into areas of their lives that could be private or very sensitive. Your research should never knowingly cause anyone harm, whether psychologically or physically, either at the time of data collection or at the point of reporting and publishing research. Without the consent of participants, or without the publicly available nature of much online discourse, we would not have anything to analyse. Data are only data because we treat them as such, and first we need to be sure that we *can* treat discursive practices as data.

Chapter 3 raised some of the ethical considerations that go along with discursive research in the context of developing your research question. As noted there, what you might find is that your ideas about research questions can change once you start addressing the practical and ethical considerations. An idea to examine children's playground activities at school, for example, might involve more time to develop trust with schools and gain consent from schools, parents and children than you have available (this might be more feasible for a doctoral study than an undergraduate project). So you may need to be more creative in your ideas for data sources. It is also worth remembering that even sensitive or personal topics are not necessarily off-limits. Hepburn and Potter (2003) demonstrate how such areas can be accessible if people are approached in the right way. One thing to bear in mind when seeking consent to collect data from participants is that DP focuses on discourse and social practices; on people interacting, rather than people as individuals. In that sense, it can help to reassure people that the analysis will focus on the small details of talk, and on their interaction as an example of how people talk in different settings.

Gaining ethical approval is typically sought through a university or research organisation, and procedures will vary depending on where you are located. This usually involves completing a form, and preparing information sheets, consent forms (see Box 4.3 for an example consent form), and any advertisements that you might use to recruit participants. You will need to be very clear about each stage of your research project, including details about the participants, what kind of data you will be collecting and what you will be doing with it, before ethical approval will be considered. It can be frustrating at times to have to consider this in so much detail – and this is particularly the case if the project depends on successfully gaining funding – but it is an important stage and ensures that you work through exactly how the research will proceed. It can help you to work through the practicalities of your research and identify any issues that might need to be adapted.

When using video data, some specific ethical implications will need to be considered:

- You need to capture the actual words that people use, in the setting that they use them. This means that you need a detailed audio and/or video record of their talk (i.e., their voice and their words). Taking notes or summarising a 'gist' of what they have said is not sufficient for DP analysis. So as a basic requirement, you need to gain permission from participants to record and use their talk as data, and you need to do this in advance of the day of recording. You *should never* secretly video- or audio-record anyone; this is not only disrespectful to others and unethical, but also potentially dangerous (if the people you are recording become violent or aggressive, for example).

- When analysing your data, you will begin to collect together instances of a particular action or feature of the talk (e.g., reference to a category of person), and so large sections of the data might feature as part of the coded corpus. One person's talk is also interwoven with the rest of the interaction, so individual contributions are not easily separated. For these reasons, it is not easy to extract individual participants' contributions at a later date. It is advisable, then, to be very specific about the time period in which participants can withdraw from the study (for example, up to one week after recordings have been collected, or even before the equipment is returned to the researcher). While many studies can suggest, and at times ethics committees can require, that you allow for participants to *withdraw at any time*, in practice you cannot withdraw one person's data once the analysis is complete and your report published. One way in which I deal with this issue in my research on family mealtimes is to give the family members full control over the recordings. The video cameras I use allow them to easily review what has been recorded, and delete anything that they do not want to be used.

- When disseminating your research (see Chapter 8) – whether in a poster or oral presentation, or written up in a journal article or book – it is increasingly common to see images or short sections of video that can help to clarify or exemplify a particular analytical point. If possible, therefore, seek permission to use still images or short sections from the video recordings for presentations and publications.

- While you are collecting this data for a specific project, it is likely that there will be a number of issues or areas you might focus on in the analysis, and so a good chance of the possibility of *secondary analysis* of the data. If possible, therefore, seek permission to use the data for subsequent analyses (see also section on storing and archiving data).

The process of gaining ethical approval and discussing your research with potential participants can be time-consuming and challenging. People who initially seemed keen to take part in the research might have reservations later on and decide not to continue. Finding anyone suitable, or gaining access to socially marginalised settings (such as where there is no public access, or where people interact with one another in intimate or exclusive locations), can require patience, openness and a willingness to try different approaches. It may help to involve someone you have met and gained a working relationship with, who can help you to access any other participants that might be recorded (a 'gate-keeper'). Sometimes, however, you will have to compromise on your ideal data setting. At the end of the day, research takes second place to people's rights to privacy and choice, and there is almost always something else that we can do to find the data that best fits our project.

Data collected from mediated sources – such as textual interaction on the internet – also brings with it a set of ethical considerations, even if you may not meet people directly or video- or audio-record their interactions. For example, you might want to analyse the discussions in an online forum where a sensitive topic is being discussed. You will need to make a decision as to whether you will inform the forum moderators and members about your research: will you seek their permission to use the text as data? How will you gain that permission? Would seeking permission actually cause more harm? These are challenging questions to consider, and while there are no simple answers, it is important that you work carefully through any decisions made about the research, particularly at the data collection stage.

Box 4.3: Sample consent form

This is an example of a consent form that I have used when collecting data from families to record mealtimes in their homes in the UK. It is given to the adults in the family and a simplified version can be given to older children. Note that to take part in the project, the participants must consent to all items in this list, though the last two items are optional (and have a clear yes/no indicator so that participants can opt in or out of these). Different ethical priorities or considerations may require different levels of consent or participant involvement in other cultures or institutions.

Consent form: Everyday mealtime project: video recordings in the family home

I confirm that I have read and understood the information sheet for the above project and the researcher has answered any queries to my satisfaction.

I understand that my participation is voluntary and that I am free to withdraw from the project at any time up until the return of the video equipment, without having to give a reason and without any consequences.

(Continued)

(Continued)

I understand that I have full control over which of my family mealtimes are recorded, and which are returned to the researcher to be included in the project.

I understand that any personal information recorded in the investigation will remain confidential and no information that identifies me will be made publicly available; though I understand that it is not possible to anonymise any audio or visual details on the video and that myself and other members of my family may be recognised visually or audibly.

I understand that the video data and anonymised transcripts will be retained for at least five years in order for further analyses to be conducted, and to combine my data with that from other families.

I consent to being audio and video recorded as part of the project.

I consent to being a participant in the project.

I consent to still images from the video being used for academic presentations or published reports. Yes/No

I consent to short video clips being used for academic presentations. Yes/No

Name (please print):

Signature:

Date:

Recording data: video and audio equipment

The equipment needed for data collection depends primarily on what kind of data you are aiming to use for your project. If you are collecting data from the internet, then see Box 4.4. For face-to-face interaction, the most common form of data is video or audio recordings. If you have a choice between audio and video, always collect video recordings, as this provides you with details about the physical space and people's movements within that space, as well as the discursive practices themselves. It can also help you to identify who is speaking and when, particularly if you are recording more than three or four people at a time (and they have similar voices). Distinguishing who has laughed or coughed, for example, can be almost impossible by audio recordings alone, unless that person has a very distinctive voice. DP analysis relies on understanding the detail of what and how something has been said, and this includes an examination of the visual aspects of the setting: such as eye gaze, bodily orientations and gestures.

DATA COLLECTION AND MANAGEMENT

The basic equipment you will need is:

- A video camera or audio recorder to record the interaction (this can be part of a mobile device such as a smartphone or tablet)
- A tripod or fixing device to hold the video camera steady
- Memory cards or external hard-drive to save the data
- Power cable or batteries for the recording device

Depending on the type of video recording equipment you use, you may also need an external microphone. This is a separate microphone that plugs into your recording device, which may require a separate power supply, so make sure that you have fresh batteries in these before you start recording (and make sure that you switch it on before you record, and off once you have finished).

The growth of digital and mobile devices has made the process of capturing video and audio data relatively easy. The emergence of smartphones, tablets and other portable computing devices, alongside the rise of social media and video-sharing platforms online (such as YouTube), means that people are already documenting their lives in different ways. It is more commonplace to see video cameras being used; in fact, this has led some to argue that we now live in a 'surveillance society'. Regardless of the political implications of this, for researchers interested in discourse and interaction, it means that recording people is no longer treated as an unusual or overly obtrusive activity. It also means that you are likely to have access to video recording equipment on your own smartphone or tablet. In many cases, the quality of image and sound will be of a high enough standard to allow you to use these for your own data collection. See Box 4.5 for a checklist of technical specifications and practical tips for setting up the recording equipment.

Box 4.4: Collecting online data

The various stages and complexities of setting up video cameras or audio equipment may be daunting, and you may be tempted to think of using online data as an easier way of finding some data for your DP project (see also Box 4.1). While in some ways the process is simpler, using online data is not the easy option. It is a different way in which people interact with each other in everyday life, and for that, it is becoming increasingly convoluted. For instance, people may be connected through numerous social media sites and interacting on these while also engaged in face-to-face conversation; so the

(Continued)

(Continued)

line between online and offline interaction is blurred. Research in this area is in the early stages and the full benefits of this area for DP analyses have yet to be realised. In terms of data collection, your main concern will be to find and use data that are *publicly accessible*; that is, from a source that anyone can access without a password. This might include textual data (such as discussion forums) or talking data (such as videos on YouTube or a news channel). For textual data, you will need to copy and save the text *in its original format* (e.g., with emoticons, images and text layout) in a word document. Keep a note of the website/url from where you accessed the data, and on what date and time you downloaded it (internet data can change at any point in time). For talking data, you may need to find some way of downloading the sound or video files to be able to use them when you are not connected to the internet. You could also make use of an archive of existing data that has been collected by other researchers. As the move towards 'open data' develops, this may become an increasingly common way in which we use data for DP research. The 'Talkbank' (talkbank.org) site is worth investigating for this purpose, and has specific data collected from child language learning settings.

Box 4.5: Video technical specifications

- As a basic requirement, you will need one video camera. Where possible, use two video cameras to capture different angles of the interaction. Place these at angles to each other, and consider how they might be positioned to best capture different facial expressions or bodily movements.

- Aim to have sufficient memory space on your storage disk/memory card that will allow you to collect multiple interactions without continually needing to download the files onto a computer.

- Record in a format that will allow for high-quality recordings but not so large that the video files are unmanageable or take up extensive storage space.

- Use a tripod to position your video camera carefully. Some small tripods have flexible legs that can be used to secure the camera from a different angle.

- If you are unsure about the battery time of your video camera, record if possible near a power socket, so that you can plug the camera into the mains electricity while recording.

There may be occasions, however, when audio recording is more appropriate, perhaps because you do not have access to video equipment, or the topic is deemed too sensitive to include visual images, or else the data only exist in audio form (such as a telephone conversation). In this case, all the notes above about selecting the best quality equipment still stand.

You should also take time to practise with your recording equipment. Set it up in different locations in your home, for example, to find out how to position the camera or recorder for the clearest visual recording and to capture the sound well. Different rooms and surfaces will have different acoustic implications. Large rooms with lots of hard surfaces (e.g., wooden floors) and no soft furnishings (e.g., sofas, curtains, rugs), for example, can increase the chances of echo on the recording. Busy cafés or other public spaces are likely to have lots of external noise (from people, electronic devices or traffic) that will make it challenging to capture just the interaction that you want to capture. Remember that our perception of sound filters out noises that we are not attending to, but a video camera picks up all sound according to its volume rather than its relevance to our perception. We do not always hear a ticking clock, for instance, or can 'tune out' of background noise, but a video camera is not as sophisticated as our ears and brain. Recording in a public place can therefore raise practical as well as ethical challenges: you will need to consider how you will gain good quality recordings, while also being aware that not everyone in that public place will have given consent to be recorded.

Other technological developments are opening up new ideas for discursive and interactional research, such as 'smartpens' (e.g., by Livescribe, Neo or Echo), which not only digitally transfer your handwritten notes to your computing devices, but can also in some cases audio-record at the same time. This kind of tool can be used to capture people talking while making notes during a meeting, for example, and can be combined with video recordings to capture the visual details as well (see Wright, 2014, for an example of this used in beer-tasting competitions).

Storing and archiving digital data

Once you have collected some data – whether audio, video or text-based – and are almost ready to transcribe it, you will also need to consider how to store and archive your data for future use. If you are using DP for a short class project, or an undergraduate dissertation, you may feel that there is no need to store or archive your data beyond the point at which your report or analysis is complete and has been assessed. There may be ethical requirements for you to use your data only for your current project and for it to be destroyed as soon as the academic year has finished. Indeed, in some institutions it is commonplace to state on consent forms that data will be destroyed within five years, the assumption being that data should not be kept and was only to be used for a specific, named project. Since around the beginning of the 2000s, however, there has been a shift towards the need for long-term storage and sharing of data through open-access policies. 'Open access' data are data that can be used or accessed by other researchers to gain the maximum benefit from the data set. The widespread use of digital data means that it is relatively easy to transfer even large video files from one device to another. Multiple copies can therefore easily be made, and this means that data can physically last longer than in previous, older formats. For those working on Master's projects and beyond, the issues surrounding open-access are worth considering in more detail (see Corti et al., 2014). In terms of storing and archiving your own data for any size of DP project, there are some important steps that you need to take:

1. Always store your video/audio data in at least two locations: such as a laptop or computer hard-drive, as well as an external hard-drive or cloud storage. This will be invaluable in case of technical failure and worth the expense of back-up storage.

2. Always label your data files with information about the date, time, location and/or the participants. For example, '310715 Smith breakfast SWScot' tells me that the video was recorded on 31 July 2015, by the Smith family (pseudonym), at breakfast, and they are based in south-west Scotland.

3. Store your data in a file format (such as .mp4/MPEG-4 for video data) that will retain all the detail of the original recordings, while also enabling the files to be opened on different computing systems (e.g., PC or Apple Macintosh). Avoid compressing the files as this can reduce some of the video or audio quality.

4. Always password-protect the files (whether on your computer, laptop, external hard-drive or cloud storage).

5. Never share the files (i.e., original recordings or unanonymised transcripts) via email, phone messaging or social media sites, unless it is a small section that is being used for presentation or publication purposes. Doing so can leave 'traces' of the files on different computer servers or personal devices that could be accessed by someone else. If you need to share data, use an encrypted or password-protected file-sharing website or USB memory stick.

The processes involved in storing and archiving data can seem lengthy, particularly if you are only dealing with small amounts of data. But they are examples of good practice, and it just takes time for them to become a routine part of research. Start small and gradually build up to maintaining your data in a manageable and organised format. Do not try to do it all at once or it may become overwhelming. It is also easy to underestimate the extent to which technology can be superseded by new versions in a short space of time. So while we can use new technology to our advantage, we also need to bear in mind how shifts in technology have the potential to reduce the shelf-life of our usable data.

Box 4.6: Checklist for storing and archiving video- and audio-recorded data

- Ensure that you have consent from participants to store and archive the data.
- Consider how and when you will transfer the recordings into other locations (e.g., laptop, computer, external hard-drive).
- Decide on how many storage locations you will use, and always store in at least two places in case of equipment failure.
- Ensure that all storage locations are password-protected and stored securely.
- Ensure that all video/audio files are labelled clearly with time and date of recording.
- Keep a record of all labelled files with details about participants in a separately stored file to ensure anonymity is maintained.
- Check whether you will need to back up the data in the future (i.e., if some formats are likely to degrade or become technologically obsolete in a few years' time).
- If you choose to destroy your data, ensure that all copies are destroyed and that this is done completely (physical destruction of hard-drives may be needed, or use software to permanently erase the original files).
- If sharing data, ensure that this is encrypted (encoded securely, so that it needs a 'key' to unlock or decode the information in the file) and, where possible, share using a secure website or with a copy on an external hard-drive.

KEY POINTS

- The data collection stage can be one of the most exciting but also the most unpredictable and challenging stages of our DP project. Be prepared.
- DP can use many different types of data, though there are heated debates around using researcher-generated data which may impact on your research choices.

(Continued)

> *(Continued)*
> - Consider and seek approval for ethical issues before you begin collecting data.
> - New technologies provide interesting opportunities to record data in different ways and in different settings.
> - Good quality data are essential to a good DP project. Take your time to do it properly.
> - Always create copies of your data files and organise them carefully.

Recommended reading

Corti, L., Van den Eynden, V., Bishop, L. & Woollard, M. (2014). *Managing and sharing research data: A guide to good practice*. London: Sage.

Heath, C., Hindmarsh, J. & Luff, P. (2010). *Video in qualitative research: Analysing social interaction in everyday life*. London: Sage.

5

TRANSCRIBING AND CODING DATA

Chapter contents

Why transcription is the first step of analysis	91
The golden rules of transcription	92
Making detailed notes on your data	93
How to transcribe (in three steps)	95
Coding the data	107
Software to aid transcription and coding	109

Once you have your video or audio data recording, the next step in the analytic process is to convert this 'raw' data into a word document that will enable you to code and analyse the data in full. This is called transcription: the process of converting audio and video data into a written document. In this chapter, we will briefly discuss why transcription is an important part of the analysis before working through the practical details: how to format it, where to start (and when to stop), and adding in additional features such as intonation, pauses, overlaps and visual details. We will then consider how to code your data: how to search and select those instances that you will analyse in detail. Note that if you have textual data – such as from an online discussion board – then you will not need the transcription process, though you will still need to format your data. In that case, you can read Box 5.1, then skip to the 'coding the data' section of this chapter. For the rest of you with video/audio data, you have a little work to do first, and this will help you to become more familiar with your data and better able to analyse it. A good transcript is the key to a brilliant analysis, and it offers a completely different insight into the choreography of social interaction.

The process of transcription should not be, as many people suspect, a dull and repetitive process. If it is, you are probably doing too much for too long (see 'the golden rules of transcription'). On the contrary, it is the process through which we first really see the benefits of the zoom-lens approach of DP: we can be unashamedly meticulous, focused and geeky about our data. We can examine the minutiae of discourse and interaction and the implications of this for social interaction and psychological concepts. Here we also see DP's close relationship with conversation analysis and a focus on the organisation as much as the rhetoric and word choice of interaction. Transcription can be considered as similar to travelling by canal boat (also known as a narrow boat, or barge). When you first step onto a slow-moving boat like this – which sometimes travels at no faster than walking pace – it can feel frustratingly, mind-numbingly slow. Once you become accustomed to the speed of travel, however, other things become clearer. You are more likely to notice things in the environment around you that you might have otherwise overlooked, had you been going faster. So it is with transcription. It forces us to slow the interaction down to a speed that will enable us to type up what and how things were said. Because of this practical need to slow down the recording, we then begin to notice features of the interaction (a 'tut' or a sigh, for example) and aspects that might then become our analytic focus. And we realise just how beautifully messy, but highly effective, spoken interaction really is.

Box 5.1: Formatting textual data

If you are using textual data from the internet (such as a blog or discussion board), you already have the words typed out and your initial task then is to format this data. The first thing to do is to copy and paste all parts of the text that you are going to use as data and put this into a word document. Remember to label the document clearly so that you know where and when you sourced the data. You will need to make decisions about whether to include any graphical or pictorial images that accompany the text – such as emoticons or avatars in discussion boards – these are often an important part of the local context of the interaction in that setting. The second step is then to add line numbers (see notes below) so that the textual data is set out clearly. If your data is taken from a discussion thread, then the initial post and replies might be included in one 'extract', so that you can see the interaction within that thread as a turn-by-turn sequence. Include the dates and times of posts, as well as the name of the person who wrote the post (which are often included automatically in the discussion forums) so that you can track through the progression of the interaction, from when it started (and by whom) to when it finished. Your aim with formatting textual data is thus to include as much of the original information as you can, while still creating a clear and readable transcript.

Why transcription is the first step of analysis

Transcription is a theoretical process as well as a practical one. It is theoretical in that we make decisions about what will be transcribed, what will be included in the transcript and how it will be formatted. Even prior to this, we have already made decisions about what research question to use, what counts as 'data' and what we will record, and then which parts of this recording we will transcribe. Each of these decisions will be based on our assumptions about what it is we are studying and how we are going to make interpretations about the discourse. They also involve practical issues: the position of microphones can impact on the audibility of people's voices and other sounds, and thus on the quality of the transcription. In Chapter 2, we saw the differences between transcripts that might be used by different forms of discourse analysis and the implications of these for our analytic focus. As such, the transcript has the potential to illuminate certain features and conceal others. If we include pauses but not hand gestures, for example, then we will analyse in terms of what the pauses are doing with little understanding of how these are related to the visual aspects of the interaction. A transcript typically only makes available those people who are talking in the interaction. If someone is present but silent in an interaction, then they are often missing from the transcript, though this is where the inclusion of images in published transcripts has an added benefit. So the transcript is another step in this theoretical and analytical process. This means that we cannot treat it as a neutral, impartial record of the event; it is always bound up with the research context.

In a similar manner, we might also treat the transcript as never really 'complete', and that it might change depending on what aspects or areas of the data we are focusing on at that moment. For instance, if we are interested in how people take turns in a political debate then we may pay more attention to these in our transcript and overlook other details, such as facial gestures or voice intonation. This does not mean that the transcript is just a subjective interpretation of what is going on, but rather that we need to be clear in how we transcribe as well as making sure that our research process is coherent from start to finish.

It should hopefully now be clear that transcription is not a stage that we must hurry past before we can get stuck into the 'real' analytical work. It is a crucial part of the analytical process; a means by which we can become absorbed in the data, begin to notice features of the interaction and gain an understanding of 'what is there' in the data. This is also why we cannot work with notes or a rough gist of what was said. These would leave us unable to produce the detailed analysis of DP. An orthographic (words only) transcript may be easier to read at first but it, too, can gloss over the features of social interaction that can make all the difference in terms of how we analyse and interpret the talk. If we see just the words spoken, but not how these were uttered, then they are more likely to be interpreted in terms of an individual speaker rather than a rich social context.

They appear as if a written, grammatical language, not a live and kicking *discourse*. We need to see the interaction played out on paper, the nuances of spoken words captured in clear detail. This stage of transcription will prove invaluable later on. Those who have the resources to pay for someone else to transcribe their data may be saving time initially, but this is often time that must be taken at a later date.

The golden rules of transcription

Before we get started into the practicalities of converting your audio and/or video data into a written transcript, here are some golden rules to save you time and help prevent transcription from taking over your life.

- *You do not need to transcribe all of your data.* Depending on your time and schedule, therefore, it may be more efficient to make detailed notes (see Box 5.2) on all your data, and transcribe those sections which you have identified as being of analytical interest.

- *Create an electronic version of your transcript from the start.* Do not be tempted to write it out by hand first, then type it up later; you are simply doubling your transcription time if you do that.

- *Allow sufficient time to transcribe.* It can take at least six hours to produce an orthographic transcript from one hour of video or audio data. This time can vary according to things such as: how many people are talking in the data, how fast you are as a typist, whether there is a lot of overlapping or unclear speech and the quality of the recording. To produce a Jefferson transcript, it can take anywhere between 10 and 20 hours for every hour of data. While these estimates might seem eye-watering, the more time you put into transcription, the quicker you will be able to move forward in analysis and identify issues to focus on.

- *Use different headphones.* This can be really helpful if you are struggling to hear certain sections of the recordings; different headphones can have different sensitivities to sound.

- *Work in short bursts and alternate transcript work with other activities.* Taking frequent breaks will enable you to become more attuned to details in the talk and less likely to miss the details. Transcription can be a tiring process and it is always better when you come back to it refreshed.

- *Do not use punctuation as you would for written text.* While it may feel strange at first not to use commas, full stops and capital letters, it is important that the speech is presented as it is said, not how it might appear grammatically or in written prose.

- *A good quality transcript is the key to a good quality analysis.* You cannot analyse something that isn't in your transcript, so you need to make sure that you are thorough and detailed; even the smallest words or features of interaction (such as 'mmms', 'ohs' and short bursts of laughter) can be highly consequential for analysis. Note that for a good quality transcript, you need first to have a good quality recording; see Chapter 4 on this issue.

- *Paying for a transcriber or transcription service is not the easy option.* While this may help if you have vast quantities of data, it will not remove the need to read through and check the transcripts for accuracy, as well as adding in Jefferson details.

- *A transcript is never 'complete' or finished.* Don't despair; this isn't the same as saying that you will need to transcribe forever. It means that a transcript is always a partial representation of the video/audio recording, just as the recording itself is a partial representation of the interaction it sought to capture. What you are aiming for, then, is a transcript that will be good quality and 'good enough' for a DP analysis, detailing the features that are relevant to the issue that you are aiming to analyse.

Making detailed notes on your data

As noted above, you do not always need to transcribe all of your data. While it may provide a comfort and satisfaction to have all your data transcribed, unless you have the funds to pay for someone to transcribe for you, this can often take up more time than you really have available. This is a decision you will need to make on the basis of how much data you have recorded, how much time you have and how quickly you can type. Even for a transcription geek like me, there will come a point when transcribing more of the data does not add any extra value to the project. So before you begin transcribing any of your data, consider first the option of making detailed notes on the whole corpus.

Having a written document that details the contents of a video or audio recording but without taking the time to transcribe it in full can be helpful for two main reasons. First, the process of producing these documents can allow us to get a quick overview of our whole data set in approximately the same time that it takes to watch or listen to it in real-time. Second, it can be a really useful resource to search when we're analysing different topics, so the more detail we add, the better, and you can always go back to the notes and add in further details as you become familiar with your data set. Skim reading through a word document (and using the 'find' function to search for certain words) can be a lot quicker than trying to watch or listen to your data to find examples of instances where a particular pattern occurs.

Making notes in this way allows you to be as detailed or as broad as you wish, and this may depend on what stage you're at with your research. For example, I have been studying family mealtimes for a few years now, and often focus on food assessments, so in my detailed notes I typically write down the specific assessment words that people use (see Box 5.2 for an example). This does, of course, mean that I am likely to miss other things; so bear in mind that this process of making notes on the data, like transcription, is only a partial record of the data. Note that I have also written down rough timings quite frequently, so that I can quickly find the sections that I want to focus on, and transcribe fully, at a later time. The notes do not have to be grammatically correct or neat; the important thing is that I am capturing some features of the talk in a relatively quick manner, to help me identify sections later on. I have also headed the notes with some details about the recording that will help me to log and track across different data sets. Some of these details can then be used in a summary table or spreadsheet for when you store or archive your data.

Box 5.2: Data notes

Example notes from a project on weaning interactions with parents and their infants.

Lewis family: meal 001, 30 June 2014.

Length of recording: 44: 28

Present: Mum, Dad, Ellie (infant, 8 months old)

Two video cameras: one on Ellie, one focused on Mum & Dad, who are sitting next to Ellie at the dining room table.

Food eaten: roast chicken and roast vegetables. Parents using baby-led weaning where pieces of food provided for baby who feeds herself.

> Mum brings Ellie to highchair and straps her in. 'Good girl' said a few times. Mum sits down diagonally opposite Ellie. Puts plastic bib on Ellie. Dad can be heard in background, clattering plates and dishes.
>
> 1:20 Mum offers water in cup with lid & spout. Ellie drinks. 'Good girl'. Some adjustment of the table on the highchair; this is pulled up to the table.
>
> 1:50 Mum leaves to get dinner & returns with Ellie's plate. Mum talks to Dad who is off-camera.
>
> 2:30 Ellie and Mum/Dad begin eating. 'Is that good'? Dad comments: 'nice? Yum yum, mmm? 'we like roast chicken don't we?' Is that good?'
>
> 3:30 Mum offers water; Ellie still busy eating. Dad makes lots of comments about 'liking chicken, yum yum, is that nice?' Dad says there's plenty more.

How to transcribe (in three steps)

Step 1: Creating the orthographic (also known as basic, verbatim, playscript or words-only) transcript

At its simplest, the transcript provides a written document of the data. It means that you can read through the data as well as watching or listening to the original recordings. An orthographic transcript captures only what words are spoken, by whom, and in what order. You do not have to use the correct spelling, however, if words are spoken in a particular way. This means that you should type out the words spoken as they sound, rather than how they are spelt. For example, 'hello' is the English spelling for a typical greeting, but it might also sound more like 'ello', 'hallo' or just 'lo'. There are occasions, however, when using the orthographic form would enable you to see fairly quickly what is being said – to scan through the transcript at the coding stage, for example – and to use the search functions of word software to collate all instances of a particular word or phrase. An example of this is when I searched for all instances of the 'eugh' utterance for a study into disgust responses (which might also sound like 'urgh', 'ugh' or 'euw') in my family mealtime data. If I had initially transcribed it using different spellings, it would have taken much longer to identify all examples of this in the data corpus. So remain consistent with how things are actually spoken, but also be aware of how this might have implications for coding and electronically searching the data later on. This is one example of how the transcript is never really finished; there are always alternative ways in which we could represent the recording.

Box 5.3: Checklist for orthographic transcript

- Use line numbers for each line in talk.
- Write the speaker's pseudonym next to their speech. Start a new line when there is a change of speaker.
- Write out what is said by each person, without 'tidying it up' or typing what you think they meant to say. Write it *exactly* as it is spoken.
- Do not use punctuation to create sentences; we might write in sentences, but we do not talk in sentences. The transcript might look like a long string of words at this stage, but this is very typical of spoken interaction.
- Represent noticeable pauses as (pause); this can help you identify particular features of the interaction later on.

(Continued)

> *(Continued)*
>
> - Note when there is overlapping speech (two or more people talking at the same time), by typing *((in overlap))* before the words spoken.
> - If you are unsure of what is said, write your best guess in brackets, or else write *((unclear speech))*.
> - Use single quotation marks to indicate speech that is spoken as if it had been spoken by someone else, or by themselves at a previous time (referred to as 'reported speech').
>
> See Nikander (2008) if you are working with data that is in a language other than English, and if you will need to present in English at some point.

You first need to decide which parts of your data to transcribe, and to what level of detail. Whatever amount of data you have, it makes sense to start transcribing at the beginning: at the start of the first recording that you made (excluding any pilot or test data you might have collected; you can always return to this later if necessary). Remember that you may not need to transcribe all of your data if you have a substantial amount (and what counts as substantial will depend on the time you have available and your typing skills), but you should aim to create an orthographic transcript of at least half of your data to allow you to examine it more closely. The sections that you work up to a more detailed transcript can then be selected on the basis of particular features of the data that you have noted in the early stages of coding (see step 2, below).

To begin the process of transcription, play a very short section of your recorded data – around five seconds – at a time, and type this into a word document. You may have to play this several times, and possibly on 'loop play' (where the software automatically plays back a section that you have highlighted), to capture all the words in this part of the talk. Once you are happy that you have included all the words, play back the next five seconds, but include around one second from the previous play-back, so that you are overlapping each section that you listen to. For example, listen first to 0:00:00 – 0:00:05, then from 0:00:04 – 0:00:09 of the recording. This can help to avoid missing out small sections, or mis-hearing words that might cut across the short sections. Once you have transcribed one complete section of data recording, listen to the whole interaction in full while you are reading through the transcript, to check and make sure that you have included everything. This final check can often highlight small sections that you may have missed, and allows you to take a metaphorical step-back from the data after the close listening that is required for transcription.

As you are creating the transcript, it is essential that you anonymise your participants and any identifying features (such as place names or organisations), and the easiest way to do this is to create a list of real names alongside your chosen pseudonyms as you encounter each new speaker. Keep this list in a separate word document in a password-protected computer: this is effectively the key that keeps your data confidential and anonymous, so take care with this. It is not advisable to use initials (e.g., 'A', 'B') to refer to participants, as if you later decide to change this to a full name you will have to change each occurrence of the initial manually (you cannot use the 'find and replace' function in Word as every instance of that letter, in all words, will also be changed). When choosing a pseudonym, it can be helpful to keep the number of syllables consistent between the real name and the pseudonym, and consider if the person is ever referred to by a shortened version of their name. For example, if one of your participants is called Jennifer (three syllables) and sometimes called Jen or Jenny, we could use Gillian (shortened to Gill or Gilly) as the pseudonym. You may also use other techniques to enable you to create pseudonyms, such as keeping the first initial the same or ensuring that gender-neutral names or abstract 'avatar' names are matched with a comparable replacement.

Now we come to the practicalities of the transcript, in terms of how to format it and add in line numbers. This can sometimes be one of the most frustrating parts of creating a transcript, so I will go into quite specific detail here to help guide you through the process. Use Courier font, size 10 (`Courier New` or `Courier Prime`). This typeface is what is referred to as monospaced or non-proportional font, which means that each letter takes up the same horizontal space on the line. Compare that with the proportional font used in this book, and where the letter 'm' takes up a wider space than an 'i' for example. Having a non-proportional font is important for a DP transcript so that we can accurately represent where overlapping speech occurs. It is also a clear and easy-to-read font, which is important if we want our transcripts to be easily accessible for publication. Size 10 font is also the typical font size used for transcripts (so slightly smaller than the text size – 12 – for the surrounding text).

> You should also provide wide margins on the left- and right-hand side of the page. There is no set requirement for how wide these should be, but this paragraph gives an indication of what it might look like. The wide margins provide space for analytical notes, though this is less important when working with an electronic document, where notes can be added using 'comment' functions.

What you are aiming for is three columns: one for the line numbers, one for the speaker names or identifiers, and one for the discourse. Once you add in the line numbers – and see below how to do this – the first column will automatically be created for you. So for now, just focus on writing the names first, and then a second column for the talk. Use the tab function to create a gap between the name and the talk; this will keep the start of the columns in a neat line. If one person's talk continues over more than one line, press return at the end of the line, then space bar, then tab, to align the talk with the rest of that column. If another person begins speaking, then you can type in their name, tab across, and start typing up their talk. Do not use a table to create a transcript as this can be cumbersome to add in more line numbers.

Below is an example of how a transcript might look, from a section from the 'steak and fish' mealtime data that we encountered in Chapter 2. The video that corresponds to this transcript can be found here: www.youtube.com/watch?v=OtKaXw6WqYM. Note that I have just typed the words only, with no pauses or intonation, and no punctuation.

Extract 5.1

```
Lesley:   yours is fat
Bob:      mine's is quite a lot of I don't like steak
Lesley:   no don't do either
```

Now you can add line numbers, and you can start this at any point in the transcription process. There are at least two different ways of adding line numbers, and this can cause confusion when creating the transcript or when you want to cut-and-paste sections of it to another document later on. The best way to add line numbers is to use the 'line numbers' option that can usually be found under 'page layout' or 'layout'/'text layout' tabs, or in page set-up in your word document. These usually have the option to choose 'continuous'/'restart each page'/'restart each section', as well as 'none', for when you want to remove the line numbers. There should also be further options (often in a separate pop-up box) to specify what number you want to start with, and whether you want to count in 1s, 5s etc. This way of adding line numbers means that the original format of your transcript (including how many words you can fit on each line) remains unchanged. The line numbers are effectively added to a specific section of your word document, so if you have other writing in this document that you do not want numbered, then you will need to create section breaks. This process should also mean that when you cut-and-paste a section of the transcript into another word document, the line numbers are also transferred. The line numbers should appear down the left-hand side of the page like this:

1. Lesley: yours is fat
2. Bob: mine's is quite a lot of I don't like steak
3. Lesley: no don't do either

Another way of adding line numbers is through the use of a 'numbered list'; this is often found under the 'home' and 'paragraph' tabs in the document. While this might at first seem easier, in that you can more easily add line numbers to just a section of the text (by using your mouse to select and highlight the section to which you want to add line numbers), it can affect the formatting of your document. It can shift the whole text over to the right (it takes up space in the left-hand side of the page, thus bumping everything across) which if you have a lot of text on one line can result in this happening:

1. Lesley: yours is fat
2. Bob: mine's is quite a lot of I don't like steak
3. Lesley: no don't do either

Imagine this occurring on hundreds of pages of transcript, and you have just made yourself more work in terms of tidying that up (what you would need to do would be to place the cursor at the start of 'steak', press return – which creates a new line number – then space bar and tab to align the speech with the rest of that third column of text). So you can also use this approach to add line numbers, but beware that it may cause some formatting issues.

Each line should have its own number, even if it is where there is a pause in the discourse. Start a new line when there is a new speaker, a longish pause (e.g., over one second) or before you get to the right-hand margin (to create a large space at the side of the page). You might also need to adjust the length of a line depending on whether there is any overlapping talk with another speaker to ensure that this is clearly presented. You will also find that as you add in more details to the transcript (as in step 2 below) that you will be able to fit fewer words on each line. As the transcript becomes more detailed then, it will also become longer.

Step 2: Creating the 'Jefferson' transcript

The standard transcription key for DP (and other interactional) research is that developed by Gail Jefferson and is known as the Jefferson transcription system. Unless you have only a small amount of data, it is unlikely that you will transcribe all of your data to full Jefferson level. As noted earlier, this can take anywhere between 10 and 20 hours for each recorded hour of data. What you will need to do is to transcribe at least half (if not all) of your data to words-only level, then begin the coding stage. At that point, you will be in a better position to identify the sections of the transcript that you want to analyse in more detail. So if you are at this stage, skip ahead now to the 'coding the data' section, then return here for guidance on how to transcribe in more detail. Bear in mind that the process of coding data and creating more detailed transcripts can often go through cycles; you may have to do this more than once. This is because the detailed transcripts can reveal different features of interaction that might not have been noticeable in the first stages of preparing an orthographic transcript and then coding from this.

The process of creating a Jefferson transcript is very similar to that for producing an orthographic transcript; the difference is that you will spend more time on shorter sections of talk and you will use symbols to represent the phonetic features of talk. Box 5.4 details the main transcription symbols from the Jefferson system that you will need for a DP analysis (see Hepburn, 2004, for extra details to transcribe crying sounds). You should work through your coded sections of data, one at a time, and play each recording back while working with your orthographic transcript, which you have already prepared. You are not starting from scratch each time, therefore, since you already have the words typed out. Listen to short sections of the recording at a time, again using loop-play if available. You will probably need the list of transcription symbols alongside you while you are doing this, until you become familiar with them. Take your time to check and stop the recording frequently. Add in the symbols to correspond with how the talk is spoken: you are mainly focusing on aspects such as the timing of words (how quickly they are spoken, and the silence between words, whether there is overlap between speakers), the pitch (rising or falling) and the emphases placed on certain words. You can do this by concentrating on one feature of talk (e.g., pauses) at a time, or include all aspects of one short section at once. Extract 5.2 below shows the same fragment of interaction that we saw in Extract 5.1 with one extra line to illustrate the occurrence of the overlapping speech here; this is added at the exact point at which the words were heard simultaneously. This section of talk lasted five seconds, so you can see the kind of detail that can be added in just a short space of time.

Extract 5.2

```
1. Lesley:   yours is fat,
2. Bob:      °mine's is° >quite a lot a'<
3.           (1.0)
4. Bob:      I don't like steak.
5.           (0.8)
6. Lesley:   no: [don't do either
7. Bob:          [.pt disnae- (.) disnae fire my rockets
```

When using the symbols, always place them before the letter or word to which they apply, although there are occasions, such as when placing overlaps, stretched talk or breaths, when they will be placed in the middle of words. In these cases, place them where you can hear them between the sounds in words. For example, when people

TRANSCRIBING AND CODING DATA

appear to be laughing as they are talking, it can look like: 'laugh(h)ing thr(h)ough t(h)alk', also sometimes referred to as interpolated laughter. The '.pt' in Extract 5.2 is a 'lip smack' sound, and is underlined in the transcript as it was particularly noticeable in the audio. The 'disnae' is a shortened version of the words 'does not', spoken with a fairly strong Scottish accent. Focus at first on becoming familiar and confident with using the symbols. Your transcript is a working document, remember, and to be used alongside the recorded interaction, so it does not have to be 'perfect'. Do not worry at this stage as to whether the symbols are relevant for your analysis; what matters here is that you are building a more detailed picture of the interaction *in written format* so that you can analyse it more completely.

Box 5.4: Jefferson transcription notation for DP (taken from Jefferson, 2004a)

(.)	A micro-pause (less than two-tenths of a second)
(1.2)	A pause or silence, measured in seconds and tenths of seconds
=	Latched talk, where there is no hearable gap between words (can occur within a turn at talk, or between speakers)
::	Stretched sounds in talk; the more colons, the longer the sound, as in rea::lly l::: ong sounds
CAPITALS	Talk that is noticeably louder in contrast to the surrounding talk (sometimes shouting)
Underlined	Emphasised words, or parts of words, are underlined
°	Degree symbols enclose noticeably °quieter° talk, with double degree signs indicating °°whispering°°
> <	'Greater than' and 'less than' symbols enclose talk that is at a faster pace (>speeded-up< talk) than the surrounding talk
< >	'Less than' and 'greater than' symbols enclose talk that is at a slower pace (<slowed down> talk)
↑↓	Upward arrows indicate a rising pitch in talk, downward arrows indicate falling pitch

(Continued)

(Continued)

£	British pound sign indicates smiley voice or suppressed laughter
#	Hashtag indicates 'creaky' voice such as when someone is upset.
[ ]	Square brackets indicate the start (and end) of overlapping talk
hh	hhs indicate audible breaths. A dot followed by hs (.h) indicate audible inbreaths; without the dot (as in hh) is an outbreath. Within a word (as in 'ye(h)s'), this indicates laughter while talking ('interpolated laughter'). The more hs, the longer the breath.
Huh/heh/hah	Laughter can be represented with outbreaths that have vowel sounds within them.
?	Strongly rising intonation (not necessarily when asking a question)
, .	Commas indicate slightly rising intonation, full-stops indicate falling indication at the end of words
'yes'	Single quotation marks are used to indicate reported speech or thought
(( ))	Double brackets (sometimes without italics) contain details about other features that have not been transcribed, e.g., ((waves hand))
(Unclear)	Words in single brackets are the transcriber's best guess at what was being said, or (unclear) or (inaudible) if it really can't be heard clearly

[Acknowledgment: From 'Glossary of transcript symbols with an Introduction'. In G. H. Lerner (2004), *Conversation analysis: Studies from the first generation*, pp. 13–23. With kind permission by John Benjamins Publishing Company, Amsterdam/Philadelphia. www.benjamins.com].

Your first encounter with a Jefferson transcript can be fairly overwhelming and confusing. It can be hard to know what to read first and how to read it. This is why creating a Jefferson transcript for yourself can help you to become familiar with the symbols and how they 'sound'. Reading out the extracts and paying attention to the symbols can help you to 'hear' the talk as it was said. This detail is there for a reason, however, so spend a bit of time getting used to transcripts in this format. Reading journal articles that include Jefferson transcripts will help too.

One final word of advice about pauses before we move onto even more advanced transcription – the timing of pauses can be done in two ways. There is the technical way to do this, where you use the playback tool to indicate the length of the gap between sounds (see section on software). Use this if there is a particular section of talk where pauses appear to be crucial to the interaction, or if pausing is an aspect of your analysis that is particularly important. The non-technical way is sometimes referred to as the mississippi method of counting seconds (some people also say 'one-one-thousand' but I prefer mississippi; it has a nicer rhythm to it). Each syllable of miss-iss-ipp-i counts as two-tenths of a second (represented as (0.2) in our transcripts), and so when we add one, two or three to the end of mississippi, then we are counting one second, two second, and so on. Use a watch to help you find the correct pace at which to count. Start saying 'mississippi one, mississippi two' (and so on) when someone stops speaking, and stop when the next sound in your data appears; this is the gap (pause) between the two sounds. For example, if you get to 'miss-iss', then that is 0.4 of a second; 'miss-iss-ipp-i' would be 0.8 seconds. The point of this is that it should be a quick and dirty way of timing the pauses between sounds that will enable you to create your transcript with sufficient detail, and you can always go back and check the crucial pauses with the technical method later on.

Step 3: Adding extralinguistic details (visual gestures)

Once you have become familiar with transcribing the linguistic (words spoken) and paralinguistic (aspects of speech delivery, such as intonation, etc.) details, then the next stage is to include what has been termed extralinguistic detail. This includes the non-verbal aspects of interaction, from eye gaze, to hand or bodily gestures, bodily orientations of different speakers and the interaction between objects and people in their environment. This step is obviously only relevant for those with video data, and it is typically reserved for more advanced DP analyses. If you are using DP for an undergraduate (bachelor) class or dissertation, then getting to Jefferson level transcript should be sufficient. Unless you're really keen, of course. Either way, this third step is extremely useful, analytically, but it does take time and effort. So if you are not proceeding further, then you will need to pay more attention to the visual aspects of the recorded data *in the video alone*, without having included these in the transcript.

Knowing where to start adding in these transcription features can be a daunting process: we could, in theory, include all visual aspects of an interaction. These might involve:

- Eye gaze (e.g., gazing at objects or people)
- Facial movements (e.g., smiling, eyebrow raise, lip curl)
- Hand gestures and touch (e.g., pointing or open palms, touching self or others)
- Posture (e.g., how the body is orientated, leaning, or position of head and shoulders)
- Interaction with objects (e.g., passing an object or pointing to something).

Remember, however, that not all of these will be directly relevant to your analysis, and you may find that you need to return to your transcripts once you've begun analysing coded sections in detail, to add some more refined features to the transcript or to focus on another feature. This is why a transcript may never be 'finished'. Nor should you try to capture everything. There is immense detail and intricacy in social interaction, even in just one minute's worth. This is one of the ways in which conversation analysis has been particularly influential for DP: to illustrate the orderliness of talk and interaction, and of the relevance this has for how we understand discursive practices. What you will find is that it becomes almost impossible to read a transcript if there are too many notes about visual details. Our task, then, becomes to maintain an awareness of this complexity without being overwhelmed by it. We can do this by focusing on one feature at a time.

Let us illustrate how this 'layering' of extralinguistic features might look on our transcript, by detailing the eye gaze of Bob and Lesley, who feature most prominently in the short section of mealtime talk that we have been using as an example. The simplest way that we can add in these details is by describing them in words, and using overlap markers to indicate where and when these occur:

Extract 5.3

```
1.  Lesley:   [yours is fat,
2.            [((Lesley leans forward slightly and
3.            looks at Bob's plate))
4.  Bob:      [°mine's is° >quite a lot a'<
5.            [((Bob looks down at his plate))
6.            (1.0)
7.  Bob:      [I don't like steak.
8.            [((Bob looks down at his plate))
9.            (0.8) ((Bob glances to Linda then Lesley))
10. Lesley:   no: [don't do either ((looks at Bob))
11. Bob:          [.pt disnae- (.) disnae fire my rockets
12.               [((Bob looks at Lesley))
```

The advantage of including detail in this way is that it is easy to write in features as and when we notice them in the video. In written form, these words can then be searched using the 'find' tool in Word. The transcript begins to look quite cluttered, though, and the frequent placement of overlapping brackets can lead to confusion at times as to whose eye gaze or gestures are being described. It also leaves us open to

TRANSCRIBING AND CODING DATA

the risk that we might label behaviour in a particular way, and that this might lead to one interpretation over another. This is less obvious when describing eye gaze, but if we had added descriptions of other facial gestures, such as 'disgust' face (rather than: 'lip curl, nose wrinkle, downward turn in mouth'), then that might assume or make relevant a particular emotional response. This is not the same as saying these things are not relevant, just that we have to be careful about how we describe them. Here we see how the social constructionist approach to discourse applies to our own practices as well; we need to be aware of how easily we can make one interpretation seem more 'obvious' than another.

Another way to include extralinguistic features in transcripts is to make use of lines (dotted, dashed and solid lines) to indicate the start and end of a movement, or the shifting of eye gaze from one person to another (or from an object to a person). For example, a series of dots (….) can indicate that a person is moving their eye gaze to look at, or shift their bodily position to face towards another person. A solid line then denotes the period in which that gaze or bodily orientation is fixed on another person. A series of dashes (- - -) can indicate gaze towards an object, and commas (,,,,,) can also be used to indicate a turning or shift of eye gaze away from a person. This way of transcribing visual details was devised mainly by Charles Goodwin in the early 1980s, though it has been adapted and used by others since then. It is often combined with screen shots (or 'frame grabs') to illustrate how that visual detail works within the interaction as a whole. Now look at how our mealtime extract might look if we transcribed it that way (note also that the line numbering system has been added using the 'section break' method):

Extract 5.4

```
1
2  Lesley:     _____
3              yours is fat,
4  Bob:        ___ ........
5
6
7  Bob:        °mine's is° >quite a lot a'<
8              .. -------------------------
9              ((Bob looks down at his plate))
10
11
```

```
12
13         (1.0)
14         ----
15
16 Bob:    I don't like steak.
```

```
17         ------------------
18
```

```
19          (0.8)
20          .._..__  ((Bob glances to Linda, then Lesley))
21
22
23
24 Lesley:  no: [don't do either
25          .._____
26 Bob:        [.pt disnae- (.) disnae fire my rockets
27             ..._____
28
29
```

In Extract 5.4, the images are placed immediately below the line in the transcript to which they relate. There is one image embedded within another one – the smaller image in the bottom left of the frame is taken from the opposite camera angle. From left to right in the main image there are: Bob, Edith, Linda and Lesley. So Bob is sitting opposite Lesley, and Edith is sitting opposite Linda; they are seated at a circular table. In the transcript, the solid line on Lesley's turn indicates her gaze at Bob (her father). Bob's gaze is then either at Lesley, his plate, or at his wife Linda (briefly). Even with this very short, five seconds of interaction, adding in the eye gaze of just two people – and we have not included Linda's or Edith's eye gaze at this point – the transcript becomes very complicated. So examine how the discursive practices of people are bound up with everything else in the interaction, and with how capturing visual features can enhance your understanding of just how psychological concepts are invoked and made relevant in social settings, but use these sparingly in your transcripts, publications and presentations.

Coding the data

Coding your data – and we are referring here to data as both the recorded interaction (the video or audio file) as well as the transcript you create – is the process in which you sort the data into smaller sections for analysis. It is a means of making the data manageable, as even with small amounts of data you are unlikely to be able to (or need to) analyse it all. It is not to be confused with the coding that is done in forms of qualitative research where meanings are attributed to the data and the aim of the code is to capture some 'essence' of the data. By contrast, the DP coding stage is the process of searching for particular features or areas to be analysed, using your research question as a guide. For instance, you might code data to identify those sections where people invoke a racist or xenophobic identity to examine how and where these are accomplished in your data corpus.

The relationship between transcription, coding and analysis is an iterative one: while we may begin them in that order, more often than not each stage becomes intertwined with the others. For instance, while analysing a section of transcript that we had first identified through an early coding stage, an issue that we might have at first thought to be simple becomes more complex. When I first began analysing mealtime conversations, I thought that a focus on 'food assessments' might be one small part of my PhD. Not long after the analysis on food assessments began, that 'small part' seemed to explode: suddenly I realised there were many different avenues to explore (such as how assessments are constructed, where they occur in mealtimes, who uses them, and so on). I am still researching this topic now. So this phenomenon of a topic or issue 'exploding' into many other issues – and it does feel like an explosion, in that it can derail your analytical focus temporarily and create a sense of confusion – is a good sign that your analysis is developing and you are identifying new ways of approaching the data. It does mean, however, that you may have to go back through your data and code it for some of the different, new issues that you have recently identified.

To code your data, you first need to decide what feature or aspect of the data to search for. It may be all the 'firsts' in an interaction – when someone first begins talking to someone else, or when someone enters a room, for example – and in that sense you may identify those instances through their location at particular time points in the interaction. Alternatively, you may want to focus on how a particular psychological notion (such as blame, embarrassment or deference) or a particular social action (such as flirting, criticising or seeking advice) is accomplished. Note that you will see later (in Chapter 6) that psychological notions and social actions are often difficult to separate. In such cases, they may feature at any time in your data corpus, so you will need to search thoroughly and in an organised manner.

As you search through the data, create a new file or folder in which to store those instances that you have coded. This will be a data set: a smaller, sub-set of your whole data corpus. You may want to store just the transcripts, or also include the video or audio clips that accompany these, and software can be used to help with this process through the use of synchronised transcripts (see section below). As you code each instance (or 'extract'), be sure to label it in some way, so that you know exactly where in the data corpus it was taken from. This might include some information on the date of the recording, the participants and the timestamp to indicate exactly where in the recording it is located. This process can be time-consuming, but do not skip over details; this data set may form your final analytical extracts and be used for many weeks or months ahead.

When identifying instances to include in a data set, you should be as inclusive as possible. You may come across a section of the data that you are not sure about, and there are often fine lines between what is and what is not a particular social action or psychological concept. Take flirting, for example. It is not always easy to identify what counts as 'just' a compliment or whether an eyebrow raise or smile, at just the right moment, is flirtatious or not. Always include these borderline cases. It is far easier to remove them from your data set later on than to search through the whole data corpus again. Similarly, when cutting-and-pasting that instance from your transcribed corpus into your data set file (or the section of audio/video), always include a few lines or seconds before and after what you think is the core of the instance. This is important as it helps us to preserve something of the immediate interactional context, and thus enable us to analyse that fragment appropriately.

Once you have your data set, you may well go back to the transcription stage and transcribe these selected instances – those fragments of data – in more detail, if you have not done so already. You can then begin to analyse those fragments. That is, you do not have to wait until you have Jefferson transcribed them before you begin analysing them all. Sometimes it pays to transcribe a few in detail, begin analysis on those, then you can make a decision as to whether you need to code again, change your analytical focus, or else continue with the transcription and analysis. The key here, therefore, is to take your time when working through these stages. Do not try to rush through to complete and write up the analysis. Be flexible in terms of what your analysis might focus on and what aspects of your data you will code and transcribe. This is the stage in which we really begin to see that our research may produce unexpected results, that we need to work with what is in the data, not what we expect or hope to find.

Software to aid transcription and coding

There are many different types of software tools that will help you with the transcription and coding processes. These include software that will enable you to:

- playback the audio/video recordings
- edit the recordings
- transcribe the data
- 'automatically' transcribe (voice recognition software)
- code the data

Some of these are essential, in that it would be extremely laborious (involving pens, plenty of paper and a photocopier) without them. Just as the tape-recorder sparked a whole new approach to interaction in conversation analysis so developments in technology are not only facilitating DP research, they are also changing the field. Here, then, is your quick guide to what you need.

Playback software

Your essential kit here is software that will enable you to play back your video or audio recording (you will not need this, obviously, if you have textual data). There are many free options available, but aim for one that will play back different formats and can be used on different computer operating systems. This will be essential if you are holding a data session (see Chapter 6) or presenting a video or audio clip (see Chapter 8). For video, VLC media player is a good, free all-round universal player. This has the useful option of allowing you to slow down the playback speed as well as allowing the video to 'float on top' of other documents or windows open on your screen. VLC also has some editing functions, such as saving a snapshot image of the video and creating effects to blur or distort the video images (this can help to anonymise, though you might lose crucial details, such as eye gaze direction or facial gestures). For the Mac, QuickTime also allows you to play a section of video on a loop. As noted above, this is really useful for transcribing short sections at a time. VLC can also allow you to convert your files into different formats. For example, by converting your video file into an audio-only file (such as a .wav format) you can open this file in audio software such as Audacity (free software). Audacity is a very useful tool, enabling you to listen back to the audio at different speeds, on loop-play, measure the length of pauses (by highlighting the timeline gap between waveforms, i.e., between the end of one sound and the start of the next), and create short audio clips for saving separately.

Editing software

Being able to playback your recorded data – so that you can transcribe and analyse it – is the basic requirement, but being able to edit your data will be your next step for organising and working with your data. For example, you might want to create short sections of video or audio, so that you can save these separately to compile a corpus and use for presentations or data sessions. You might also want to select a single frame or screen shot from your video to use as an image. Two versions – Apple's iMovie and Windows movie maker – that are typically part of basic software packages on computers and laptops are both user-friendly and offer many features that will do most of the things that are needed for simple video editing and exporting. For instance, they can allow you to cut out sections of the video, apply blurring or edge-detection (to create a line-drawing effect) and merge two videos together (with one inset into the other, as in Extract 5.4 or seen side by side; this is very useful if you have used two video cameras for the same recording, from different angles). You can also add subtitles to the video and separate out the audio waveform. Another very useful tech gadget is to find software that will allow you to edit photo images, for use in presentations or publications. ToyViewer, for example, is available to download for free, and can alter the photograph so that only edges remain (using the contour tools). The effect is more like a line-drawing or cartoon, which can help to anonymise the participants while preserving the facial features and embodied gestures. There are other video editing software that can be used, often designed for professionals (such as Apple's Final Cut Pro and Adobe Premiere), though these can be expensive and will require some training time.

Similarly, image editing tools such as Photoshop, Comic Life and Snagit can provide you with hours of fun in preparing still images for presentations or publications, but don't let that get in the way of your analysis. A bad analysis cannot be saved by pretty pictures.

Transcription software

The basic software that you need to transcribe are the playback software (see above) and a word document. This is transcription at its simplest, and will suffice for most and many occasions. I have transcribed this way for many years and find it suits me well. All I need is the word document open in half of my computer screen, and the audio or video playback software open in the other half (or 'floating on top' of the word document). There are other forms of software, however, that can do this and a bit more. For example, Express Scribe, Audio Notetaker or Inqscribe software enable you to incorporate audio or video files into the software, and transcribe alongside the playback. They have free and paid versions – you pay a little more for extra features, such as using a foot pedal to allow you to pause and rewind playback of the recording while still typing continuously – so that you can try out the free version to see how it works. A particularly useful option here is being able to add 'time stamps' to your transcript, so that you can pinpoint exactly where in the audio or video that part of the transcript occurs. Inqscribe also allows you to export subtitled QuickTime movies, using your transcript as the subtitles, which can then be played on any playback software. If you do decide to use transcription software, remember to check how to export your transcripts into other documents – you may not be able to add Jefferson transcription symbols within the transcript software, for instance – so that you can easily edit and transfer across different operating systems (e.g., Windows or Apple) or import into other software packages (such as MAXQDA or ATLAS.ti) without losing any transcription features or timestamps.

Voice recognition software

For some years now, the allure of voice recognition software has beckoned to those who dread the thought of many hours of transcription. As technology improves, this may be a potential time-saver for those with large data sets, although it does require investment of time and money to use its full potential. The most prominent voice recognition software at the moment is Dragon, and it works by being trained to recognise one person's voice. This means that you will not be able to simply download your video or audio files and let it transcribe. You may have to 're-voice' them first so that all the words spoken are in your voice (which you will need to train the software to recognise). It will provide a words-only transcript, but if trained correctly and using good quality headsets (for a clearly audible voice recording), it may be an option for those seeking a long-term solution.

Coding data

There are software packages that can assist the process of coding and organising your data to make it easier to find sections from your transcripts and fragments from your audio or video files. Many of these must be purchased, but there are usually reasonable discounted rates for those in education (whether students or tutors) so they can be a useful investment if you are going to be working with recorded data for more than one project. The main ones that are currently available are ATLAS.ti, MAXQDA and NVivo. As with the transcription software noted above, these can allow you to watch (or listen to) the recording alongside the transcribed file, add in timestamps and cut short sections. They do much more than this. You can add codes and labels to organise your data and identify repeating patterns or areas of transcript/recording that are related to a particular topic or aspect of interaction. Synchronising your transcript with your recording also helps not only with locating sections of data, but also with improving your analysis by ensuring that you 'stay close to' the original recording and do not rely on just the transcript. Note that none of these software packages will do the coding for you, but with a little practice they will be a very useful way of organising, searching and exporting your data.

KEY POINTS

- Transcription is a theoretical and analytical as well as a practical process.
- You do not have to transcribe all of your data if you have a large volume of data.
- Focus on writing down the words only, then build up by adding phonetic/intonation details, then visual details.
- You can begin to code your data before you transcribe to Jefferson level.
- Coding involves searching and sorting your data for instances of particular features; it provides a way of selecting out sections of data for close analysis.
- Coding can occur multiple times in the transcription and analysis processes.
- Many software packages are freely downloadable and can assist you in the transcription and coding stages of analysis.

Recommended reading

Paulus, T. M., Lester, J. N. & Dempster, P. G. (2014). *Digital tools for qualitative research*. London: Sage.

Rapley, T. (2007). *Doing conversation, discourse and document analysis*. London: Sage. Particularly Chapter 5.

6

ANALYSING DATA USING DP

Chapter contents

Doing discursive psychology: stages of analysis	114
Advanced DP analyses	133
Validating the analysis (aka 'how do I know when I'm doing it right?')	135
Analytic pitfalls to avoid	139
Holding a data session	142

Here you are, with lots of words to analyse, and possibly not quite sure where to start. Facing a detailed transcript and being expected to analyse it can be a daunting and overwhelming place to be. When you first look at your transcript, you might at times wonder if there is *anything* to analyse in your data or, conversely, whether there is *too much* to analyse. In this chapter, we will break down the analytical process into manageable chunks and provide scaffolding to help you gain confidence and competence as a DP analyst. DP provides a way of analysing what might appear to be an overwhelming mass of words on a page: it provides a lens through which these words appear organised and coherent. So we are going to work through the process of using that lens and help you to make sense of the words (your data) in front of you. The aim of this chapter is therefore to demystify the process of analysis. It will first lead you through the stages of analysis, with a summary table of the discursive devices (see Chapter 7 for further discussion of these). It will help you to get started and, even more importantly perhaps, how to stop. The chapter will also discuss more advanced analytical issues, and ways in which you can ensure you are producing a 'good' DP analysis. Finally, there are suggestions for holding a data session with other researchers, to help you see how you can develop your analysis through group discussion and interaction.

In many ways, each stage of your research is part of the process of analysis, since we make decisions about what features of interaction to record, the process of transcription, which sections to code, and how to select your extracts for close analysis. So this is really the part where the analysis becomes very detailed and concrete, and in many ways this is the part of the book that most clearly distinguishes DP from other forms of discourse analysis (see also Chapter 2). As with many analytical approaches, DP does not have a clearly defined, universal, step-by-step approach. There is no recipe to be followed. It has been likened to a skill such as riding a bike (Potter & Wetherell, 1987): a theoretical framework rather than an analytic method. That said, when starting out in analysis it can be useful to have a supporting structure to help guide us along.

Doing discursive psychology: stages of analysis

It will be helpful if you have your own data extract in front of you, with video and/or audio files where available, as you work through this chapter. This will allow you to practise each stage of analysis as you go along, pausing and taking a break when you need to, and spending time becoming familiar with each task. You may have been developing your own research project and worked through the previous chapters, in which case your research question will help to guide you as you work through the analysis. You might, however, have been given a data extract to analyse for an assignment or class activity, in which case you may not have been involved in collecting or transcribing the data, and you may not even have been given a research question. In that case, you might have no idea of where (and how) to get started. Either way, it doesn't matter if at first your focus is quite broad, or if you find yourself getting distracted by different issues. You should just concentrate on getting started, slowly but surely, and don't rush to get to the end. You should also familiarise yourself with the theoretical principles of DP (see Chapter 1) to ensure that you adopt an appropriate social constructionist stance on discourse. For those of you who don't yet have any data to work through, see Box 4.1 (Chapter 4) to find some data to practise on, or use the 'steak and fish' data extract referred to in Chapters 2 and 5.

The following stages of analysis will take you through the process of DP analysis, but they come with a caveat: doing DP is not a simple step-by-step linear process. It can involve moving backward and forward through different stages (see Figure 6.1 below for an overview of the DP analytical stages). The stages are provided as scaffolding, to get you started on analysis, until you build in confidence and competence. While you might need to follow these stages meticulously at first, you should find that as you become more skilled in analysing data, the process becomes more fluid and iterative. Around stage 3, you might also need to familiarise yourself with the DP devices before you apply these to your own data (see Chapter 7).

We will work through the data extract that we first saw in Chapter 2 (the 'steak and fish' example) to illustrate how the analysis should be carried out at each stage. This has been transcribed to include paralinguistic details about pausing, speed of talk, overlapping speech and emphases on specific words. The extract was also chosen from a longer section of mealtime interaction as a starting point for analysis, given that it includes people talking about likes and dislikes of food and detailed descriptions of foods they are eating. This is characteristic of how DP works with data: we focus first on one extract, one single short piece of interaction, and examine this in detail. Only when we find something – a psychological concept, for instance – that is being invoked or orientated to, and have a

ANALYSING DATA USING DP

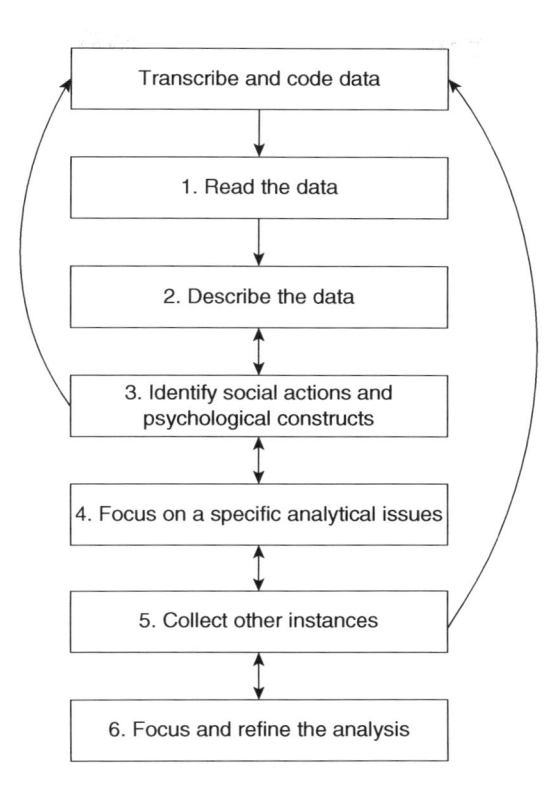

```
        ┌─────────────────────────────┐
    ┌──▶│   Transcribe and code data  │◀──┐
    │   └──────────────┬──────────────┘   │
    │                  ▼                  │
    │   ┌─────────────────────────────┐   │
    │   │       1. Read the data      │   │
    │   └──────────────┬──────────────┘   │
    │                  ▼                  │
    │   ┌─────────────────────────────┐   │
    │   │     2. Describe the data    │   │
    │   └──────────────┬──────────────┘   │
    │                  ▼                  │
    │   ┌─────────────────────────────┐   │
    │   │ 3. Identify social actions and│ │
    │   │   psychological constructs  │   │
    │   └──────────────┬──────────────┘   │
    │                  ▼                  │
    │   ┌─────────────────────────────┐   │
    │   │4. Focus on a specific analytical issues│
    │   └──────────────┬──────────────┘   │
    │                  ▼                  │
    │   ┌─────────────────────────────┐   │
    │   │    5. Collect other instances │──┘
    │   └──────────────┬──────────────┘
    │                  ▼
    │   ┌─────────────────────────────┐
    │   │  6. Focus and refine the analysis │
    │   └─────────────────────────────┘
```

Figure 6.1

sense of how this is involved in a particular social action, do we then move to find other examples in our data corpus. In this way, our research is inductive (also termed bottom-up or data-driven) and rigorous, staying close to the issues that are arising in the data and grounding our analyses in specific examples.

Extract 6.1: The data excerpt: 'steak and fish'

```
1.  Bob:     mine's is >qui- a lot of<
2.           (1.0)
3.  Bob:     I don't like steak.
4.           (0.4)
5.  Lesley:  no: [don't do either
6.  Bob:         [.pt >doesna< (.) doesna fire >ma
7.           rockets it just disnae<
8.  Lesley:  I like fish::=we >never have enough<
9.           fish:
10. Bob:     w- we:ll. See that fish you bu::y, (0.4)
11.          <don't buy that> see that thing that
12.          gets like- (.) incarcerated in some
13.          kin'a-
14.          (0.8)
15. Bob:     <chemically:> (0.2) compound (.) >thing<
16. Edith:   mm
17.          (0.2)
18. Bob:     THA- (.) you get it like- >it doesn't
19.          look like a fish< that thing we had the
20.          other night
```

When you start to analyse data, it is important to analyse a small amount at first. Doing too much at once can be overwhelming and could lead to a limited analysis. About one side of paper is sufficient to get started, and there should be enough detail in this (particularly if we've coded an extract that overlaps with our research question or area of focus, see Chapter 5) to be able to get started. You can use up to around three or four sides of paper if you are working with others – see the section on 'holding a data session' – because you will be able to cover more ground when working collaboratively. Note that the extract shown above is very short, but it should be sufficient to illustrate the stages of analysis for the purposes of this chapter. It can also give you a sense of how detailed psychological business can be accomplished in just a few seconds of talk. You will also note that Extract 6.1 includes words and features of intonation (i.e., paralinguistic details), but no extralinguistic detail (such as eye gaze, facial or bodily gestures). We can add these in later as and when we need to; what is important here is that when analysing the data we refer not only to the transcript, but also to the original recording.

Stage 1: Read the data

This stage might seem very obvious, for we need to have watched, listened to or read through our data to have been able to transcribe it. It might also seem so simple that you might not even think of it as an analytical stage. Do not be fooled, however, as the first stage of reading through the data can often help you to notice things that you had not seen when transcribing or coding the extract. Just as the process of transcription can slow down the pace at which you listen to the audio (or video) file, so a careful reading of the data should slow down the pace at which you consider each line of text, and the words within these. Remember that 'data' refers here to both the original video and/or audio recordings of the discourse as well as the transcribed extract. When you are working with textual data, you will have only the text and no audio or video.

When you have video or audio data, then, you should first watch and/or listen to this a few times before you move to your transcript (so if you are working with textual data, you can skip to the next paragraph). Remember to focus, at this point, only on that part of the recording that matches the transcript that is front of you. This might be less than a minute, or just a couple of minutes' worth of interaction. Play through the data at a slower speed if possible (see the section on software for transcription, in Chapter 5, for how to do this), to avoid you skimming through it too quickly. As you watch the video, pay attention to visual aspects – where the speakers are, who is looking at whom, whether there are any hand gestures or body movements, and so on – as well as verbal aspects. For example, consider how words are said and where the talk occurs in relation to gestures or body movements. This will help you to familiarise yourself with the interaction as it happened, and playing this over and over can sometimes make features of the interaction stand out more clearly. For instance, if we are used to hearing particular words or phrases we might not notice them as being particularly unusual. It is only when we focus on them *as they are said as part of interaction* that we can begin to question their taken-for-granted status.

Once you have become more familiar with the video/audio data, you can then move to your transcribed data. Read through your extract at least two or three times to gain a sense of the sequential nature of the discourse; what comes first and what happens next. Take your time to become familiar with the transcription symbols and how these relate to the way in which the words were spoken. This is where it really pays off to have done at least some of the transcription yourself, as then you will already have a close familiarity with your data and the transcription symbols. If you have textual data, you may not have features of intonation, but there may be peculiarities in the way in which words are written (such as the use of capitals, ellipses, emoticons, and so on). This might also give you time to notice any patterns or repetitions (for instance, the slight mirroring of 'I don't like', line 3, and 'I like', line 8, in Extract 6.1) or phrases that appear to stand out (such as 'disnae fire my rockets' or 'incarcerated' in Extract 6.1). You do not need to write anything on the transcript at this point, focus instead on becoming familiar with the *content* and *organisation* of the data: what is said, and in what order.

This first stage, ironically, is often the point at which novice DP researchers can panic, if they think that nothing appears to be of interest in the extract they've chosen, or if they think they have found something and then rush to identify a 'theme'. So the first lesson is: don't panic. There is *almost always* something to analyse in your data, even if the extract you start with may not be the ideal choice. The second lesson is: don't rush to find a theme. This stage is about becoming familiar with your data and getting used to using the DP lens. Unlike many qualitative approaches, DP (and other forms of discourse analysis) focuses more on issues or social practices rather than themes.

Stage 2: Describe the data

Once you have become more familiar with your extract, you can then begin to make initial notes on the transcript. The aim of this stage is to focus your attention on describing, in detail, what is going on in the interaction; to begin to use the DP lens to focus on how discourse is constructed/ive and how it is situated (the first two principles of DP; see Chapter 1). We cannot do this effectively just by listening to or watching the data; seeing the transcript typed out on the page is essential for examining the turn-by-turn detail of interaction. This is why the first step of reading of the transcript is important. It allows us to examine exactly what was said, how it was said, and when it was said: so your aim is to focus on the *what*, *how* and *when* of different parts of the interaction. This helps us to avoid making assumptions about the data. By describing it in detail, we focus on what is actually going on rather than what we assume is going on. A common mistake when first analysing discourse is to move too quickly to make interpretations or analyses of the data (see also the 'pitfalls' sub-section of this chapter). Whether through habit (we might try to work out what our friends 'mean' when we talk to them) or through an urge to do the analysis quickly, it can at first seem obvious about what is going on in the talk. This usually leads to weak analyses or analyses that are not consistent with a DP approach, so take it one step at a time, and you'll save time in the long run. As you become more familiar with DP analysis, you will find that stages 1, 2 and 3 merge together, and that you will start to make notes as you are reading and will be quicker at identifying social actions. Getting started, however, it can be helpful to separate out these stages to ensure that you work through carefully and rigorously.

In this second stage, then, we move from reading the transcript to making our first notes about the data. This is part of the process of examining the interaction in terms of social actions (which will be stage 3), but before we can identify 'social actions' we first need to be clear about what exactly is going on in the interaction. When making initial notes on the transcript, it can be helpful to start working through the transcript line by line, in sequential order, to help us to get started and ensure that we do not miss out any aspects of the data. Sooner or later, however, we will start to look backwards and forwards through the text in a more fluid manner. As we noted in Chapter 1, one of the core principles of DP is that it treats talk as situated sequentially and within a particular interactional and rhetorical context. In order to interpret one turn in talk, then, we also need to examine what *comes before* and what *comes after* the turn in talk that we're focusing on. This is what is referred to as 'indexicality', when the interpretation of a word or phrase is dependent on the context of its production; in this case, what occurs immediately before and immediately after that section of discourse. This is why DP needs to examine interactions within the context in which they were produced (whether this is a family meal, an online discussion forum or a telephone helpline).

For this stage, you need to focus on describing in detail what is going on in the interaction. As you work through each line of the transcript, make notes about the talk or text in terms of:

- **What** was said/written: focus on the type of word or phrase that was used, for example, in terms of word form (is it an adjective or noun?) and cultural context (is it a culturally-specific word or slang phrase?). How does it draw on specific categories of people or objects? This helps us to focus on the *content* of the discourse and on *what* is being *constructed*.

- **How** it was said/written: is there anything about its prosody or delivery (e.g., rising intonation, stretched-out talk, loud or whispered talk, 'smiley' voice)? Does it overlap with other talk or actions? What else is going on in the interaction? Is there any laughter, crying or other displays of affect (note that we do not refer to these as emotions, as that would imply a known internal state)? This focuses us on the *style or structure* of the discourse, on *how* the talk is constructed.

- **When** it was said/written: look at where the word or phrase is positioned within the speaker's turn at talk (i.e., at the beginning of their turn, or following another specific phrase), and within the surrounding interactional context (i.e., the preceding and the following turns). This focuses us on the *organisation* and *situatedness* of the discourse.

You might find it more comfortable to work through the data on paper, with written notes on the transcript itself and in the margins. This is why we use wide margins and double-spaced transcripts, to leave room for analytical notes. Or you might prefer to work in an electronic word document, using the comment function to add notes. Either way, don't worry at this stage about whether you need to interpret something or make any 'meaningful' notes. You do not need to write something for every line of talk, and you may need to go through the extract a few times to gain some practice. The most important thing here is that you are starting to 'do noticing', that is, to slow down the pace at which you look at interaction, focus on the details and begin to describe the talk clearly. In doing so, you should focus on **what is said** and **what happens** in the discourse. Do not try to identify why someone said something, or what they might be thinking or feeling. If you find yourself making interpretations that infer cognitive or emotive states, then stop to question what it is about the discourse that triggered that interpretation. Sometimes interpretations like these can alert us to important aspects of the interaction, so we can use them to our advantage, not be concerned that we aren't 'doing it right'. Remember too that most notes that you make on your data will not necessarily end up in your final written analysis, but they are an essential stage in the analytic process and can help you to develop ideas about the data.

Figure 6.2 is the 'steak and fish' excerpt with my initial notes on it, to give an example of what this note making might look like.

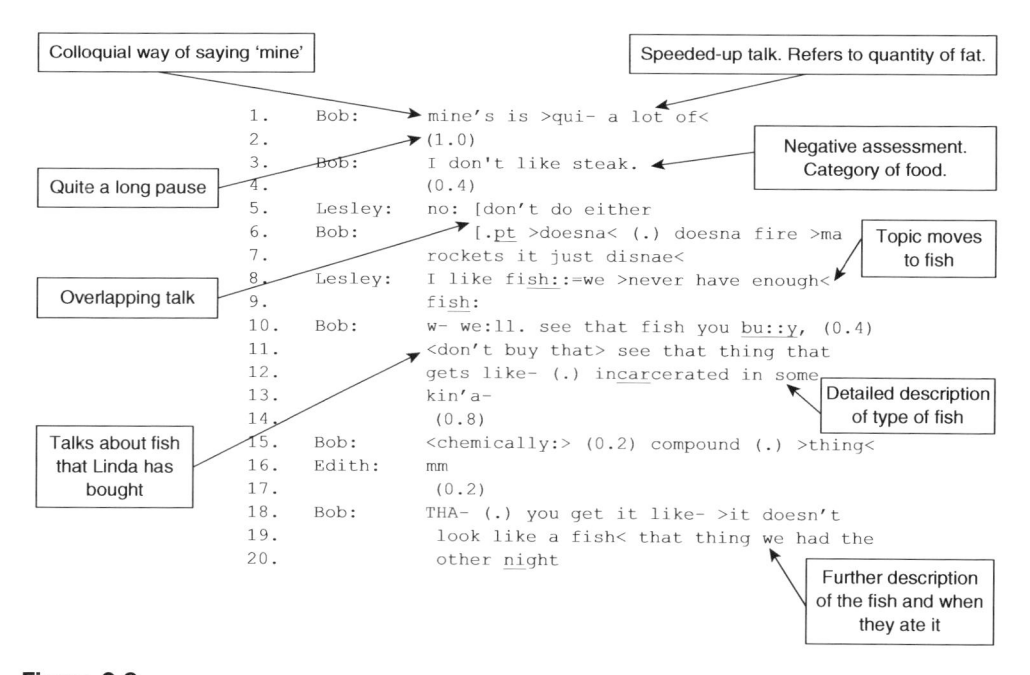

```
 1.    Bob:      mine's is >qui- a lot of<
 2.              (1.0)
 3.    Bob:      I don't like steak.
 4.              (0.4)
 5.    Lesley:   no: [don't do either
 6.    Bob:         [.pt >doesna< (.) doesna fire >ma
 7.              rockets it just disnae<
 8.    Lesley:   I like fish::=we >never have enough<
 9.              fish:
10.    Bob:      w- we:ll. see that fish you bu::y, (0.4)
11.              <don't buy that> see that thing that
12.              gets like- (.) incarcerated in some
13.              kin'a-
14.              (0.8)
15.    Bob:      <chemically:> (0.2) compound (.) >thing<
16.    Edith:    mm
17.              (0.2)
18.    Bob:      THA- (.) you get it like- >it doesn't
19.              look like a fish< that thing we had the
20.              other night
```

Annotations:
- Colloquial way of saying 'mine' (line 1)
- Speeded-up talk. Refers to quantity of fat. (line 1)
- Negative assessment. Category of food. (line 3)
- Quite a long pause (line 4)
- Overlapping talk (lines 5–6)
- Topic moves to fish (lines 6–8)
- Talks about fish that Linda has bought (line 14)
- Detailed description of type of fish (lines 12–13)
- Further description of the fish and when they ate it (lines 18–20)

Figure 6.2

We can then continue through the transcript in this way, line by line, and as we do so we can begin to gain a sense of the social actions that may be unfolding in the interaction.

Our aim in the second stage, then, was to break down the interaction into small chunks, to start to see how discourse is put together, like an engineer taking apart a piece of machinery to understand the component parts. It is in the next stage of analysis that we will use the discursive devices to help us identify what actions are being accomplished.

> ### Box 6.1: Activity: Familiarising yourself with the discursive devices
>
> Before you begin stage 3 of the analysis, you might want to work through Chapter 7 to familiarise yourself with the discursive devices (sometimes referred to as the DP devices). The devices themselves are like a set of tools that are used to examine particular features of discourse, and like many tools, they require some practice to become comfortable with how and when they should be used, and to become sensitised to their flexibility and complexities. Just as with learning other skills, the more time you spend practising, the more competent you will become. So do not be put off if it seems strange or awkward at first. This is a natural process of working with something new. If you have not already done so, go to Chapter 7 for a full set of descriptions and worked examples for each of the devices, separated into basic, intermediate and advanced sections.

Stage 3: Identify social actions and psychological constructs

The third stage of analysis is the one that most distinguishes this process as DP analysis, by focusing explicitly on the interplay between social actions and psychological constructs. It is therefore probably the most important stage and the one that requires the most care and effort. We will zoom in on small sections of the data at a time, just two or three lines for example, and work closely with these. We will continue to use the first two principles of DP – how discourse is constructed/ive and how it is situated – and in this stage we will also add in the third principle: how discourse is action-orientated. This stage of analysis, then, is the process of explicating social actions: of showing what actions are accomplished through discursive practices, how they are accomplished, and how psychological business is managed in the process of doing these actions.

So what is a social action?

Social actions are the kinds of things that we do in talk and interaction all the time: make requests, ask questions, flirt, discuss the weather, complain, praise someone, make promises, and so on. We are never 'just talking'; there is always something else going on. Sometimes these social actions are referred to as the 'functions' of talk, though the term function suggests something a bit more rigid and formulaic (as if by using word X then function Y will be the resulting outcome). By using the term *social action* instead, the emphasis is on the combination of discourse and the interactional context (including who is speaking and how things are spoken) and the subtle ways in which actions are enacted across a number of turns in talk. In other words, it is not just that a single word can have a particular function, but that sequences of words and phrases, used when people are interacting with each other, together combine to perform a social action. In other words, the social action is the outcome of interaction.

One of the skills you will learn in doing DP, then, is to be able to recognise the kinds of actions that frame our talk and social interactions. What you will see is that social actions are produced through the subtle and intricate ways in which we talk and interact with other people. For example, just saying 'I do' or 'I will' does not make a marriage; these words must be said in the right context, with the appropriate people, and following a particular script. As such, it is not possible to identify the actions in advance of the analysis. We cannot simply point to the transcript and say, 'look, here's a complaint'. The words on their own are not actions: they *become actions* through being used in a particular context. While we might have an intuitive sense that someone might be trying to persuade us, or flatter us, or blame other people, we need a rigorous analytical approach to help 'unpack' the actions in talk and to examine how psychological matters are being invoked as part of these actions. If we break this process down a little, to examine talk in terms of its component parts, then we can start to identify the actions that are being performed and how these are put together. Examining the discourse in terms of 'social actions' can take a bit of practice; it requires a different approach to talk than we are probably used to and being an expert at talking doesn't make us immediate experts in analysing talk. So we need to analyse the interaction using participants' orientations – to examine how they make sense of each other in talk – not our categories as analysts. For this reason, then, identifying social actions is our goal, not our starting point.

In order to help us to analyse discourse in this way, DP makes use of what have been referred to as 'discursive devices'. These are features of discourse, ways of talking and writing, that are recognisable and recurrent across different interactional contexts, and which help to perform social actions. These devices are the tools of DP, as it were, to enable us to examine the discourse *as discourse*. They shine a spotlight on particular parts of discourse and are particularly useful in terms of examining social actions and psychological concepts. For example, a footing shift can mark the change in speaking *as an individual* to speaking *on behalf of oneself and an/other person/people*. Sometimes this can be achieved through using a different pronoun. I have done this a few times in this book, for instance, when I move between talking about what 'we' will do in a chapter, to 'your' data, and also to personal accounts of what 'I' have found to be useful. The point with discursive devices, then, is that they can help us to use the DP lens, to make the shift from describing our data in everyday language, to analysing it using the DP framework. Since the initial development of DP in the late 1980s and early 1990s, researchers have been slowly adding to the list of devices (see Table 6.1), and so there is every chance that

Table 6.1 Discursive devices

Device name	Description and example function	Examples in talk (bold indicates target feature)
Basic		
Pronoun use & footing shifts	Using different pronouns (I, we, you, us, one) can highlight the relationship between the speaker and the account they are providing. Footing shifts refer to the way in which we might speak as the author, animator or principal of the discourse.	I was like, **you** know when **you're** dead upset.
Assessments/ second assessments	Assessments (evaluations) in interaction are often followed by second assessments; these are typically upgraded if they agree with the first assessment. There is a 'preference structure' for assessments.	This is **nice.** Yeah, its **lovely** isn't it.
Silences, pauses and hesitations	Silences/pauses can indicate trouble in interaction; if there are too many pauses or too long a gap between speakers.	**(1.2)** vs **(0.2)** pauses
Hedging	Hedging talk often precedes a dispreferred second assessment (i.e., a second assessment that disrupts conversational norms); it can also be seen in accounts, and can function to highlight the delicacy of an issue.	**.hh (.) em (.) and I- (0.2)** I'd just moved into...
Extreme Case Formulations (ECFs)	A phrase or word that is semantically extreme; i.e., invoking the maximal or minimal properties of an object, person or event. Can be used to justify or strengthen an argument, add credibility and manage one's identity.	The **best friend I ever had.**
Minimisation	Treats the object or account as minimal, often using the terms 'just', 'only', 'little', 'bit'. Can be used to downplay the significance or importance of something.	It's **just** a little something.
Lists and contrasts	Listing is a regular feature of interaction, and three-part lists add a particular rhetorical strength to an argument. They are often used in political speeches for this reason. Contrasts can be setting up an either/or state of affairs, or contrasting the speaker's intentions/desires with an alternative 'reality'. In both cases, they can be used to manage accountability and identities.	They hadn't bothered coming, or they'd stayed for another drink, or whatever they've done. I'd love to be able to do that, **but** I just can't.

(Continued)

Table 6.1 (Continued)

Device name	Description and example function	Examples in talk (bold indicates target feature)
Intermediate		
Affect displays	Displaying affect (i.e., an emotive or physical state) in interaction is often organised within the unfolding interaction, e.g., immediately preceding or following a particular action in the interaction.	When there is audible sighing, crying or moaning.
Consensus and corroboration	These are accounts that suggest that many people or everyone agrees with what you are saying (consensus) or that someone else provides an independent witness (corroboration). Both of these are key ways in which people can attend to the factuality of what they are saying, and reduce any sense of their own investment in the account.	**Everyone** who ate it said they liked the cake.... **He told me** 'that was the best cake I've ever tasted'.
Detail vs. vagueness	Giving specific details of an event or person vs being vague or unclear can manage investment ('stake') in the account and thus the speaker's entitlement to tell the account or to be asked questions about it. It can also be used to suggest particular observational skills on the part of the speaker (i.e., their identity as being accurate and observant).	It was quarter to ten last Thursday vs one evening last week.
Disclaimers	These are inserted statements before the main account to try to mitigate the speaker's stance on a particular issue. They make visible a particular interpretation of what they are going to say, then explicitly deny this. These often work alongside category membership-type issues (i.e., when a speaker's identity is being explicitly addressed)	**I'm not sexist but**... **I've nothing against X but**...
Metaphor	Metaphors can be subtle or more striking, and they can frame an account in a particular way, opening up issues of agency and blame, as well as speaker categories and footing.	**It was** a scene from a horror movie.
Narrative structure	Presenting an account in a sequential order and within a particular temporal structure; often highlights things that need to be known first. The plausibility of an account can also be increased by embedding the account in a narrative sequence.	By 9 o'clock I'd had enough and went home.
Reported speech (aka active voicing)	Where speakers report the words or thoughts of others as if they were directly spoken; adds authenticity to an account.	I said, **'oh do you know what,'**
Script formulations	This is where an account appears as if it is a regular or frequent occurrence (as if scripted, or following a script); can present the account as normal and expected.	She's **always there**, she'll help you out.

Device name	Description and example function	Examples in talk (bold indicates target feature)
Advanced		
Agent-subject distinction	Speakers often make relevant their agency within a particular course of events; i.e., how they are positioned as active or passive, and their associated responsibility or accountability for these events. This is also related to what Edwards and Potter (1992) refer to as 'empiricist reporting', where academic articles are written in the third person to remove any sense of researcher agency or subjectivity.	**I went** with them vs they made me go with them. **Data from** fifty participants was collected using an online questionnaire.
Emotion categories	Speakers often make reference to their own or other people's emotional states. In discursive research these are analysed in terms of their interactional function, as a discursive accomplishment rather than as indicating an underlying emotional state.	That was like, quite **upsetting**…. She was so **angry** with me.
Category entitlements	Using a category to refer to a person or category-bound activity (e.g., age, gender, job/career, family position); inferences can be made from either categories of persons or activities and who might or might not be expected to engage in such activities.	**My daughter**…. I thought **she was older than 60**. You'd expect **the builder** to come on time, wouldn't you?
Modal verbs	Modal verbs are those that infer obligations, abilities or likelihood of something; as such, they can be used to manage responsibility or accountability for one's own or other people's actions.	You **shouldn't** have to worry about that.
Stake inoculation	Similar to category entitlements, this is where speakers construct their talk to defend against the claim that they might have a stake in what they are saying (i.e., that they might be biased or subjective).	I **wouldn't usually be fooled** by such schemes, but this one was really believable.

new researchers might identify new devices that can be used in subsequent research. You never know, it could be you.

For now, though, let us look at the most common devices used in DP research. These have been broadly separated into three groupings in Table 6.1: basic, intermediate and advanced. The reason for separating them is that many new researchers to DP can be overwhelmed by the list of devices at first, and can have trouble knowing where to start. We will start, therefore, with the basic devices. These are the ones that are a fairly regular occurrence in everyday talk and interaction, and therefore most likely to be the ones to identify first in your data. The intermediate ones are less common but should be straightforward to identify when they are present. The advanced devices are a mixture of features of discourse but most of them require more experience of DP to be able to analyse data using them effectively. Think of these as your power tools, to be used once you've become more comfortable with the way of doing DP and when you're ready for something that requires more skill, but which can also give you extra analytical insight.

Now, the trick with using the devices is to examine them while also paying attention to the constructed and situatedness of the discourse. Consider how and where they feature in the data, as much as you note *which* devices are being used. So we are not just 'spotting' the devices (see 'pitfalls' sub-section), but instead are using them as a means to interpret and analyse the data and provide an explanation of what is going on. As with stage 2, you can work on your data transcript on paper or electronically. Rather than working through line by line as we did in stages 1 and 2, however, focus on a few lines at a time. This will enable you to examine how different devices enable specific social actions to be accomplished, and to work across the interaction as a whole. You won't need to use all of the devices and, as noted above, it may help to focus on the basic devices first. What you can do, then, is to identify any of the devices that appear to be prevalent in the section of data that you are focusing on. Your annotated transcript may then look something like Figure 6.3.

The first thing we might notice in the extract in Figure 6.3 is the three assessments (lines 3, 5 and 8). If we consider how these assessments are formed (in the form of 'I like X' or 'I don't like X'), they are subjective assessments; that is, they construct the assessment in terms of a personal reaction rather than attributable to the food (e.g., 'I don't like steak' rather than 'the steak is horrible'), because of the use of a personal pronoun ('I'). All three assessments also refer to a category of food rather than a particular item: 'steak' or 'fish' rather than 'this steak' or 'that fish'. It is worth noting that immediately prior to this extract, Lesley had been commenting on how much fat was on each of their pieces of meat, and this may be what Bob is referring to on line 1 (i.e., 'quite a lot of'... fat). The one-second pause on line 2 also suggests trouble, because it is a reasonably long pause (anything over one second long is quite a long time in everyday conversation). As Bob appears to stop mid-sentence, in that he doesn't quite finish what he was saying (line 1), the pause works to 'hold' his turn. So Bob's negative, subject-side assessment, category-focused assessment ('I don't like steak') is then situated

ANALYSING DATA USING DP

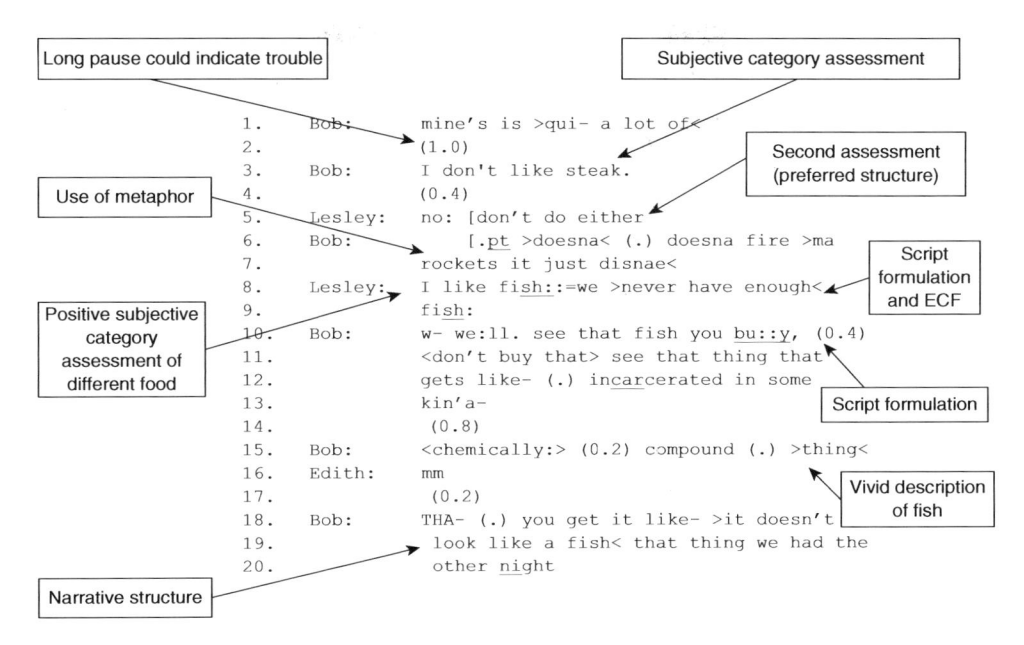

Figure 6.3

```
1.   Bob:     mine's is >qui- a lot of<
2.            (1.0)
3.   Bob:     I don't like steak.
4.            (0.4)
5.   Lesley:  no: [don't do either
6.   Bob:        [.pt >doesna< (.) doesna fire >ma
7.            rockets it just disnae<
8.   Lesley:  I like fish::=we >never have enough<
9.            fish:
10.  Bob:     w- we:ll. see that fish you bu::y, (0.4)
11.           <don't buy that> see that thing that
12.           gets like- (.) incarcerated in some
13.           kin'a-
14.           (0.8)
15.  Bob:     <chemically:> (0.2) compound (.) >thing<
16.  Edith:   mm
17.           (0.2)
18.  Bob:     THA- (.) you get it like- >it doesn't
19.           look like a fish< that thing we had the
20.           other night
```

Annotations: Long pause could indicate trouble; Subjective category assessment; Second assessment (preferred structure); Use of metaphor; Script formulation and ECF; Positive subjective category assessment of different food; Script formulation; Vivid description of fish; Narrative structure.

following this trouble-marked pause. One of the issues that we might investigate further is whether the social action being accomplished by this assessment is a *complaint* or simply a *report of an internal state*. These two actions can actually be combined, and so this is an early interpretation about what might be going on here. We do not have to come to any conclusions at this stage; what we are doing here is identifying possible social actions and the construction of psychological states. At this point, a possible social action could be a complaint and the psychological state seems to be food preferences.

If we look further at the extract, we can also note that Lesley provides an assessment on line 5 (in the form of 'don't do either'), so this works as a second assessment in that it follows soon after an initial assessment by another speaker. It agrees with the first assessment so it is produced without an extensive delay and is unmarked by any hedging or accounting for the assessment (which we might expect if it disagreed; see Pomerantz, 1984). While Lesley utters this, Bob then adds elaboration to his assessment (lines 6–7), and because of the overlapping speech early in Lesley's turn, we could argue that Bob is not responding to Lesley's turn but simply continuing his own. Staying with the focus on Lesley's turns, she then introduces another assessment ('I like fish', line 8) followed immediately by a claim that 'we never have enough fish'. This is an extreme case formulation (ECF, see Box 6.2) because it suggests that no amount of fish would ever be enough. Produced together, these are an interesting turn in talk. They make relevant a different food preference from the one previously discussed (i.e., fish rather than steak) and, as such, shift the focus from what the family are eating at the present time to what they might eat (in either the past or the future). By prefacing the ECF with an assessment, however, Lesley invokes and makes relevant her claimed food preferences for the purposes of talking about the family's food habits. In doing so, a psychological state (in this case, what someone 'likes' or doesn't like to eat) is used to perform a social action: a potential complaint that the family's eating pattern does not match her own food preferences.

These are early, tentative interpretations about the data. What they do, however, is to illustrate how we can use the discursive devices (here, we used assessments, pauses, and an extreme case formulation) to help develop our interpretation and understanding of the data.

We would then continue to work through our data in this way, bit by bit, and make notes about what kinds of social actions are being performed and which psychological states are being invoked, managed or negotiated within the interaction. You should aim to work through a reasonable amount of your data in this manner. There are no fixed guidelines about how much of your data set you should use at this stage, but you need to cover enough to generate a number of possible analytical issues. This could be, for example, around a quarter or a half of your data set. The aim of this third stage is to identify possible analytical issues to focus on – selecting one and finding examples of that in the whole data set in the next stage – so repeat this process of examining a small section of data until you have found a number of possible areas. For example, in the mealtime clip above, I identified a possible complaint about food, and also the use of food assessments, framed as individual food preferences. So these might be two areas (both of which deal with psychological issues: responsibility for food choice in the family and preference for particular foods) that could be developed into the focus of our analysis for this data set.

Box 6.2: The joy of ECF

The extreme case formulation (ECF) device is often incorrectly and over-used by new researchers to DP, primarily because it can appear to be quite obvious and common across numerous data sources. So this is a quick how-to guide on ECFs to help you use them with academic precision rather than wanton abandonment.

To summarise: ECFs are semantically extreme words (nouns, adjectives, adverbs) or phrases. They can be used for a number of social actions: to defend a claim, to support 'object-side' ('out-there-ness') accounts (i.e., attending to factuality), or when accounting for a behaviour. They can be used to normalise one person's behaviour and pathologise another's. They were first noted by Sacks (1992: lecture 3, fall 1964), with key analyses also provided by Pomerantz (1986) and then by Edwards (2000; see also

> Whitehead, 2015). An ECF is similar to hyperbole in linguistics, but distinguishable in terms of the way in which they work in an interactional context (Norrick, 2004). That is, ECFs only *become* ECFs through indexicality (see Chapter 1) in that they are *hearably* extreme; that is, they are typically orientated to *as* non-literal descriptions, as going to extremes. They are, however, what Edwards (2000: 352) terms 'factually brittle'. It would be easy to challenge and undermine them with a single exception to the extreme case they imply and yet they still maintain their rhetorical power *even when* they are challenged and are subsequently softened to a less extreme version.
>
> An ECF is *not*, however, an assessment such as 'very good', 'excellent' or 'awesome'. These are positive assessments but *on their own* do not mark the target item as special in any way. Like any DP device, the ECF should not be treated as a 'thing' that can be easily defined and then spotted in your data. They are ultimately a participants' resource, something that is used to perform particular psychological business, such as defending a claim or showing investment in an account of events. When checking whether or not something is an ECF, then, you need to: (1) consider whether it is an end-of-the-line, semantically extreme version of events, and (2) examine how it features in the interaction: what social action is it accomplishing? How does it manage a speaker's investment in their account? How is it responded to in the subsequent interactional turns?

I noted earlier that the third stage of analysis should not be rushed. You will need to go through various sections of your coded data corpus working through the analysis in this way, examining social actions and psychological business. Sometimes this can be helped with time away from your transcript doing another research task, such as reading or transcription, so that you move from one research process to another in an iterative manner and allow each part of the research to inform the other parts. Reading other published reports of DP empirical research can also help to shed light on your data, even if the topic area or data set used is very different from your own. I also find that reflecting on the data (and often, just one small phrase or section of the interaction, and 'playing' that over in my thoughts) while I am engaged in other things can often bring new insights. Sometimes this happens when I'm travelling or engaged in a completely different activity, such as walking the dog. It can also happen when I'm talking to other people or listening to other people's conversations on the train (yes, eavesdropping). The point is that analysing data isn't just about time spent looking at your transcript. Since DP is all about understanding the discursive practices that make our individual lives relevant to social practices, then immersing ourselves in social settings can help us to stay grounded in the practical relevance of our data. You can find comfort, therefore, in knowing that you can still analyse when you are socialising and doing all the things you usually would do; just don't forget to return to your data!

Stage 4: Focus on a specific analytical issue

By the time you reach the fourth stage of analysis, you will have read and worked through your data extract many times. Even in just a short section of interaction (say, 30 seconds for audio or video data, or a few lines of interaction in an online forum), you may be surprised at how many social actions are being performed, and how psychological business is relevant for topics that on first appearance might seem quite commonsensical or trivial. Once you have worked through some possible interpretations of social actions and psychological concepts in your data, you then need to develop a structure from your initial notes. This is the stage of moving from notes on your transcript to a focus on a specific analytical issue, the one which might then turn into the focus of your report or research paper. Remember that this is an iterative process and that we might follow up one issue only to find that it develops into another issue and we follow through a different part of our data. It is around this stage (and the next one) that I find things can start to get explosive: we may think we're focusing on one issue (such as 'food assessments in mealtime talk') that at first seemed quite specific and narrow, only to find it explodes into multiple issues (such as 'subjective versus objective assessments', 'food preference talk', 'assessments as part of food offers', and so on). Each of these issues might also be refined further: how children rather than parents use food preference talk, for example. What we had thought, at first, to be a simple topic suddenly becomes much more detailed and intricate. This is one of the reasons why our research question can change when we're using DP, and in the first stages of our research, you might find that your research question is a guide rather than a rigid focus. It is also one of the reasons why DP research can be so interesting and exciting to take part in; you never know where you might end up.

The best way to manage this stage of analysis is to write down all the emerging analytical issues in a separate word document or piece of paper. You might do this as you are working through stage 3, by noting down any features or aspects of the talk that appear to be particularly interesting or relevant for your research question. This might be quite an overwhelming list, and you might, like me, be sure that you will return to all of these issues one day (even if the lists are many years old and in your 'archived data' folder). The point here is to see the potential in your data, to gain an understanding of the range of analytical issues you might focus on, and how these might overlap or relate to each other.

Once you have your list, then you can return to the research literature and your own research question. What was it that inspired this project in the first place? What were you looking for or aiming to analyse? What does the literature suggest is an important (or missing) area of research? Consider each possible 'issue' in your list in light of these considerations. Which might be the most fruitful for analysis? Which ones, ultimately, are you most interested in or intrigued by? There are no hard-and-fast rules for which analytical issue to focus on, but remember that you will need to report these decisions and choices in the writing-up stage. So consider each one carefully, and make an informed choice on the basis of existing literature and your own understanding of the data so far. You should then identify one or two issues to focus on first.

Stage 5: Collect other instances of this analytical focus in your data corpus

You should now have an issue or focus for your analysis. In our worked example above, this might be 'how and where objective assessments feature in family mealtime talk'. Already, then, we have focused down our research question to something even more specific, and we should be prepared for this potentially changing again. The next step is to read and search through the rest of your data corpus to collect together more instances of this issue. Not all of your data will be fully transcribed, so work with either the transcripts or the original recordings. Just ensure that you are thorough and take a systematic approach so that you are as inclusive as possible. In the meal example above, I would identify all sections where a subjective (e.g., 'I like fish') or an objective (e.g., 'the steak looks fatty') assessment is used. As when coding the data, when you select out these sections always include a few more lines of interaction before and after the target section, erring on the side of caution and including more interactional context until you are sure what is and what is not relevant.

This is the equivalent of a second stage of coding and you may have to go back through your original corpus (rather than your first coded corpus) again to check that there aren't any instances that you might have missed the first time. Also be flexible with your search as some instances might be ambiguous (some descriptions, for example, are treated as assessments in interaction) and others might use different words or phrases than you might expect, so just using the 'search' function of word documents could miss valuable examples. You are aiming to compile another, new, word document that contains all of the transcripts for the sections of data that include your specific analytical focus. This may mean that you need to do a little more transcription at this stage – to represent those sections of the recording that you have identified in this stage, but which have not yet been transcribed – and as such that can help you to gain a fresh look at the data through blending the transcription/coding/analysis stages.

Stage 6: Focus and refine the analysis (aka 'how to stop analysing')

At this final stage of analysis, you should have a word document – with associated video/audio files where relevant – which includes all of the possible segments of data that incorporate your specific analytical focus. Your task, then, is to repeat stage 3: to work through each data segment and analyse it in turn. You may find that some segments seem to follow a pattern, while others might seem very different from the rest (these might turn out to be deviant cases; see the section on validating analyses). If you are struggling to analyse or make sense of some segments, it is fine to leave these and come back to them later. You should aim to get a sense of how the whole of this new corpus 'works': are there any patterns across the data segments? Is there coherence in how your analytical issue fits with the data? What new insights can you gain from analysing lots of examples of the same sorts of issues?

This is now the time to start writing out your analysis, even before you have 'polished' it up and come to any conclusions. It may seem counter-intuitive to be writing before you have finished your analysis, but the writing process can help to refine certain aspects of the analysis, and can flag up issues that perhaps don't really 'work'. In the same way that a story can be refined and clarified in the telling, so the writing up of the analytical notes can show more clearly what adds depth to the analyses and what is merely noting devices in the data.

Once you have gone through your list of data segments, making analytical notes and checking your analysis against the original recordings, then you can start to select some for writing up. There are no fixed rules about which ones to select: at this stage you should choose the data segments that featured the most analytical insights and which you found most interesting and engaging. Later on, there will need to be a more careful selection process to ensure that the data extracts we use in our written reports are representative of the coded corpus. For now, though, your aim is to start writing and not to spend too long at this stage pondering which segment to focus on. Copy and paste one of your data segments – the ones you have just been working on – into a new word document. You need to create a clear space to begin writing, to allow you to write as much as you want or need to, without cluttering up your documents with your analytical notes. Underneath the extract, begin writing out your analytical notes: what did you notice about the data? What social actions and psychological states are being managed? How are these achieved through the use of discursive devices? This stage of writing out your analysis can take some practice, and you will probably have to draft and re-draft many times. This is something that even very experienced researchers do. It is part of the process of refining our analyses and working through different interpretations and conclusions about the data. So do not worry if it looks very sketchy at first. What you are doing here is beginning the process of 'fixing' your analysis and working towards producing your final report, which is where we will continue in Chapter 8. Box 6.3 provides a student perspective on this process.

Box 6.3: Transitioning from note-taking to dissertation writing

'At first, the analysis phase can seem like a really daunting process, especially when your data set is so lengthy. However, I soon found that I had much more confidence in formulating my analytical notes, purely because I was able to work from such an extensive data set. With in-depth data, I was able to make highly detailed notes, focusing on key patterns and consistencies among the data, as well as highlighting differentiations within the data corpus: something which was

> fundamental in my own study of social identity construction. Although the revision of notes can be somewhat monotonous and time-consuming, I found that perseverance allowed the transition into the actual dissertation writing to be far more manageable, as my notes were so enriched.'
>
> Robert McQuade, undergraduate student (2010–2014), University of Strathclyde

Advanced DP analyses

The six stages of analysis outlined above are the scaffolding that will hopefully enable you to get started with DP and continue to develop your own competence and confidence in using this approach. At some point, however, you may be ready to advance a little further, and to tackle more complex issues that allow you to develop your DP skills in terms of both theory and analysis. The nature of discursive work is such that the field is developing all the time – empirical research is applying analyses in new areas, developing new discursive devices and pushing the boundaries of our understanding of psychological issues (see also Chapters 9 and 10) – so immersing yourself in the literature is crucial at this stage. This could be literature that not only relates to your topic area, but also to DP or other discursive or interactional research. This can be daunting at first in that there can seem so much to read. That is why this chapter has shown you how to apply the principles and analytical devices of DP without the need to do mountains of reading first. Many of you will, of course, have read and will want to read research in this area. Reading widely in DP and other research in your topic area will enable you to really develop your analytical skills and produce a much better report at the end.

While reading (lots of related research) is the crucial first step to developing advanced DP analysis, you will also need to examine areas that the previous stages do not address in detail. There are potentially many such areas, of course, and critics of DP might well have an extensive list of their own. Areas might include, for example, the boundaries between the individual (as psychological, physical, emotional, for example) and the social or regional vocal accents and how these might be attended to interactionally. Below are three areas relating to advanced analytical issues that might help inspire you to develop your own analyses further.

Subject-object relations and embodiment

As we saw in Chapter 1, DP emerged out of a concern with the cognitivism of much of (social) psychological research, and as such the early studies in DP often focused on core aspects of cognition research: attitudes, memory, attributions, emotions and so on. In more recent years, however, researchers in a number of different research disciplines have been considering the relationship between people's physical bodies and the world around them.

This kind of work is sometimes referred to as embodiment or embodied action (the state of being in a physical body and the related processes and practices that this involves) as well as affect (emotional reactions or experiences). This is an intriguing area as it requires us to re-consider the inside/outside dualism of psychology, and with how certain aspects of the physical body (such as emotions, pain, hunger) are treated as purely visceral states and separable from discourse or social worlds. It also relates very closely to the issue of subject-object relations: the ways in which discursive practices create a separation between people (subjects) and things in the world (objects). See Chapter 9 for suggested DP reading on 'emotions' and Chapter 10 for future developments of DP in this area.

Gestures and multimodality

Given its close alliance with conversation analysis, DP has also increasingly drawn on the use of technology to capture the visual aspects of interaction. It is easier, for instance, to record gestures and facial expression as well as the interaction between people and physical objects in the environment. This has opened up challenges to transcription (see Chapter 5) and of how we might analyse the extralinguistic features of interaction. The DP devices, for instance, rarely refer to aspects of interaction that are not primarily discursive. So there is an opportunity here for DP to develop in areas that address the multimodality of psychology in everyday life; of how our social actions are not just about what we say, but how we say these things in a specific environmental context. Even online interaction involves physical objects and the management of different identities in offline and online settings. How then might your analysis deal with other aspects of the social setting that are included in your data?

Change and temporality

Research tends to be treated as a 'snapshot' of time: a static moment. Yet DP has the capacity to offer a much more fluid and longitudinal approach. We could consider, for example, the issue of individual change versus consistency. Is a person treated as being the same over a lengthy period of time, in terms of their identity or behaviours, for example? How is consistency versus change treated as being more or less accountable in relation to certain topics or issues? How do discursive practices change over a period of time? Given that DP is based on the assumption that discursive practices are produced within a particular interactional and social context, then we might argue that discourse is context-dependent rather than person-dependent. This has sometimes led critics to suggest that it leaves no space for the notion of personality or consistent traits; that people might be observed using the same phrases or ways of talking across different interactional settings. By considering discursive practices in terms of processes rather than static objects, we can offer sophisticated analyses of everyday social life and the management of psychological business.

Validating the analysis (aka 'how do I know when I'm doing it right?')

By this stage, your analysis should be developing nicely and you probably have a large folder on your computer with video/audio files, transcripts, coded transcripts and analytical notes. So far, so good. You may, however, have been wondering about something along the lines of 'how do I know when I'm doing DP correctly?' and 'how do I know that I'm not just making this up?' These relate to issues such as the quality of the analysis (how good it is) as well as the broader issues around providing evidence and justification for your analyses. These might collectively be understood in terms of how we might validate or warrant our analysis, to ensure that it can stand up against scrutiny.

From a positivist approach, these issues would be referred to as reliability and validity. These terms (and the way they are used) rest on the assumption, however, that there is an objective world against which we can measure our own analytical claims. One of the things you will have noted about DP is that it is a relativist approach, based on the premise that there is no absolute 'truth' or single version of reality. As such, when we refer to validity we are not referring to whether or not our analysis is 'correct' or whether it is the only way in which the data might have been analysed. Instead, validity should be understood in terms of *how grounded our analysis is in the data and the phenomena we are researching*. In other words, our analysis must provide a coherent, plausible and insightful interpretation of that data. Does our analysis stay focused on the object we are investigating? Does our analysis provide an authentic representation and interpretation of the data?

A similar rationale applies to the concept of reliability. In positivist terms, reliability might refer to the extent to which others could replicate our research and find the same results or come to the same conclusions. It relies on the notion that there is a stable world (reality). With discursive research, however, no data are ever the same. Even if we choose an identical situation, with the same participants and words spoken, there will always be subtle variations in talk that can have important implications for the function of discursive practices. So when we refer to reliability in DP terms, we are concerned here with the extent to which others might come to the same conclusions, on examining our data and analyses. In other words, is our analysis convincing to others, and does it provide a way of understanding the data that goes beyond our own personal interpretations?

Like other relativist, critical and/or social constructionist approaches to research, DP uses a different set of criteria for warranting analytical claims, which is consistent with its theoretical and epistemological underpinnings. There are five key procedures and techniques we can use to ensure that we are staying true to our data: (1) transparency in methods, (2) participants' orientations, (3) coherence and deviant cases, (4) identifying by-products and the consequences of discourse, (5) analytical insight and contributing to the literature. These procedures and checks enable us to ensure that our DP analyses are valid and reliable and we will discuss each of these in turn here. See also Box 6.4 for a checklist to help you validate your own analysis.

Transparency in methods

One of the most important things we can do as researchers is to be clear about our procedures, both at the stage of conducting the research and in the reporting stages. This means that we should be careful in the decisions made at each stage of data collection and analysis. Who might our participants be? Where will we collect the data (and where will the cameras be located)? How much data will we collect? Each decision has consequences for the quality of analysis and our research conclusions, so it is important that we take our time to carefully consider all options, and ensure that these are aligned with our research questions and theoretical position. Reporting these methods clearly – even if at the reporting stage you will not need to note each minute detail of decision-making (see Chapter 8) – is important for what is termed 'transparency'. This means that our procedures are clearly set out so that other people can understand exactly what we did and why. At the reporting stage, this also means being transparent about our data: this is why we include transcripts in journal articles, books and presentations. If we are making analytical claims about the data, then it is important to be able to make visible those claims using examples from the 'raw' data. This is why transcripts are included in published reports and, where possible, still images from videos or sound files on websites. As technology develops, so the opportunities to have closer links between the research data and the reader will hopefully increase. Including transcripts in published work also provides opportunities for 'reader validation', where readers can check the validity of the interpretative claims being made, as sophisticated users of discourse themselves.

Participants' orientations and next turn proof procedure

One of the things that distinguishes DP from other discursive approaches is a concern with how discursive practices have particular actions in specific interactional contexts. This means that we are not trying to identify the abstract 'meanings' of words or provide an expert diagnosis of what someone is saying. Instead, the aim is to examine how participants (i.e., the people whose discursive practices we are analysing) themselves orientate to and make relevant different interpretations of discourse. This is what is known as an 'emic' approach: taking an insider's, rather than an outsider's, perspective. While we are not aiming to get 'inside the participant's head', we should focus on analysing discourse in terms of how people within the interaction make sense of it. For example, if we are not sure about our interpretation of something (in Extract 6.1 above, is Bob's 'I don't like steak' utterance a complaint, for example, or a taste assessment), then we should look to see how it is treated by the other participants, either in the next immediate turn or in the unfolding interaction soon after. This is what is referred to as the 'next turn proof procedure', where the 'proof' of the interpretation is based on what happens in the next turn. The point is that we should not look to validate our analytic interpretations in terms of whether we think it is correct or 'sounds right'; instead, we should look to see how our analysis is supported by the data and in the way in which participants make visible their interpretation of each other's talk.

Coherence and deviant cases

Your analysis should be coherent: it should be clear and understandable, with each part of the analysis fitting together in an organised way. An analysis often has many parts with each part focusing on a different aspect of the discourse (such as the structure or content of the interaction). Separately, they may not add much insight, but taken together they should provide a coherent narrative, an interpretation of the data that is consistent, clear and structured. We might think of the analysis like a jigsaw puzzle, with all of the separate pieces fitting together in just the right way to provide a bigger picture. It is not so simple as that in practice, of course, but the analogy highlights the need for us to think of our analysis as comprised of many parts, with each part being important, but not sufficient on its own (see 'device spotting' in the 'pitfalls' section). You should therefore be thorough in your analyses. While you may not transcribe all of your data in Jefferson detail, you should ensure that your analysis fits with all relevant sections of your data (i.e., the coded corpus) and not just a small selection.

As you conduct your coding and analysis of the data, therefore, you are likely to come across sections of the data that do not fit the pattern you have identified or which do not seem to be coherent with the rest of the analysis. These are known as *deviant cases* (similar to the notion of 'outliers' in statistical terms): they are instances in the data that do not fit the pattern or analytical interpretation that you have just made. On first glance, then, you might think they are a problem and we need to ignore them (or worse, pretend that you did not see it in the first place). Do not be fooled, however, as the deviant case is actually a really useful analytical tool and can often be the saviour of your research. What the deviant case does is to mark some exception (a deviation) to the analytical pattern or observations you have previously made, but in doing so it can often confirm the validity of your analyses. So here we see the beauty of the deviant case: it can give your analyses a whole new strength. An example of a deviant case might be in terms of structure of the interaction (such as if someone does not return a greeting when you say hello) or about the content of the interaction (such as if someone uses a very different rhetorical device to support their account of their behaviour).

Identifying by-products and the consequences of discourse

In identifying a pattern or rhetorical strategy in discourse, we then examine the function(s) that these serve. For example, using a subjective category assessment (such as 'I don't like steak') can serve the function of turning down the offer of food without making any comment about the food itself (the refusal here is apparently based on our taste preferences, not a problem with the food, for example; though it may, of course, open up a different kind of complaint about not attending to personal preferences). While discursive practices have particular functions in interaction, however, they can also produce by-products or introduce new problems or issues that need to be dealt with. This might also be likened to the idea of an emergent property, which is a property of a system as a whole, but not present in the component, separate parts. In the example above, a by-product of using a subjective category assessment is that it suggests a fixed food preference that is unlikely to change. This then creates a dilemma for the person should they find themselves eating steak on another occasion (whether intentionally or not); how do they then account for their consumption? So identifying one function of discourse can often reveal other by-products. Identifying these by-products and the consequences of different discursive practices can be another way in which we can ensure our analysis is valid and coherent.

Analytical insight and contributing to the literature

DP analyses should provide insight into the data and phenomenon that you are investigating; it should add something new and different, provide an alternative way of looking at the phenomenon. You should not, therefore, be able to come to the same analytical conclusions if you had not first undertaken DP. This is the distinction between description and interpretation; it needs to provide another layer of understanding that could not have been reached by other means. When you are starting out in DP analysis this might seem a tough challenge, to add something new and insightful. Remember, however, that your data are unique (even if others have conducted research in a similar area), and that there is always something that you can add to the literature. Your analysis should also, therefore, be grounded in other research, whether related by topic or other discursive work. It should not be treated as isolated or separated from other work. It should refer back to earlier research and demonstrate how you are building on that research (whether by providing additional insights or alternative interpretations). In that way, you can ensure not only that your work adds something new and provides a fresh insight into a phenomenon, but also that it adds to a growing body of research, of which yours should now be part.

Box 6.4: Validation checklist

- Do the methods (of data collection and analysis) match the research question?
- Does the research connect with or adequately refer to existing research in this area?

- Is the data collection procedure clearly described and documented?
- Have ethical issues been appropriately considered?
- Is the analytical procedure clearly and fully described?
- Is the selection of data/extracts clearly justified?
- Is the analysis systematic and organised?
- Is there appropriate discussion of issues in the data with reference to extracts?
- Are any deviant cases (where relevant) discussed in relation to the analyses?
- Is the analysis coherent and insightful?
- Do the conclusions align with the analyses?

Analytic pitfalls to avoid

One of the daunting aspects of doing any analysis is the fear of not doing it 'right' or making a mistake. This is the equivalent of falling off your bike or crashing your car, if we use the analogy of learning DP as similar to a craft skill (we're using the word 'craft' in its loosest sense here; dropping a stitch – the knitting equivalent of falling off your bike – doesn't quite have the same gravitas). After the first lesson in how to get started (stage 1) and your second lesson in how to stop (stage 6), your third lesson is what to do if you do fall off and how to get back on again. Knowing what can go wrong won't necessarily prevent you from making these mistakes, but it should make you more aware of being able to recognise these *as mistakes* and so put you in a position to be able to fix them for yourself. Besides which, it won't be as catastrophic as crashing a car, so the odd mistake as you practise will not do you any harm.

With DP (and other forms of DA), there are a number of pitfalls that, with a little practice, we can avoid. Antaki et al. (2003) noted the following six pitfalls, and these neatly encapsulate many common problems that can be encountered when starting out in DP analyses:

1. 'under-analysis through summary'
2. 'under-analysis through taking sides'
3. 'under-analysis through over-quotation or through isolated quotation'
4. 'the circular identification of discourses and mental constructs'

5. 'false survey'
6. 'analysis that consists in simply spotting features'

We will use Extract 6.2, taken from an interview with a first-year university student (Louise) about friendship (see www.heacademy.ac.uk/resource/tqrmul-dataset-teaching-resources-louise%E2%80%99s-interview for access to the video data), to illustrate each of these pitfalls.

Extract 6.2: Friendship interview

```
1.  Louise:   like our flat mate I do try n make the effort
2.            with her cos I just think
3.            (0.3)
4.  INT:      this is the [the quieter one yeah
5.  Louise:               [must be yeah must be so hard for her
6.            (0.6) cos we're all quite (.) bubbly (0.3)
7.            characters n (0.6) °(that)°
8.            (0.4)
9.  INT:      n is she unhappy?
10.           (0.6)
11. Louise:   she ↑doesn't seem to be(0.2)cos I've spoken
12.           to her about(0.3)things li:ke (0.5) how are
13.           you finding it here n stuff n she (0.2) quite
14.           ↑likes it
```

Pitfall (1) is where you might find yourself describing or summarising the data – perhaps even pointing out some features of the interaction – but without adding anything new or providing any interpretation. For example, we might say of Extract 6.2 that 'Louise notes that she tries to make an effort with her flatmate and that she and her friends are quite bubbly and outgoing'. We might also point to the careful way in which Louise appears to be talking about how she has spoken to her flatmate, with a few short pauses and rising intonation. In doing so, we aren't providing any analysis because there is no interpretation being made, no discussion of psychological states or social actions being performed in the talk (the description of Louise's efforts do not count as a social action because these are things that happened *prior to* the interview and the discourse we are analysing).

Pitfall (2) is what can happen if you find yourself taking a moral or political position on what is being said by participants. There may be a temptation to make a judgement or assessment of the discourse; to either align or distance yourself from it. With Extract 6.2, we might say that Louise is right to try to include her flatmate or that she sounds like she is being a good friend. In data that are more emotionally charged – such as when dealing with traumatic or dangerous social encounters, such as reports of abuse or recorded interactions where people are being physically threatened – the stakes can feel higher and we may want to take a moral or political stance in order to defend someone or argue against a political regime. It is appropriate to make choices in the research that you conduct, to deconstruct racist rather than anti-racist discourse, for example. You can apply your analysis to support a particular issue in social policy or public debate, and in that sense to use your analyses for a political goal. But these decisions should come before and/or after the analysis; the analysis itself should be balanced and free of any attempts to 'spin' the analysis in a particular direction.

Pitfall (3) is where you provide more quotes than interpretation (it is often recognisable by large sections of direct quotes and very little written analysis) or else provide a quote and let it 'speak for itself'. This is tempting to do when you are very new to DP and perhaps do not have the confidence to make your own interpretation of the data (or you are worried about misinterpreting or reading 'too much' into the data). In Extract 6.2, we might cut-and-paste parts of the extract and then present this as 'here Louise accounts for how she tries to include the other flatmate in group activities'.

Pitfall (4) is perhaps one of the toughest challenges for new DP researchers and there are two parts to this. The first is that, in rushing to identify a 'discourse' or pattern in the data, you might find yourself listing the features of a pattern or discourse and then claiming that you have identified a pattern and the features that define it. In Extract 6.2, for example, we might say that people justify their behaviour around friendship in terms of individual characteristics (being 'quiet' or 'bubbly', for example), and that being quiet is important in friendship because Louise made reference to this issue. In doing so, we are identifying a possible pattern and saying that it exists because we have found it; hence it is a circular argument. Similarly, we might make inferences about the cognitive or emotional state of someone through reference to their use of cognitivist (e.g., liking something) or emotional (unhappy) talk. Not only is this a circular argument in that it provides no evidence to support these claims (it only states the conclusion as if it were the evidence for the conclusion), but it also makes the assumption that talk is a direct link to cognition, which goes against the theory underpinning DP (see Chapter 1 for a detailed discussion about this).

Pitfall (5) is what can happen if you extrapolate too far from your findings; if you notice something in your data and then interpret this as an indication of what happens in other settings and to a broader context. With Extract 6.2, for example, we might say that it is important to make an effort with new friends otherwise they will feel excluded. While we might want to, and think it important to, show how our research has a wider relevance (and indeed it does), making claims that go beyond your data set is not the way to do this. What we need to do instead is to show how our analysis provides an insight into a small part of a bigger picture; one study cannot find all the answers, but it may well provide some answers and a handful of more important questions yet to be explored.

Pitfall (6) is similar in some ways to pitfall (1), but here you might find yourself spotting the discursive devices and showing how and where these occur. This can be very satisfying when you are starting out in DP: 'Look – there's an extreme case formulation', or 'I found a three-part-list!' All well and good for practising your skills at focusing on DP devices and for training yourself to look at interaction with the DP lens, but this is not in itself analysis. In Extract 6.2, for example, you might have spotted an example of direct reported speech on lines 12–13: 'how are you finding it here'. Just spotting this, however, does not tell us anything about how it functions in this extract; to add more, we might analyse it in terms of how it constructs Louise as a caring flatmate, and as if this were just one example among many that illustrate this as being the case. You need to take the next step, therefore, to examine how these devices are used in the interaction to accomplish particular social actions and make relevant specific psychological concepts.

So beware of the pitfalls, and don't despair if you fall into a few along the way. This is very common and is not a reflection on your skills or competence with DP. Even proficient researchers sometimes get caught out. It makes us human. The main thing is that if (or when) you do fall down, dust yourself off and keep going. Your analysis will be all the better for being able to recognise when you are going wrong.

Holding a data session

One of the most effective ways to become competent and confident as a DP analyst is to take part in a data session with other researchers. Ideally, do so on a regular basis if possible, whether this is weekly, monthly or even just a couple of times a year. This will provide not only the intellectual support of working with others in your field, but also exposure to different ways of interpreting data and enabling you to refine your own analytical skills. Ensure that some of those taking part in the data session are familiar with, or experienced in, discursive research (and DP specifically); at least one other person needs to be competent so that you can stay focused on discursive analyses. It can also be helpful, though, to have a range of perspectives and levels of competence in a data session. New researchers often come with fresh questions and different ideas from those who perhaps are more familiar with the literature. Trying out your analytical ideas in a data session is a great way to develop your skills and competence. You can test out your initial observations among a group of people who are similarly there to discuss the data, without fear of being 'wrong' or looking stupid. So plan a data session at the early stages of coding and analysing your data, as they work best as a means to explore different possible aspects of your data. If you wait until you have almost finished your analysis, you are likely to be less open to new ideas.

Data sessions can also be valuable not just for the person who brought the data, but for the other group members as well. It enables you to hone your analytical skills and you never know when you might gain insights to your own data through examining someone else's data. Box 6.5 includes suggested guidelines for holding a DP data session.

> ### Box 6.5: Suggested guidelines for holding a data session
>
> - A data session might involve between two and twenty people, but between four and ten is optimal, to enable everyone to be able to take part in a full discussion of the data.
> - Agree on the language to be used in the data session in advance if it is an international group or involving visitors from other countries.
> - The data session should focus on just one piece of data (usually provided by one person or group of people, if working collaboratively), to stay focused on a particular issue.
> - Prepare sufficient transcription to cover around 2–4 sides of paper (double-spaced, wide-margins). Any more than this and it can be difficult to discuss it all and to collectively stay focused on certain sections of the data. Bring paper copies of the transcript for everyone in the data session; circulate electronic copies in advance if you can. Without the transcript, it can be very difficult for participants to make any comments on the data or to examine the detail of the discourse. If confidentiality is an issue, you can request that all transcripts be returned at the end. Regardless, everyone should be respectful of the data and not use them for other purposes.
> - If the data are taken from a video or audio recording, the clip should be played and shown on a large screen if possible (i.e., through a data projector), or at least on a laptop or tablet that can be seen and heard by everyone.
> - Data sessions might be structured in many ways, but a typical session could run like this (plan for about a 1.5 to 2 hour session):
>   1. Play the video or audio clip (where possible) and read through the data. Play the data three or four times to enable people to have time to read and get familiar with it. This might take around 10–15 minutes.
>
> *(Continued)*

(Continued)

2. Allow time for people to make notes individually, in silence, to give time for ideas to develop. This might take around 15–20 minutes.

3. Discuss the data by, for example, making analytic observations, comments about issues that might be explored further, or noting similarities with other data sets/research settings. You might prefer to allow people to speak by going round each person in turn, or raising hands to allocate a turn-taking order. Or you may find that an unstructured discussion works well enough (this can be the case if you have only three or four people present, for instance). Decide at the start of the data session how you will structure this discussion, and on any etiquette that you wish to follow as a group.

- Encourage everyone to comment on the data and offer analytical suggestions, and use these as either stand-alone comments or as starting points for discussion on a particular issue. The data session is not a time to critique or assess other people's analyses; no one should be judged or have their contributions treated as less valuable than others' contributions. Similarly, no one should feel obliged to speak if they are not confident to do so or do not have anything to add to the discussion. Data sessions at their best are collegiate, supportive and intellectually stimulating settings. Refreshments help – sharing food can help to lighten the atmosphere and provides a good distraction if the discussion is slow to get started.

KEY POINTS

- Analysing DP is a skill to be learnt rather than a recipe to be followed, but there are six interrelated stages that can be used to help scaffold the analytic process.
- Good analysis takes time: don't rush it!
- The stages of transcribing, coding, analysing and writing up your data are iterative and interwoven; be prepared to go back through your data as your analysis develops.
- Gain confidence with DP analysis before you move on to the advanced issues.

- Validating the analysis means checking for quality, rigour and coherence.
- There are common pitfalls when analysing data and these can help you to distinguish 'good' from 'poor' analyses.
- Working in a data session with other researchers can be a really valuable way of developing your analytical skills.

Recommended reading

Edwards, D. (2005). Moaning, whinging and laughing: The subjective side of complaints. *Discourse Studies*, 7(1), 5–29.

Wood, L. & Kroger, R. (2000). *Doing discourse analysis: Methods for studying action in talk and text*. London: Sage.

7

DISCURSIVE DEVICES

Chapter contents

Basic devices	147
Intermediate devices	158
Advanced devices	169

In Chapter 6, we worked through the process of DP analysis, from the first reading of the data to refining the analytical focus. We also first encountered the discursive devices: the core analytical tools of DP that enable us to examine the discursive production of psychological and social actions. In this chapter, we will examine the devices in detail, with detailed descriptions and worked examples, to help you to familiarise yourself with each one. The devices have been highlighted in **bold** type in the worked examples to enable you to more easily identify them. They have been split into three sections: basic, intermediate or advanced. This separation of the devices is somewhat arbitrary in that they might have been clustered together in different ways, but this ordering should match onto the level of competence you are likely to need when using them. You could think of this chapter as your DP training ground. As with any kind of exercise, little and often works best, so you don't need to tackle it all at once. With each device, read through the worked example, then consider whether they are identifiable in your own data, and have a go at using them to begin to make interpretations about what is going on in the interaction.

The important thing to remember is that these devices cannot be used like tools in a mechanical sense; we do not simply identify the existence of a phrase or word in interaction and then immediately point to its function or outcome. Similarly, this is not like a chemical reaction or mathematical equation where x (assessment) + y (second assessment) = z (agreement). The devices are to be used, instead, as instruments that can sensitise us to the subtleties of interaction. We might then use the analogy of a Sherlock Holmes detective, who uses various techniques (ways of observing the world, a sensitivity to details) and devices (the magnifying glass, the fingerprint kit) to examine a situation and interpret what is going on. So, as DP analysts, we also need to use the devices with some care and skill, and this is why we need to practise. Each interaction is unique, and this is what makes DP analysis so interesting. Not only can we find something new each time, but it also provides a different perspective on the social world that you can practise and apply every day.

Basic devices

We will start with what have been broadly clustered as the basic devices: these are the ones that are typically easier to identify and which are fairly common in everyday interaction. In that sense, their relative frequency provides for greater opportunities to practise them. They are as follows: pronoun use and footing shifts; assessments and second assessments; silences, pauses and hesitations; hedging; extreme case formulations; minimisation; lists and contrasts.

Pronoun use and footing shifts

Pronoun shifts involve identifying when and where speakers use different pronouns to refer to themselves or other people. The most common ones are: I, you, he, she, it, we and they. They can also be used in terms of ownership: my/mine, his, hers, its, ours, theirs. Pronoun shifts are an example of the broader category of footing shift: this is a concept originating in Erving Goffman's (1979) work and refers to the movement across participant roles that are produced in the talk. For example, one can speak as the *author* of our talk (i.e., saying our own words), the *animator* (i.e., the 'sounding box': speaking as if relaying someone else's words), or the *principal* (i.e., the agent or person responsible for the talk). The great thing about footing shifts is that they allow us to understand the *layers* of frames of reference in discursive practices. That is, we are rarely just speaking 'as ourselves'; our words also draw on issues about who is responsible for what we say, whose words we are using and who is saying it. So pronoun and footing shifts can be used to manage identities of the speakers, and accountability for what is being said. They can also be found when the factuality of an issue might be in question, to position the speaker as believable or simply reporting 'the facts'.

Worked example

Extract 7.1 illustrates the use of pronoun shifts in discourse, taken from research examining how people account for having chronic fatigue syndrome (CFS). The section is from an interview where Angela (someone with CFS) is talking with her husband, Joe, to the interviewer (Mary) about what happened when her illness began. See Box 5.4 in Chapter 5 for a full transcription key.

Extract 7.1: Taken from Horton-Salway (2001: 250, extract 1)

```
1.  Mary:    mm and how did it (.) can you remember much about
2.           how it started?=
3.  Joe:     =heh heh
4.           (.)
5.  Angela:  it started off with=
6.  Joe:     =it started with a sore throat=
7.  Angela:  =I had a sore throat and I had the very worst headache
8.           I've ever had in my life (.) it was one evening=
9.  Joe:     =go back to where we believe it was caught at the
10.          swimming baths
```

The different pronouns in this extract provide a way of orientating to a particular subject or object. For instance, the neutral third-person pronoun 'it' refers to Angela's illness but does so without labelling it too specifically (we can compare 'it' with 'your illness', for example). It also treats the illness as a 'thing', an object or real state of affairs. By referring to it in this way, Mary invokes the reality of the illness without making any specific claims about what 'it' might be. So *neutral third-person pronouns* can be used to make a vague, undefined reference to something while still treating that 'thing' as real. The other pronouns are first-person (I, my) and second-person (you). Note that in the English language, the same word (you) is used for second-person pronouns, whereas in other languages (such as the French *tu* and *vous*) we can make a distinction between singular and plural uses through word choice alone. This makes the English 'you' more ambiguous, though there are regional variations where speakers might say 'youse' (or 'yous') colloquially to indicate more than one person. Use of the first- and second-person pronouns can be seen in this extract to position the illness as located within an individual – something that Angela had, and to which Angela was subject – but also as something that Angela might be individually responsible for, or at least having primary access to the experience of the illness ('I had a sore throat', 'I had the very worst headache'). We then see a footing shift on line 9, in which Joe invokes the first-person plural pronoun (we); this then re-orientates Angela's account to include him as part of the 'accounting for the illness' social action. The *author* of this line might then be both Joe and Angela, even though Joe is the *animator*. So while Joe is not claiming to also have the illness, the shift to 'we', rather than singular 'I' or 'you', brings him back into the picture. It presents the illness as a mutually understood event;

something that they were both involved in, and thus which Joe might also have access to, as part of that experience.

Assessments and second assessments

As with pronoun use, assessments are defined primarily linguistically, that is, they are identified as those instances in which a description is provided that makes a specific judgement or appraisal of something (and that something could be a person, object or event, for example). Assessments are sometimes referred to as evaluations in the DP literature. Second assessments are assessments that *follow* or are found soon after an initial assessment, and they typically follow what is called a preference structure. This is where there is a normative pattern for agreements (i.e., second assessments that match the evaluative direction of the initial assessment; see Pomerantz, 1984, for more details). This means that second assessments which agree with the initial assessment are typically produced soon after, with no hesitation or prefacing and may *upgrade* the initial assessment, whereas second assessments which *disagree* with initial assessments are typically preceded by a pause or hesitation, are often prefaced in some way and may partially agree or disagree with the previous assessment. Assessments can also be presented as if the reason for the assessment was located within the subject (termed 'subjective assessments', the person doing the assessment), where personal pronouns are used (e.g. *we loved the film*), or as if located within the object or the thing being assessed (termed 'objective assessments', e.g., *the film was brilliant*). Assessments therefore not only invoke our stances in an interaction – how we might be assumed to be a particular kind of person, or have a particular kind of opinion, for example – but also invoke our involvement in the thing that we are assessing. In other words, giving an assessment also makes a claim that we have experienced or have knowledge of the thing that we are assessing.

Worked example

Extract 7.2 is taken from a family mealtime, where Laura has cooked a chicken dinner for her daughter (Beth, 11 years), brother (Bill) and Bill's wife, Doris. The family members are coming to the end of the meal.

Extract 7.2: Taken from Wiggins and Potter (2003: 522, extract 4)

```
1. Doris:   that was lovely Lau:↓ra [thank ↓yo:u
2. Bill:                             [because eh-
3. Beth:    it is [love↓ly
4. Laura:         [>did you enjoy that< there is
5.          [some >d' you want<
```

```
6. Bill:      [she ↑said-
7. Laura:     there's a bit mo:re if you ↓want (0.6) >there's
8.            a bit< more ↑sauce?
```

There are two assessments in this extract – 'that was lovely' (line 1) and 'it is lovely' (line 3) – that display an orientation to the food as being the source of the assessment (with the use of the third-person pronouns 'it' and 'that'). These are what might be called 'objective assessments' in that they foreground the object (they are not, however, objective in the sense of being more accurate or truthful). As such, they work well here as compliments, because they locate the 'loveliness' of the food as being in the food itself, not the consumer. Note, then, how there is also a subjective re-formulation of the assessments on line 4: Laura asks if 'you enjoy(ed) that' (though we do not know here if the 'you' is plural or singular), which shifts the focus back onto the person eating the food. The assessments work here then as compliments about the food and as demonstrating an appreciation (in combination with the 'thank you' and the direct naming of Laura on line 1) to the cook. Laura's re-formulation then avoids taking too much credit for the food and treats the assessment as an indirect request for more food. So there are a number of social actions going on in this very short clip. We can also identify a second assessment here (from Beth, line 3), which is produced soon after the initial assessment (by Doris, line 1). This conforms to the preference structure for agreement in assessments – there is no hesitation from Beth and her assessment is not prefaced or softened. Doing dispreferred actions as preferred can often be the source of humour in television sitcoms, for example where a character might violate the norms of interaction and this is treated as awkward or observational humour (see Stokoe, 2008).

Silences, pauses and hesitations

The noting of silences, pauses or hesitations – those gaps in interaction when there is no speech – is possibly one of the transcription features that most clearly flags up a transcript as having been prepared for conversation analysis or DP. Silences are typically measured in tenths of a second, with (.) indicating less than one-tenth of a second pause, (0.2) indicating two-tenths of a second pause, and so on. The term 'pause' is most commonly used in DP research because it suggests that the lack of speech is a temporary state and that the conversation will resume at any point. 'Silence' potentially suggests something more intentional or meaningful, so this might refer to a much longer pause (for instance, where the pause is more than just a few seconds long). Referring to something as a 'hesitation' suggests that there is a deliberate withholding of talk by a speaker, so this term is used with caution. When transcribing, we also need to be careful as to where a pause is indicated on a line at talk; if it is within a speaker's turn at talk, then it can appear as if the pause is *theirs*,

DISCURSIVE DEVICES

and thus it is expected that they will continue speaking immediately after the pause (see also Chapter 5 for further discussion on this). Pauses are really important, then, in terms of clarifying the delivery of talk and noting any patterns or structure in the organisation of interaction. For instance, Jefferson (1989) suggested that in everyday conversation, a pause of one second or more was noticeable and could indicate interactional trouble of some kind. In institutional talk, where there is more likely to be a certain pattern to the way in which people respond to each other, then pauses may be longer or differently structured. There is no standard set of functions that pauses or silences can be used for, however, but they can alert us to something particularly interesting going on in the interaction.

Worked example

Extract 7.3 illustrates how pauses can be slightly longer than expected (cf. Jefferson, 1989) when used in institutional talk, but that they can also highlight other social actions and psychological business being managed. This extract is taken from an audio-recorded weight management group, within the National Health Service in Scotland, involving people who are attending for weight issues. The group leader (Melanie) is a dietitian and has been talking to the group about a 'balance of good health' diet and how that might compare with their current food intakes.

Extract 7.3: Taken from Wiggins (2009: 378)

```
1. Melanie:    can you see: (.) >wh- ↑whats th' difference
2.             about< (0.6) what you eat at the ↓moment
3.             compared to that kind'v bal↓anc:e
4.             (2.4)
5. Paul:       act'lly not a ↑thing cos that's:: (.) what we eat
6.             (0.6) >ah m'n< (0.8) we don't eat >a lot of fat(ty)<
7.             foods:,
8. Melanie:    righ',
9.             (0.4)
10. Paul:      an::d,
11.            (0.8)
12. Paul:      I don't take su:gar in ma- (0.4) coffee >anythin'
```

```
13.             like tha',<
14.             (1.0)
15. Paul:       its s:kimmed ↑milk we use (.) °but°=
```

There are a number of pauses in this extract, including some short ones (such as (.), (0.4), or (0.6)) and longer ones ((2.4) and (1.0)). The short ones can occur within someone's turn, such as the (0.4) on line 12, as well as between people's turns, such as the (0.4) on line 9. In that sense, we cannot simply spot a short or long pause and be able to identify whether it signals a hesitation or trouble of some kind; we also need to examine where it is and how it is embedded with the surrounding talk. The (2.4) pause on line 4, for example, occurs immediately after Melanie's question to the group. Given that the group consists of a number of people (around 10–12), this pause could be accounted for in terms of it being addressed to many people (not just one person) and so it may take time not only for people to answer, but also to make sure that they will not be interrupting someone else by answering first. So longer pauses may be more likely in institutional question–answer sequences than in everyday chat with friends. We can also note how there are some slightly longer pauses in Paul's turn on lines 10–15. These serve the purpose of 'holding' his turn, in combination with their placement after the stretched-out 'an::d,', which also has the comma that marks continuing intonation. Pauses also indicate where there might be a change of speaker. For example, someone else might have started speaking at line 14, given that Paul's immediately prior turn looks like it is 'complete' and there is a one-second pause. Since no one else does, then Paul continues to give a little more detail about his account.

Hedging

Hedging is what occurs when a turn in talk is marked in some way as provisional, tentative or conditional on some other events. This is something that can be seen in academic work as much as in everyday talk, for instance, when we 'suggest' our results or state that 'we would argue that…'. It has also been considered in literature on politeness strategies. Hedged talk is thus talk that helps to manage a speaker's accountability, in that it avoids making a specific or certain claim about something, and can be softened or retracted in the event of disagreement. Hedging often appears alongside other discursive practices, such as pauses or hesitations, or particular terms such as 'well-prefaced' accounts (where a turn begins with 'well, …' and typically marks a disagreement with the prior turn). It can also be used alongside delicate issues, such as in the worked example below.

Worked example

Extract 7.4 provides an illustration of the different forms of hedged talk that can be seen in social interaction. This extract is taken from a focus group with UK psychology

DISCURSIVE DEVICES

undergraduates, who were asked to discuss the issue of asylum. SG is the moderator, P2 is one of the participants.

Extract 7.4: Taken from Goodman and Burke (2011: 115, extract 2)

```
1.  P2:   wher::eas: (2.0) if (.) ↑you know you are part
2.        of av- (.) a minority then (.) .hh
3.        (1.5)
4.  P2:   ↑the:n I think yeah people ar:: (.) are more
5.        (.) you can- you can say it I think .hh
6.  SG:   °okay°
7.  P2:   but at the same time I think that
8.        (1.3)
9.  P2:   ↑I don't know I think that if:: >if a person< (.)
10.       from minority groups: does: (1.3) say e::: (1.3)
11.       I don't know (.) if they oppose kind of asylum seeking
12.       .hh ↑you think (0.2) >I don't know< it's re:- it's
13.       confusing 'cause' (2.3) y- it has to be (.) er I think
14.       it's taken more as in (0.2) okay (.) i:t's like (.)
15.       econom- it must be econ↑omic reas↓ons rather than
16. SG:   right
17. P2:   like (0.2) anything other -like any ra:cial issues
```

As can be seen from the highlighted words and pauses here, there is no single way in which discursive practices can be understood as being hedged. They can be identified, however, through the way in which a turn in talk appears hesitant, includes a number of (longish) pauses within a speaker's turn, and uses words such as 'I think', 'I don't know', 'could be' or 'sometimes'. In Extract 7.4, for example, P2 appears to be talking around the issue and not giving a direct answer. Talking about asylum, racial issues and minority groups is a delicate issue; there is the risk that the person might appear racist or prejudiced. The hedging therefore enables the speaker to raise these issues while also distancing themselves from any particular stance. It softens the impact of the discourse and marks the talk *as delicate or sensitive* in some way.

Extreme case formulations

Extreme case formulations, or ECFs, are words or phrases that are both semantically extreme and orientated to as extreme (Edwards, 2000; Pomerantz, 1986). They go beyond phrases such as 'very good' or 'excellent', which make a positive assessment of something but do not necessarily frame this as being an extreme case. So to work as an ECF, a word/phrase must be treated as, or hearable as, going to extremes. That is, it does more than just exaggerate or emphasise something. It is used to defend a claim or demonstrate investment in a particular account. They go beyond description and are used to manage a speaker's identity in relation to what they are saying; as being a particular category of person, for example. As such, ECFs might seem at first to be easy to 'spot' – in that we look for an exaggeration of something – but we need then to check how they are situated within the local interactional context to be certain whether they are being treated as an extreme case. In early work on ECFs, they were identified primarily in those situations when someone was making a complaint (Pomerantz, 1986). In later work, it was argued that despite being 'factually brittle' (Edwards, 2000: 352), in that it would be easy to argue against an ECF being the case, they are typically unsoftened because they are designed to be *heard as* going to extremes. In other words, they are typically not produced as a 'fact' but work instead to manage a speaker's stake or investment in what they are saying. See Box 6.2 for more information on ECFs.

Worked example

In Extract 7.5, there are three examples of ECFs in a short space of time. This extract is taken from an interview with a man ('R9') who had been a refugee in the UK for seven years and had recently moved to Glasgow. He had just been asked why he moved to Glasgow, and he then proceeds to give accounts of what happened to him following his move.

Extract 7.5: Taken from Kirkwood et al. (2013: 755, extract 4)

```
1. R9:   yeah >for instance< you know I was attacked twice
2. INT:  °oh really°
3. R9    I came he::re (.) in (.) Glasgow having all my teeth
4. INT:  really
5. R9    and as you see now all this part ((points to gap in
6.       teeth)) (.) is fully gone
```

```
 7. INT    °yeah°
 8. R9     and (.) now I was attacked twice
 9. INT    geez=
10. R9     =in the ↑city
11. INT    god
12. R9     and I did nothing to nobody
13. INT    geez=
```

The ECFs featured in this extract are first used as a contrast pair – between 'all my teeth' (line 3) and 'fully gone' (line 6) – which works to emphasise the damage done by the attacks (line 1). Note also that the participant provides further evidence by pointing directly to his mouth so that the interviewer can see this for himself. The ECFs work not just as a description of dental records, but also as a way to manage the speaker's claim as having being brutally attacked twice; it adds not only to the plausibility of his account, but also implies the force behind the attack, even if this was not explicitly stated. The third ECF – 'nothing to nobody' (line 12) – then further adds to this management of the speaker as being a victim and blameless in the series of events being described. It would be very easy to challenge this ECF – he must have done *something*, even if it was just to say 'hello' or to look at someone – but it works here to emphasise the speaker's investment in the claim as being genuine. The interviewer's responses (lines 2, 4, 9, 11 and 13) then orientate to the account *as genuine* and as hearably extreme.

Minimisation

In its simplest form, minimisation is present in discursive practices through the inclusion of words such as 'just', 'only', 'little bit', and so on. It is the practices through which the volume or extent of something is treated as minimal or insignificant. It is important to note, however, that some of the words used for minimisation can also have other uses, so we need to do more than simply look out for these words in the data. The word 'just', for example, can also be used to mean 'exactly', as in 'it's just right' or 'recently', as in 'we just got here'. Where minimisation does occur, this can be used to downplay the importance of an object, event or behaviour. It can therefore be used to manage one's accountability for something: to minimise the extent to which it could be treated as serious behaviour (for example, in police interrogation or court testimony). As such, it tends to be found in discursive practices when people are describing something or have been asked to account for something. Minimisation can also be used in combination with contrasts (e.g., contrasting one smaller thing with something much larger); see 'lists and contrasts' devices below.

Worked example

In Extract 7.6, we see the use of a minimisation device being used in an online discussion group for people who have recently had (or are about to have) bariatric surgery. In the first 'post' of this extract, one of the forum members is asking other members what to eat in the post-operation period. Note that all the exclamation marks were in the original text taken from the online discussion forum.

Extract 7.6: Taken from Cranwell and Seymour-Smith (2012: 875, extracts 2 and 3)

1. Post 16, Jenny
2. Hey!!! I just had surgery on the 8th!!!!! I am SO Sore!!!!!!!!!
3. But I am excited!!!!!! And I am never hungry!!! Should I eat
4. **just** to eat, or don't worry about it?!?!!
5. Post 17, Liz
6. Hey Jenny congrats!! YES you have to eat!!! I know it's a fight
7. I am having aswell, but what the doctors told me was even if
8. **I just take** a couple of bits of my protein food, but NEVER miss
9. a meal completely.

There are two instances of 'just' being used here as a minimisation device. In the first example, Jenny is asking a question about what to do (i.e., what to eat following surgery) and managing the dilemma of whether she might be eating 'just to eat' (line 4). Given that bariatric surgery is aimed at helping people to effectively manage their weight, then eating for the sake of it (with no other purpose) is potentially a risky thing to say in this forum. The minimised 'just' helps to soften this issue, and combined with the rest of this post, suggests that a small amount of food might be all that is needed. This is then confirmed in the response by Liz who explicitly tells Jenny that she has to eat (line 7); in doing so, she orientates to Jenny's turn as being reluctant to eat when she isn't hungry. Note then, the minimisation device ('I just take', line 9) by Liz. Not only does this also downplay the amount of food that she eats herself – thus rhetorically working against the counter-claim that she might be eating too much or being greedy – but it also specifies the type of food (protein) that is 'taken'. So the minimisation device works alongside these other constructions (and you may also note the potential ECF on line 9: 'NEVER') to both provide support for Jenny while also accounting for Liz's own food intake.

Lists and contrasts

The use of listing in talk – where items are presented together in a sequential order as if reading from a list – are a particularly useful rhetorical resource in everyday and institutional discourse. Lists typically appear as three-part units (the 'three-part list'; Jefferson, 1990), and this normative pattern is fairly robust across different social settings – so much so, that in the absence of a specific third part, people will often use 'generalised list completers'. For example, a three-part list might be something like: 'he went on, and on, and on' and an example with a generalised list completer (in **bold**) could be: 'there were wolves, raccoons and **all sorts of animals**'. One of the great things about three-part lists is not only that they serve to emphasise something and make it seem more factual or 'real', but they also project a completion point. In other words, they indicate to the other speaker that the person's turn is likely to come to an end: the third-part is so normative as to be expected. This has been evidenced in, for example, political speeches where the audience applause coincided precisely with the end of the three-part list (Heritage & Greatbatch, 1986). The use of contrasts is a related rhetorical device that also works to emphasise one thing over another and highlight the relevance of a particular feature. It occurs when one aspect of discourse is directly compared with another, to emphasise particular characteristics or the distinction between one or more objects.

Worked example

Extract 7.7 provides an illustration of both listing and contrasts. This data is taken from a research paper that analysed audio recordings of antenatal classes in the UK, where expectant parents went for advice and support during pregnancy and in the lead-up to the birth of their child. In this clip, the class leader (CL) is discussing expectations of what is achievable for parents in the first week after the baby is born.

Extract 7.7: Taken from Locke and Horton-Salway (2010: 1219, extract 3)

```
1. CL:   If you are up and dressed by lunchtime in the
2.       first week after the baby then you are doing
3.       really well, and that is what you should be aiming for.
4.       Not cooking, not shopping, not washing, not racing out,
5.       taking care of yourselves. If you think back, my eldest
6.       child is 17, and we had to stop work at 28 weeks.
7.       You had to go and be signed fit to carry on working
```

```
8.      beyond 28 weeks. So consequentially most people didn't
9.      go beyond 32 weeks because it was too much of a hassle
10.     had to go every week to be signed fit. Which is **what**
11.     **we had to do.**
```

There are two examples of contrasts here, though it is difficult to highlight these in bold as the contrast works across the discourse rather than being tied to specific words. The first contrast is between what should and should not be the activities for new parents (lines 1–5, specifically lines 4–5). The lowering of expectations – being 'up and dressed by lunchtime in the first week' (lines 1–2) is further emphasised through the contrast with seemingly everyday activities (cooking, shopping, washing, line 4). The second contrast is between 'what we had to do' (lines 10–11) and parental expectations in the present time with regard to how long you can work during pregnancy. Again, the contrast serves to strengthen the current situation through exemplifying what it could have been like. The use of a list (line 4), although it has more than three-parts, additionally supports the rhetorical features of the contrast. Discursive devices can thus be seen to work collaboratively together in interaction, and should be analysed as such.

Intermediate devices

Having established some familiarity with the 'basic' discursive devices, this section provides descriptions, worked examples and practice tasks for the intermediate devices. These do not typically occur so frequently in talk, or may require a little more skill to apply them, but they are all the more powerful in how they can manage psychological business in interaction. The intermediate DP devices are: affect displays; consensus and corroboration; detail versus vagueness; disclaimers; metaphor; narrative structure; reported speech; script formulations.

Affect displays

Affect displays involve the apparent display of emotion, such as laughing, crying or sighing. Unlike emotion categories, which use words to describe emotions or emotional states, affect displays are those that invoke *the emotion or embodied practice* itself. Some of this work focuses on conversation analytic concerns such as explicating the sequential production and organisation of laughter (e.g., Jefferson, 1984) and crying (Hepburn, 2004), though it has also been used to examine how issues such as 'gustatory pleasure' are produced and made relevant in talk (Wiggins, 2002). In DP, the concern is not to make claims about whether or not an emotion has been 'experienced', but rather to examine how displays of affect work to manage psychological business at a particular moment in social interaction. This device can be analysed, then, for where and when it is located in talk and interaction, and how it is orientated to or made relevant. Past research examining affect displays (see references above) have noted that they are typically highly organised in interaction; orientated to by both the speaker and others in interaction as socially relevant.

Worked example

Extract 7.8 is taken from a study that examined calls to a child protection helpline in the UK (CPO = child protection officer). In this particular fragment the caller becomes audibly upset, as shown by the ~ in the transcript to indicate 'tremulous' or wobbly voice.

Extract 7.8: Taken from Hepburn and Potter (2007: 93–94, extract 2)

```
1. Caller:   But he's very very violent. An' I'm-
2.           I'm scared of my own son.
3. CPO:      Are you
4.           (.)
5. Caller:   Yes.=I am. Yeah.
6.           (0.5)
7. CPO:      How long've you been scare:d of him for:.=
8. Caller:   I've been scare:d of ~'im~ (0.2) (right across::)
9.           (0.8) a ↑long t(hh)°°ime.°°
10.          (0.3)
11. CPO:     ↑Mm::, hh
12.          (3.5)
13. CPO:     °Take °°ye time.°°
14.          (5.1)
15. Caller:  Hhh
```

One of the issues noted in Hepburn and Potter (2007) is that calls to this service can often be highly charged and emotional, given as they are dealing with potential cases of child abuse. What is important for the CPOs is therefore that they gather sufficient information from the caller in order to be able to follow up the case and intervene where necessary. If callers become upset, however, there is a risk that they will terminate the call and thus the helpline organisation cannot take any further action. Being sensitive to potential 'affect displays' is therefore an important skill for CPOs, shown here in lines 11–14 where the silences and quietly spoken 'take your time' (line 13) give space for the caller to continue, while also gently affiliating with the caller, and acknowledge and validate the upsetting nature of the call. Being able to examine affect displays, where and how these are produced, and how they are attended to by others in the interaction can thus provide unique insights into how psychological business is handled. In this case, the psychological business is 'being upset' and the delicate family issue of a mother claiming to be scared of her own son.

Consensus and corroboration

The related concepts of consensus (reporting something as if many or all people are in agreement) and corroboration (reporting something as if supported by an independent source) are particularly useful in building up the factuality of accounts. As with other devices – such as reported speech – they work by invoking other people in support of whatever it is you are claiming. They are often used in accounts that manage attributional and accountability issues, of the untangling of complex social relationships or the unpacking of an event. So this is a device that might feature in institutional accounts (such as in newspaper reports or political rhetoric) or when the factuality of an account is under question. Consensus in itself can provide corroboration; if many people are in agreement, then this supports the factuality of the claim. With consensus, however, there is a risk that it could be challenged as collusion: that the 'many others' or 'all' who support your account may not be working independently. In the case of witnesses or court cases, this could have serious implications. This is where corroboration comes in, as it only needs one apparently independent account to provide support for and validate the account. This is, however, at greater risk from being challenged: it is much easier to undermine one independent witness than many.

Worked example

In Extract 7.9, we see an example of consensus being used alongside a contrast device. It is taken from an interview with people where they were shown news media clips and asked how they made sense of competing views, particularly in relation to political debate.

Extract 7.9: Taken from Dickerson (2000: 388–389, extract 3a)

```
1.  N:  that Margaret Margaret what's her name? Margaret
2.  ?:  =Beckett
```

```
3.  N:   Margaret Beckett I think is a (.) is an idiot
4.  M:   well she made an idiotic remark I think (.) by saying
5.       that the `government's clapped out'
6.  S:   well anyone can say that (.) Joe Bloggs on the street
7.       can say that really=
8.  M:   =yeah hehhehe (colloquial dialect)`gavernment's clapped
9.       awt '
```

The consensus terms used here – 'anyone can say that' (line 6), 'Joe Bloggs on the street can say that' (lines 6–7) - work to diminish the status of the politician's (Margaret Beckett's) remark. Not only does it suggest that it was an 'idiotic' (line 4) thing to say, but also that it didn't require any special skill or knowledge, in that 'anyone' can – and be entitled to – say that. The term 'Joe Bloggs' is a British colloquial term to refer to a hypothetical 'average' person. This further supports the claim that it was an idiotic remark, in that any 'average' person could say it. Consensus is provided here from 'anyone' and 'Joe Bloggs' – in themselves also drawing on vagueness and lack of specificity – even if in practice it would be easy to find someone to challenge that claim. Note, however, that the extract here also includes an extreme case formulation: 'anyone can say that'. As such, what is also going on here is that this turn in talk is hearably going to extremes, emphasising the point in a manner that is not designed to be taken literally. As noted above, it would be easy to find one person to refute the claim (i.e., one person who *wouldn't* say that), but that is not the point. The point is that this turn makes a particular case about the politician in a way that undermines the status of her speech.

Detail versus vagueness

The opposing categories of vivid detail or systematic vagueness can be used to manage a number of psychological concerns in social interaction. They are often involved in what Potter (1996) has described as constructing the 'out-there-ness' of an object or event; producing it as a fact or reality, independent of our accounts. Using detail in an account can be used to add credibility to your category as a 'reliable witness' or someone whose report is more factual. This can be useful on occasions when our category entitlement as trustworthy is under threat. Alternatively, being 'systematically vague' – i.e., vague or lacking in clarity on particular issues – can be a way of inoculating against claims that you might have a stake in what you are saying (see also 'stake inoculation' device). In other words, there are times when being *too detailed* and specific might appear as if you are too heavily invested in the account. Trying too hard, as it were. Sometimes details can be challenged or seen to be inaccurate, and so vagueness can be more robust on such occasions; it is less easy to contradict someone if their account is not specific.

Worked example

Extract 7.10 is taken from a study examining student blogs on an educational online noticeboard, where the blogs were designed to enable students to reflect on what they know about a topic before learning more in class. Issues of student identity and of knowledge claims are therefore relevant here, and these blogs were made publicly available to fellow students and tutors.

Extract 7.10: Taken from Lester and Paulus (2011: 676, extract 1)

```
1. I don't really know much about supplements. I've always
2. had the impression that vitamins are good for you. I know
3. that my mom takes a daily multivitamin and another type of
4. mineral supplement for health reasons, which was recommended
5. by her doctor. So, these types of things don't scare me, and
6. are probably something I'll consider taking in the future.
7. However, like a few people have said, things that are
8. supposed to give you energy do make me nervous. As far as
9. protein shakes go and other types of protein supplements that
10. many athletes consume, I don't know much about them. I've
11. never had any personal experience with them, but alot of my
12. guy friends have taken things of that nature in the past
```

Alongside the use of possible disclaimers (e.g.,'I don't really know much', line 1), the presence of vague references to the fact that 'vitamins are good for you' (line 2) and that 'things that are supposed to give you energy' (lines 7–8) serve to provide support for this account while also situating the account as based on second-hand knowledge. Note, for example, how the reference to 'my mom' (line 3), 'a few people' (line 7) and 'a lot of my guy friends' (lines 11–12) could be considered corroboration for her account. So the vagueness refers to what it is that vitamins *actually do*, and as such the student here is downplaying her own status as expert, but also providing an account

Disclaimers

Disclaimers are typically short phrases at the start of a turn in talk that try to mitigate the speaker's stance on a particular issue. They do so by explicitly denying a potentially negative interpretation of what they are about to say, even if the rest of their turn contradicts this. Disclaimers are often in the form of, 'I'm not racist/sexist/homophobic, but…' or 'I have nothing against (insert category of person), but…'. As such, they are often used in situations where someone's identity or category membership is under question. They can be used in conjunction with a number of other devices, such as contrasts, category entitlements and assessments.

Worked example

In Extract 7.11, a couple are being interviewed in their home about services in their local area. This is taken from a study about how denials of prejudice are often achieved collaboratively with other speakers.

Extract 7.11: Taken from Condor et al. (2006: 452, extract 3)

```
1.  Jack:    let's face it, it's not as if they're wanted here.
2.           we have enough low- life here already without
3.           importing [other people's.
4.  Hilda:             [Jack! ((to Susan)) I'm sorry about
5.           that. He's not xenophobic. It's it's not=
6.  Jack:    =it's not racist, no. We've never been racist,
7.           have we Hilda?
8.  Hilda:   No. We've got nothing against=
9.  Jack:    =nothing against the refugees. I have every sympathy
10.          for them. But you'd be mad not to ask, why are they
11.          all coming here?
```

There are a number of disclaimers in this extract, some of which (on lines 5 and 6) are working to defend against the potential for Jack's turn in lines 1–3 to be heard as xenophobic.

So in producing the disclaimer, 'he's not xenophobic' (line 5), Hilda works to resist that particular categorisation of Jack by challenging it explicitly. There then follows a series of disclaimers, which deny that what was said was racist ('it's not racist', line 6) as well as denying that *both* Jack and Hilda are racist ('we've never been racist', line 6). Similarly, the phrase 'we've got nothing against' (line 8, completed on line 9) also works to undermine any potentially negative interpretation of what is being said. And yet, what follows on lines 10–11 still marks boundaries between a seemingly homogeneous 'they' who are coming 'here'. This extract also makes use of footing and pronoun shifts to manage these claims.

Metaphor

The use of metaphors in discourse refers to the way in which descriptions equate one thing with another to make a comparison or produce a particular rhetorical effect. For example, the phrase 'your words are poison' is not a literal statement but constructs someone's speech in a way that suggests that it causes severe harm or damage. Metaphors can therefore be used to produce categories of the world, and of people themselves (hence it is linked with the category entitlement device), in that it constructs particular versions of the world that often have quite visual or figurative references. As such, metaphors can be useful to highlight some features while blurring or concealing others; they can overly simplify the distinction between one category and another. They can also, therefore, overlap with extreme case formulations, which are other devices which foreground a non-literal interpretation and could also be easily undermined or challenged. Edwards (1991) provides a detailed discussion of how the production of categories, and metaphors, can be considered discursive rather than perceptual or cognitive.

Worked example

The example in Extract 7.12 is taken from a study that examined the ways in which speakers managed their subjective investment in the complaints that they were making, that is, how they produced their complaints as properly 'complainable matters' rather than an example of how they might be characterised as moaning, whinging or generally a complaining type of person. The section of talk is taken from a phone call between friends, one of whom (Lesley) has recently had her home burgled and the police have been to her home to search for fingerprints. It is the burglar who is being referred to as the 'visitor' here.

Extract 7.12: Taken from Edwards (2005a: 17, extract 9)

```
1. Art:   How how've you settled in now after the: (p)
2.        visitor.
3.        (0.2)
```

```
4.  Les:   .hhh Oh: (.) eh hheh he .hh Well- (0.2) .h (.) I
5.         ↑mus' say this finger↓print stuff makes a me:ss but
6.  Art:   Oh:.
7.  Les:   An' I can' get the mud off the cushion: but a↑part
8.         f'm that we're alri:gh[t?
9.  Art:                         [What a ↓nuisance.
10.        (0.2)
11. Les:   Ye:[s.
12. Art:      [(Fancy) galloping all over the cushion this is
13.        ridiculous isn' it
```

The 'complainable' here is on line 5 with the comment about 'this fingerprint stuff' from the police. While this in itself is analysable – in that we might expect the burglary to be the source of the complaint, not the police investigation of this – it is the metaphor on line 12 that is our focus here. The term 'galloping all over the cushion' responds to an earlier issue noted by Lesley that the burglar had left muddy footprints all over a cushion in her house. The metaphor 'galloping' produces this in a rather comical manner; it attends to the seriousness of the issue while also dealing with the irony of being concerned about a cushion (rather than, say, the break-in and any valuables stolen). The metaphor works here, then, as a way of packaging up the event in a particular way, to manage issues such as what counts as a complaint and who should be complaining (and when).

Narrative structure

Narrative, in its simplest interpretation, is like the telling of a story. But it is more than that; it is the production of an account with a coherent, sequential order. This may involve setting the scene (where and when did something happen), the timescales (how long did it take), the order of events (what happened first), and so on. The narrative structure of an account is often also combined with other features, such as the inclusion of vivid details or vagueness in specific places; each of these helps to support the credibility of the narrative. Narratives can be used in cases where people are accounting for something that they may or may not have had a personal liability in, such as accounts of illness (e.g., Tucker, 2004) or criminal activity (Auburn & Lea, 2003). Note that this is not the same as taking a narrative approach to analysis, which involves a different set of epistemological assumptions about discourse.

Worked example

Extract 7.13 is taken from a study into the group interactions in a sex offender treatment programme, and the way in which offenders account for their criminal activities. Part of the programme requires offenders to provide an account – their story – of events.

Extract 7.13: Taken from Auburn and Lea (2003: 287, extract 2)

```
1. PO1:    Well talk us through that (unclear)
2.         (2.5)
3. Off:    Uu::hh, well we'd gone out out and we went down to a
4.         club which was about 20 mile away,
5.         uu::m (1) um by th- by the time my wife, my son, and
6.         Sally had drunk a lot
7.         I didn't drink as much 'cos I was driving, I had a 20
8.         mile drive back home (2) [sigh]
9.         so when we got home then we had a cup of coffee and
10.        I put on a, some records while we were drinking
```

There are a number of features to this narrative example, such as description of what had happened first (gone to a club), the location of this (20 miles away), and a sense of time in relation to the unfolding events ('by the time', line 5; 'when we got home', line 9). Each of these on their own would not necessarily make this a strong narrative, so it is the culmination of various features of the discourse that performs the action here. In doing so, and producing it as a 'normal night out', the speaker is also managing his own accountability and involvement in the criminal behaviour.

Reported speech (aka active voicing)

Reported speech (sometimes known as 'active voicing') refers to those features of speech that attribute the source of the talk to another speaker. This typically appears to be reporting what was said on a previous occasion. So the talk is presented as if it is a direct reproduction: not just the words of another speaker, but often presented as if it is in the same style or delivery. They can often be prefaced with phrases such as, 'and he was like…' or 'she said…'. It can therefore be used to produce a particularly vivid account, to attend to the speaker's own identity and accountability for what is said, and for footing shifts. It can help to increase the factuality of one's account, to make it seem more realistic and also to minimise one's own stake in what is being said. In other words, it can construct the speaker as if they are merely 'reporting back' and not accountable for the content of the talk.

Worked example

Extract 7.14 is taken from audio-recorded Dutch criminal trials in the closing arguments between the prosecutor and defence lawyers. Reported speech can be particularly useful in such institutional settings where the aim is to 'get the facts' and stay close to the original version of events. In this extract, you will see the English translation on the first set of each pair of lines, with the original Dutch words underneath.

Extract 7.14: Taken from Sneijder (2014: 477, extract 3)

```
1.  on the other hand I understand J a little when he says like
2.  aan de andere kant eh snap ik J ook wel een beetje dat ie
3.  zegt van
4.  yeah, but I e:h didn't behave violently at all did I
5.  ja maar ik heb toch e:h toch helemaal niet gewelddadig
6.  gedragen,
7.  eh (.) with the word violently,
8.  eh (.) bij het woord gewelddadig,
9.  you rather think of indeed (.) slapping, kicking,
10. denk je ook wel meer aan (.) inderdaad slaan, schoppen,
11. threatening
12. dreigen,
```

The reported speech here is enclosed in what Sneijder (2014) refers to as the pre-quotation and post-quotation talk; so the surrounding talk of the reported speech is as important as the reported speech itself. Framing the talk in this way then enables the speaker to partially align with the source of the reported speech ('J', line 1) as well as using it as evidence to support their case. As such, it is not only that reported speech is used to emphasise or validate a particular account, but it is also the sequential placement of the speech that adds to its rhetorical effect. This can mean, for example, the speaker prefacing or building up to the reported speech, and using it as a 'punchline' or, in extract 7.14, a basis on which to then 'unpack' the words spoken.

Script formulations

Script formulations are descriptions that present a behaviour or event as if it regularly or frequently occurs: as if following a script (Edwards, 1994, 1995). As such, they can be used to present the behaviour as normal or expected, as not unusual in any way. Script formulations can also be combined with 'dispositional formulations' (or a person script), where a person's character or disposition is constructed as if routine and predictable. Note that this can also be seen in the emotion categories device. Scripting is theorised in discursive terms, rather than perceptual ones, so it is argued that something is produced in the unfolding sequence of interaction as being scripted in a particular way. So they are produced to rhetorically defend against alternative descriptions (or formulations). Script formulations often draw on modals, such as 'would', reporting something as plural (e.g., arguments, parties), adverbs such as 'always' or 'usually', or verbs which highlight the regularity or iterative nature of something (e.g., 'gets', 'loses'). See Edwards (1995) for a summary of scripting devices. When examining discourse for script formulations, however, the focus should be on how the script works alongside the rest of the interaction; we are not simply spotting words but examining talk for its action-orientation.

Worked example

Extract 7.15 is taken from a speed-dating conversation between a man (M) and a woman (F) who are meeting each other for the first time and have been asking questions such as 'what do you look for in a man/woman?' Scripting is thus a characteristic feature of such conversations precisely because the participants are having to formulate what it is they do/are/like on a regular basis in order to try to persuade the other person that they might be a suitable future romantic partner.

Extract 7.15: Taken from Korobov (2011: 474, extract 9)

```
1. F:   not into the complaining women?
2. M:   no hh. I don't like that (.) complaining (.)
3.      I def'don't like that [n
4. F:                         [gossipy n'all that?
5. M:   oh yeah(hha) (.) no hehe
6. F:   no hh. me'neither (.) it ain't worth th'time
7. M:   f'real n'some r'jus like that (.) n'I ain't saying
8.      they're bad or [( )
9. F:                  [I-( )I'was gonna say >women say'dey
```

DISCURSIVE DEVICES

```
10.         don't like it< but they get caught up n'then it's routine
11. M:      mm::hm:: yup
12. F:      you know wt'I mean? (.) you pr'bly been w'girls
13.         that think valuable conversations'bout talkin'bout
14.         evry'body elses business [ya y'you know?
15. M:                               [yep I have girls who
16.         do that (.) who always complaining r'moaning
17.         r'naggin' or talkin'bout others just use all the energy up
18. F:      exactly (.) it uses up the energy
```

There are a number of scripted features here, most of which refer to what 'other' women are like to create a contrast between the speaker's own stance and those of other people. This is another example of how devices can work together in a stretch of talk, and how identifying them in isolation does not constitute a full analysis. In this extract, the scripting refers to what women say (line 9), what they do (lines 10 and 16), what they think (line 13), and then specific characterisations of them as 'always complaining', 'moaning', 'nagging' or 'talking about others'. The analysis could also examine how these script formulations work to produce particular gender categorisations: how women are produced in particular ways, and how the speaker's own (gendered) identity is then partly produced through contrasting with this. Note that it is F who first proposes the category of 'complaining women' (line 1) which she then uses to create distance between her own stance on the issue (line 18).

Advanced devices

The final section of discursive devices are not necessarily harder to identify, but they either occur less frequently in talk or they require a little more skill in using them in analysis. They are: agent-subject distinction; emotion categories; category entitlements; modal verbs; and stake inoculation.

Agent-subject distinction

In this device, we are considering how the agency of the speaker (or the agency of those being spoken about) is managed within the talk. Are they characterised as being agentic, as having choice, the capacity to act and make decisions or determine the course of behaviour, for example? Or are they characterised as subjects, as passive and to whom things are done? This can be as simple as the distinction between saying something like, 'I had gone to the shop' (active/agent) rather than, 'I had to go shopping' (passive/subject).

In the latter formulation, the speaker is constructed as having little (or no) choice in whether they had to go shopping. The use of the agent-subject distinction, therefore, can be particularly useful where people are managing their accountability for a behaviour or event. It is typically analysed in terms of how the level of agency is being managed in talk; that is, it is rarely as straightforward as a dichotomy between being active or not. Situations in which someone's agency might be particularly important to the consequences of the interaction are police or courtroom interrogation (Stokoe & Edwards, 2008) or neighbour mediation (Stokoe & Wallwork, 2003), for example.

Worked example

In Extract 7.16, S (suspect) is being interrogated by a police officer (P) in the UK about possible criminal damage to his neighbour's house. It could be argued that the whole interrogation can be analysed in terms of agency and accountability, and to what extent the suspect is liable for the damage (and thus can be prosecuted).

Extract 7.16: Taken from Stokoe and Edwards (2008: 104–105, extract 3c)

```
1. P:   Um: an' you kne:w (.) the do:or didn't
2.      *↓belong to you.*=
3. S:   Ye:h.
4. P:   [*(Yep.)*
5. S:   [>I w's< jus' so A:NGry you know warrame:an. (.)
6.      I'd just (be/been) insu:lted.
7. P:   Understo:od, (0.6) So- (0.2) did you- (.)
8.      when you hit the do:or (0.4) with the golf club
9.      >did you< inte:nd to- damage the door.
10.     (0.7)
11. S:  ↑↑NO! (0.4) ↑It ↑wouldn't ↑anyway.(0.3)
12.     The ↑doors as strong as oa:k
```

One of the features of the questioning from P in this extract is to present questions in a way that invite a 'yes/no' response from S. The way in which P formulates the questions is thus important in terms of having an admission from S that makes relevant particular actions. In this case, it is the hitting of the door (line 8) that is one of the criminal behaviours; and 'you hit' formulates this not only as agentic (in that S is the cause of the action), but it also suggests a category of action (hitting, rather than, say, knocking or tapping) that implies a degree of force. The question here, however, is combined with another agentic behaviour (intention, line 9) and it is possibly to this latter suggestion that S gives his strong 'no' response. Note that there is also an interesting use of an emotion category here (line 5), which we will examine in the next device.

Emotion categories

Emotion categories are those instances in which speakers verbally make relevant a particular category of emotions or emotional states. Note that this is different from affect displays, which suggest that the emotion is being *displayed* or *experienced*; by contrast, emotion categories can be delivered in a way that reports on past or current emotion states as if reporting on any other individual characteristic. For example, someone might refer to themselves as being 'so happy I could cry', or someone else as 'she's always so angry'. In DP, emotion categories are analysed as a discursive accomplishment – with how they are used, invoked and consequential in interaction – rather than whether they suggest an individual emotional 'experience'. They are often involved in rhetorical work to present a contrast with other categories, such as emotional as opposed to rational, logical or cognitively-based, or to set up a distinction between someone being genuinely emotional and 'faking it', or as having the emotion because of some external event or driven by an emotional disposition. Emotion categories can therefore be used in a range of different social actions, such as managing one's identity or accountability, managing one's stake in a state of affairs, or supporting the factuality or credibility of a claim.

Worked example

Extract 7.17 is taken from a counselling session with a married couple (Mary and Jeff), where Mary is telling her account of when she decided to tell Jeff about an extra-marital affair that she had recently ended.

Extract 7.17: Taken from Edwards (1999: 276, extract 3)

```
1. Mary:   (...) so that's when I decided to (.)
2.         you know to tell him. (1.0) u::m (1.0)
3.         and then::, (.) obviously you went
4.         through your a:ngry stage, didn't you?
5.         (.) ve:ry upset obviously, .hh an:d uh,
6.         (0.6) we: started ar:guing a lot, an:d
7.         (0.6) just drifted awa:y.
```

The emotion categories used here – 'angry stage' and 'very upset' – are both used in reference to Jeff, in relation to his reaction to Mary's news of her affair. Not only do they treat Jeff's reaction as primarily emotional (rather than, say, rational), but the repeated use of the word 'obviously' orientates to this as being a normal and expected reaction. The anger is not just anger, it is an 'angry stage', and thus constructed as if being a temporary state. The sequential placement of these terms is as important as how they are described: immediately after the news of the affair and just before the account of 'arguing' (line 6) and 'drifting away' (line 7). What is being dealt with here, then, is Mary and Jeff's accountability for the problems in their marriage. The use of emotion categories both invokes a justifiable reaction to the affair, but it also sets up a potentially ongoing issue of how those emotional reactions might then impede any repair of the relationship.

Category entitlements

Working up categories and category entitlements are one of the key ways in which identities are managed in interaction. These can be categories such as being an ordinary person, an expert in a particular skill, belonging to a particular group or geographical area, or someone who can be trusted. So categories do not always have to be broad social groupings, such as those defined by age, gender, ethnicity, nationality or some other demographic. They can be small, everyday and seemingly trivial things. Work in this area overlaps with what have been termed 'normalising' devices, such as Jefferson's (1984) examination of 'At first I thought...' sequences, and building on Sacks' (1984) work on 'doing being ordinary' (see also the stake inoculation device). What is important, however, is that these categories are consequential for that moment in the interaction; they are bound up with the social action taking place. Category entitlements are then what follows from these categories; the kind of knowledge, experiences, skills or responsibilities that the category is entitled to own. For example, the category of 'expert' is entitled to claim knowledge about a certain topic, but an 'ordinary person' is expected *not* to possess supernatural powers. Category entitlements can also be used when people are managing the factuality of claims; how they treat each other as having a stake in what is being said, and thus potentially undermining its credibility (Potter, 1996). For instance, by categorising a person in a particular way, one can support or undermine their potential claims to different category entitlements.

Worked example

Even the category of 'being ordinary' has enormous potential, and this is particularly clearly seen in reports of paranormal experiences, where people are working up not only the credibility of their account, but also the implications that this has for them as credible persons. Extract 7.18 is taken from a collection by Robin Wooffitt (1991) on people's accounts of having had some kind of paranormal experience, such as seeing a ghost, claiming clairvoyency, or experiencing poltergeist activity. The speaker's husband (David) was an RAF pilot who had recently died; she is talking here about a moment during the funeral.

Extract 7.18: Taken from Wooffitt (1991: 270, extract 3)

```
1. an' I went in there (.) er:m w-with my mother-in-law
2. and uhm:(0.4) friends that were with me
3. (1.3)
4. .hhh (.) and I was looking at the coffin
5. and there was David standing there
6. (0.3) he was in Blues
```

The presentation of this account is in what Wooffitt describes as an X/Y format, where X is the mundane and ordinary behaviour or event, and Y is the paranormal or extraordinary thing. These two formulations are usually presented in close sequential order (the Y immediately follows the X) and in doing so this highlights the contrast between the two. In the example, the speaker is doing the ordinary thing of looking at the coffin at her husband's funeral, when the extraordinary thing (seeing his ghost) is reported immediately after. So it is the combination of both the content of the talk (what is said) and its sequential order (when it is said) that does the work here of producing the account as if unexpected. The speaker's category of 'an ordinary person' is thus invoked here through a category relevant behaviour – doing something very ordinary – so categories do not always have to be directly named or explicitly stated to be invoked in this way. The upshot of the X/Y formulations is that it enables people to defend against the claim that they might have been looking for something strange or unusual by showing that the weirdness came to them.

Modal verbs

Modal verbs are those that implicate the speaker's degree of ability, obligation, intention or permission to be able to perform that activity. These are verbs such as: might, could, would, should, can, must and will. They invoke a range of different psychological issues in themselves, such as being responsible or accountable for something or being able to do something, and in that sense it might be easy to identify them in your data. They do, however, require a more sophisticated analysis: we cannot simply point to them and show that someone is managing their obligation to perform a task, for example. They are thus in the 'advanced' list because they need to be interpreted alongside other features of talk; to examine the *possible* implications of these terms, and then to interpret how they are being managed by the participants themselves. This is one of the core requirements of DP: that we examine participants' orientations in talk, rather than analysis based on our own assumptions or purely on the basis of linguistics.

Worked example

Extract 7.19 is taken from research into an online veganism discussion forum, where participants were often seeking advice or suggestions about what to eat when following a vegan diet. One of the issues that is raised elsewhere on the forum is that there may be a risk of vitamin (or other) deficiencies if one does not follow an appropriate diet regimen (e.g., when not eating enough of a particular category or type of food).

Extract 7.19: Taken from Sneijder and te Molder (2004: 607, extract 3)

```
1.  Date: 3 June
2.  From: Victor
3.  Hi, I do hope you found good info about a healthy diet as well.
4.  Veganism and a healthy diet are certainly not mutually exclusive.
5.  [... 20 lines omitted ...]
6.  And if you have a glass of fruit syrup (without added sugar)
7.  with every meal, or another source of vitamin C, then
8.  there shouldn't be any problems, certainly not with iron or zinc
9.  particular
```

The modal verb 'shouldn't' (line 8) is used here to manage the accountability that people might face when following a vegan diet: is the vitamin deficiency likely because they have not followed the diet correctly, or because a vegan diet, by definition, misses out on food groups that would provide those vitamins? This is a delicate issue in a vegan discussion forum, as the forum members themselves identify as following a vegan diet; anything that potentially troubles the 'vegan' category is thus problematic. What can be seen in this extract, then, is the forum member (Victor) constructing his response in an 'if…then…' format: if (you do this) then (there shouldn't be any problems). The implication, then, is that the vegan diet itself is not likely to cause vitamin deficiencies: it is the responsibility of the individual to eat correctly and following guidelines to ensure that they stay healthy.

Stake inoculation

Stake inoculation refers to a range of practices whereby discourse is constructed to defend against claims that the speaker might have a stake in, or be overly invested in, what they are saying. This is similar to saying that the speaker might be 'biased', 'subjective' or 'twisting the truth to serve their own purposes'. It usually occurs, however, in a subtle rather than a direct way, and so contrasts with disclaimers where the issue is tackled directly. In many ways, stake inoculation is one of the more fundamental issues of a DP analysis, though it can cover a range of different devices and, as such, there is no single way in which it can be identified. This is why it is in the 'advanced' category rather than the basic one. DP is concerned with how people *treat each other* as being factual, believable, accountable and so on, rather than with whether accounts are 'facts' in themselves. So using the concept of stake inoculation, we can examine discursive practices to see how they are put together to inoculate, rhetorically defend against or resist counter-claims that they may be less-than-factual (Potter, 1996).

Worked example

Extract 7.20 is taken from a study that involved the interviewing of paranormal investigators about their experiences of paranormal events. As noted below, however, being able to state that something was, or was not, paranormal also involves the issue of credibility as a witness (see also category entitlements).

Extract 7.20: Taken from Childs and Murray (2010: 26, extract 1)

```
1. Ad:    ↓ye::ah so I mean par- ee: <paranormal
2.        (0.2) we ca:n't say (.) b'cause we can't
3.        prove it wa:s, but we can't prove at the
4.        mo:ment, we can't prove it wa:snt,
5.        (.) neither. (0.2)
```

The phrase, 'we can't prove it wasn't' (line 4) is an example of stake inoculation whereby the speaker defends against the claim that he might be biased simply because he is a 'paranormal investigator', and thus potentially looking out for such activity. The use of the word 'proof' is also particularly helpful here, given that it hints at scientific endeavours in which evidence is required to prove a theory or assumption. So while the speaker here doesn't directly say, 'you can believe me', the use of this stake inoculation device works to help achieve the social action of being a believable or credible witness.

KEY POINTS

- The discursive devices are analytical tools that can help us to 'unpack' interaction.
- Not all of the devices will be needed for your analysis; be guided by what you find in your data.
- The DP devices often work together in discourse; more than one device is typically used to examine any section of talk.
- The important thing is to use the devices as an analytical tool to examine the social actions and psychological issues that are being managed in the unfolding sequence of interaction.

Recommended reading

Potter, J. (1996). *Representing reality: Discourse, rhetoric and social construction.* London: Sage.

Wood, L. & Kroger, R. (2000). *Doing discourse analysis: Methods for studying action in talk and text.* London: Sage. Particularly Chapters 7 and 8.

8

WRITING UP AND PRESENTING DP ANALYSES

Chapter contents

Starting to write	177
Developing and editing your writing	179
The sections of a DP report	180
Software to assist the writing and reporting processes	188
Publication issues	190

This chapter will guide you through the process of writing up or presenting your DP analysis, providing details on what to include in each section of your report, what software can help, and how to prepare your manuscripts for publication. For some of you, this will be the bit that you have been avoiding, and indeed, the idea of writing a report can be a daunting task. Where do you start? How will you fit everything in? Some of you might even have experienced 'writer's block': the paralysing fear of the blank page and an inability to get started with a piece of writing. Fear not. Just as a marathon begins with one small step, so writing is a case of starting with one word, and writing *anything* to keep you going. The important thing is that you start writing early on and that you keep writing. The trick is then at the editing stage, where you can sculpt and re-write the text until the content and structure are clearly established. Like analysis, writing is a skill that improves with practice and the more you do it, the more your writing will improve. So, grab your coffee and laptop, and let's get started.

Starting to write

The most important thing is that you get started on your writing as soon as you can. Begin when you first think of a research idea, and continue making notes and writing as you collect your data. At first, it matters less about the content of your writing; you should focus on just getting started and keeping going. Writing can also help us to develop our analyses and ideas about the data. It should therefore be considered as part of the analytical process rather than what we do at the end. With that in mind, use the following tips to help you begin writing.

Time

Don't wait for a 'good time' to write or for when you feel like you have done enough reading. If such time arises, it will usually be too late (and there is *always* going to be more to read). Instead, consider your days in terms of small chunks of time – maybe 30 minutes or one hour at a time – and find spaces in your diary where you have a chunk or two free. These can then be writing time. Short bursts of writing can be as effective (if not more so) than long hours on end. Use a timer, if that helps, to provide a fixed period of time in which to concentrate.

Space

Find a quiet space to write with minimal distractions. At the very least, you will need a chair to sit on and a table on which to rest your laptop or computer. If you don't have a quiet space around you when writing, wear headphones and listen to music that you can concentrate with. Or just wear headphones. Find a way to block out sounds and sights around you; even wearing a hat or hood can help to narrow your attention onto the screen in front of you (trust me on this one; this can also be a bonus if your house is chilly).

Reading

Rather than being a distracting activity, reading can help you to become more familiar with the writing styles that *you* enjoy reading as well as to gain a greater understanding of the topic area or analytical approach. Read lots of DP research too, so that you can become familiar with the conventions of these reports. Read lots and read widely. At a later stage, this reading will be important for demonstrating that your own work contributes to the existing literature.

Be focused

The familiar tip of breaking down a task into small chunks will serve you well here. Focus on one section of writing at a time, such as the rationale for your study, analytical notes about a data extract, or a paragraph on the implications of your analysis. Keeping it focused on one small section can help to make it feel more manageable, and it should also help you to be clearer about exactly what it is that you want to say.

Be organised

Have a place where you can store all of your writing or notes together. This might be a folder on your computer, with clearly labelled individual word documents (e.g., not just 'analysis notes' but 'analysis notes on false teeth extract'; choose something that is easily recognisable to you). You might also consider software such as Scrivener (see section below), which allows you to organise notes and writing sections in one space.

Consider your audience

Writing is always done for a purpose and there will always be an audience for whom we are writing, even if it is just for ourselves. While you are writing, therefore, think about *what* and *who* your writing is for. Is it an assignment only to be read by your tutor (and will it be assessed)? Is it to be published and likely to be read by researchers in a certain discipline? Use these questions to help you to guide your writing towards answering particular questions, such as: what will they want to know? Is it being assessed according to particular criteria? If you can find a trusted friend or peer to read your work and give you constructive and supportive feedback, so much the better.

Box 8.1: Short writing exercise

Try the following exercise to help you to start writing. Write a summary of your research project or idea (choose something you would like to research, even if you haven't started yet), and include the following: a brief description of the topic area, the focus and aims of your research project and why this is important. You should try to write around 200 words, so you will need to be concise in places. Do not worry about whether your writing is 'academic' enough. Clarity is much more important at this stage (see also Box 8.2).

Developing and editing your writing

Once you have begun to write, you have overcome the first hurdle. You can now focus on the task of writing your report or manuscript. As you do so, keep two things in mind. First, do not try to polish and refine your writing as you go along. Aim to write one paragraph (or a section) of your report at a time and concentrate on just getting the words and ideas written down. If it helps, write it as if you were explaining it to a friend or family member (someone who isn't familiar with what you are studying); that way, you are more likely to focus on being clear. It is unlikely to be perfect at this stage and this is completely normal.

The first draft is just that – a first draft – and it will probably look very different compared to the final version. Even very experienced writers go through many stages of drafting and re-drafting their writing. This is what is known as editing: we go back through our writing and change words or sentences, move parts around, add in further details and references or cut sections out. This latter point can be difficult at first. Deleting a section of text that you have spent hours working on can feel brutal. Sometimes this is necessary (and if in doubt, you can always move that piece of writing into another document just in case you find a use for it elsewhere), and taking a break from your work can help you to gain some distance from it. I mean this literally: walking away from your laptop or computer and doing something else can help you to tackle it afresh when you return. All the better if that break involves strong coffee or a nice cup of tea. You might also find it helpful to give your work to a trusted friend for constructive feedback. Do this once you have reached a point where you feel that you cannot do any more to improve it; that way, the feedback is likely to help with aspects that you have not already noticed for yourself.

The editing stage is where we sculpt our work into something that resembles the kinds of writing we see in published articles and books. It is all part of the process of writing and developing our ideas. Which brings me on to the second point: writing is not the end-point of our work. It is, in fact, central to the process of developing your analysis. Writing can help you to clarify and sharpen your analysis and this is why, as noted in Chapter 6, the writing-up stage is in many ways interwoven with the analysis stage. It is just that book chapters tend to present things as if in a linear progression (chapter 1, then 2, then 3, and so on) and as if separate from each other. In practice, it is much messier and more like zigzagging back and forth between different phases of research. This is why I encouraged you to start writing early on, even when you have only just begun your research. The benefit of this is that we typically do not need to have worked everything out before we start writing. The writing process enables us to work everything out through forcing us to be very clear and specific about exactly what we want to say.

As you develop your writing, then, take comfort in knowing that each time you draft and edit your work, you are doing exactly the same thing as every other writer – including professional authors – and this is all part of the process of developing our ideas and analyses as much as our writing skills. This process is usually hidden because we only ever read the finished, published versions of people's work. We don't see the deleted sections, the sketchy ideas, the awkward phrasing and the poor structure of the earlier versions. Likewise with your own work: you can be as messy and chaotic as you like while you are drafting your report. Nobody ever needs to see it.

The sections of a DP report

We now come to the structure of a written, academic report for DP research. The core structure is very similar regardless of whether you are writing a report for a short class project, an undergraduate or Masters dissertation or a published manuscript. There are variations, of course, according to the particular requirements of university programmes or academic journals, but for the most part these are often stylistic rather than content-related. This section should therefore guide you regardless of what writing task you are engaged in. We will work through each section of a DP report in turn, with guidance and advice on how to submit a clear and coherent report. As you write the report, keep one thing in focus: the report is not a crime or mystery novel. Do not wait until the end to reveal the main argument or analysis. Instead, state this clearly and directly at the very start; let it be the core message that you then unpack and detail in the subsequent sections.

Title

Titles should be clear, concise and tell the reader what to expect in the report. Decide on the specific focus of your research and include this in the title (e.g., 'transgender identities in older adults', not just 'identities'). Titles can also make use of colons to separate a short and snappy title from something more descriptive. They do not have to be witty or clever, but do try to engage and interest your audience.

Abstract

The abstract should be a complete summary of your research report, comprising short pieces of information from each section (introduction, method, analysis and conclusion). The aim of the abstract is to tell the reader exactly what the research is about, why it was conducted, how it was conducted, what was found, and what the implications of the study are. A rough rule of thumb is to include approximately two sentences for each of these questions. You will typically have a word limit for abstracts, and these are often around 100–150 words, so it will be good practice at being clear and concise.

Introduction

The introduction is partly a review of other research that has been conducted in a specific topic area and partly a rationale for the research that you have conducted yourself. This is the section where you will introduce theory: the assumptions about the topic area you are examining and how these relate to the methods of carrying out the research. Depending on the specific requirements of your writing assignment, you can use sub-sections to provide additional structure and to highlight key aspects of the introduction. Sub-sections are typically used in dissertations and journal articles, and you will need to use a brief heading for each sub-section to alert the reader to the specific issue you will address.

The introduction is the place where you need to provide the following information:

- What the study is about
- What existing research there is in this area (the literature review)

- How your research contributes to existing research
- Why the study is important
- Your research question(s)

The literature review – where you discuss other research that has been undertaken in your chosen topic area – is important for two reasons. First, it allows you to identify the findings and insights that have already been attained in this area and to gain a greater understanding of what knowledge has been produced to date and any gaps in this knowledge. Second, it allows you to demonstrate how your own work contributes to this area. Does it fill any gaps in understandings, for example, or select a different data context to compare with existing studies? This should also enable you to provide a clear rationale for why your research is important. Do not underestimate this: if a report does not show how it contributes to existing literature then it is at risk of missing out obvious details or arguments. You will be glad at this point that you have already been reading the literature.

When writing the introduction – and particularly the literature review – be selective in what you include and do not write about every study you find that relates to your topic area. Select those that are most central to the issue you are focused on yourself. This means you may have to write most of the introduction once you have begun analysis; that way you will know what you are focusing on. When you write about other studies, try to organise your review in terms of building up an argument or narrative. For instance, briefly explain the research that they conducted, but in terms of how it offers an insight or specific findings, what conclusions can be drawn, and so on. Do not simply list one study after another, with details about methods and results. Doing this will not only make for a very dull introduction, it will also prevent you from showing clearly where the research gaps are, and how your study fills a gap.

Towards the end of your introduction, the reader should have a clear sense of what other research has been conducted in this area and how your study contributes to this literature, even if only in a small way. You should argue about the importance of this topic: why does this work need to be done, why in this way, and why now? You will also need to be clear about your choice of methodological approach, and why it is appropriate for this study. You could detail, for instance, the theoretical assumptions taken by DP and how they fit with your chosen topic and area of interest. Note that in the introduction you are not telling the reader about how you conducted the analysis, only why this form of analysis is the most appropriate for the current study. The introduction is effectively building towards the culmination of your research question (see Chapter 3). Once this is stated – clearly, and referring back to other literature if need be – then you have set up the right context for presenting the methods of the research.

Box 8.2: The importance of clarity and coherence

The two most important things you can do to improve your report are to be clear and coherent. Being clear means detailing each aspect of your research in a straightforward manner, explaining core concepts and using simple language that focuses on your core argument or message. Some people may use lots of long or unusual words, jargon, or complicated vocabulary in an attempt to show their intelligence or gain higher marks. This usually does not work. It often backfires, and can suggest a lack of understanding of the subject area. Using simple words and clear explanation does not mean you are dumbing down or patronising your reader. Quite the opposite: with a clear writing style you are showing your ability to convey complicated issues in a simple and effective manner.

Being coherent means ensuring that each part of your report fits together in a consistent manner around a central argument or discussion point. The literature in the introduction should be relevant to the topic area and your own research, the methods should relate back to the research question and forward to the analysis, and the discussion section should refer back to issues raised in the introduction. A coherent report, therefore, is one that focuses on one or two main issues and refers to these at appropriate points throughout each section. Even if the process of conducting the research might seem incredibly messy at times, the process of writing the report is the point at which you can find order and coherence in the apparent chaos.

Methods

The methods section is where you will provide detailed information about data that you collected and how you analysed these data. It is typical to use sub-headings in this section, and often two will suffice: 'data collection' (or 'participants and data collection') and 'analytical procedure'. For much longer reports, such as undergraduate or postgraduate dissertations, it is possible that you will have a whole chapter dedicated to methodology, in which case, you can combine the theoretical justification (the rationale for choosing DP for this project) and practical details in that chapter.

The 'data collection' sub-section typically includes information on key details such as: where, when and how you recorded the interaction, who was present (i.e., who are the participants), how much data you collected and what kind of data it includes (i.e., face-to-face interaction, online discussion data, telephone interaction). Note that we refer to people in our research as 'participants', not 'subjects', to acknowledge the centrality of their role in the research. The amount of detail needed about participants can vary:

sometimes it will be appropriate to include ages, genders, sexuality or ethnicity, if these are relevant to your study. Remember, though, that DP treats context as relevant only if it is *made relevant* in the discourse and interaction, so demographical information is not always important. As a guide, then, you should include information about the participants if that information is relevant to the topic area of your research (such as national identity). It is always possible to use footnotes in the analysis section if you later need to add in details about demographics, if these are noted by participants in the extracts used.

This part should also detail the ethical issues that are relevant for your data, and at the very least should include mention of having received approval for the research from an ethics committee at your institution, and of the participants having provided written consent for taking part in the research. You should also state where and how the data were stored (e.g., on a password-protected computer and external hard-drive), and who has access to this data (e.g., yourself, your supervisor, any members of your research team). There may be additional ethical considerations (see Chapter 4 for more detail on gaining consent) to take into account if you are dealing with young or vulnerable populations, or sensitive topics. While we are ultimately dealing with talk and interaction, we should always be sensitive to the intimate aspects of people's lives that we are often studying. Regardless of whether or not we wish to analyse the individuals themselves (claiming that we are 'simply' examining the discourse, for example), this does not mean that we treat discourse as if it is some disembodied artefact lying waiting for us to investigate. Without people we would have nothing to study.

The 'analytical procedure' sub-section should then contain information about what happened to the data once collected: how did you transcribe the data and how did you code and analyse it? This means going beyond simply saying 'discursive psychology was used to analyse the data'. We need to be clear about the stages that we conducted, and what specific features we focused on. This is all part of the process of transparency (discussed in Chapter 6), of providing evidence of how the analysis was undertaken and of showing your readers how you followed specific procedures. It prevents us from being complacent, ensuring that we are clear and detailed in the steps we choose, and providing reassurance to the readers that we are being consistent with a DP approach (and not simply doing what we think is relevant or appropriate). Box 8.3 provides a checklist of the details that are appropriate for clarifying a discursive psychology analysis.

Box 8.3: Checklist for writing up the 'analytical procedure' sub-section

This section of published or unpublished reports is often woefully limited or vague about the process of analysis (some of my own publications are, alas, guilty of this too). The following checklist can be used to ensure that you do not fall into this trap yourself:

- Specify the form of discourse analysis used (i.e. discursive psychology) and use one or two references to show which literature has guided your analysis.
- State how the data were transcribed and to what level of detail: e.g., words only for the full corpus, then Jefferson-level for those sections that were identified in the coding stage.
- Describe how you coded the data: how did you select particular sections of the data? How do these sections relate to your research question? Did this process occur more than once?
- Describe how you began the analysis: what did you look for? What discursive devices did you use? Again, show how this relates back to the research question to ensure the report is coherent.
- Identify the main issues or analytical points raised by the analysis: what did you focus on and why? Show that this is grounded in the data, rather than with any presumptions you might have had about what you would find.
- Describe how you checked the credibility and coherence of the analysis: were there any deviant cases? How did you ensure that your analysis is robust?

Analysis

This is the section of your report that is likely to be the longest, given that it will contain extracts from your transcripts alongside your analytical interpretations. It is also the most important, as here you will need to demonstrate not only that you can competently analyse the discourse, but also that you can be coherent in presenting this analysis for the reader. You should typically begin the analysis section with a short paragraph to provide an overview of the analysis. Here you should refer to any sub-sections that you will use, any key points or main conclusions that will be drawn. Again, remember you are not writing a thriller here, so tell the reader what your analysis will be doing. Sub-sections can also be useful to structure this section. Perhaps you have three or four main analytical points that you want to make: you can use sub-sections to organise these and more clearly flag them up for the reader. As with the start of the analysis section, it can be helpful to briefly introduce each sub-section and, if the analysis section is quite long, conclude each section briefly before moving onto the next one.

Your analysis section will then involve the presentation of a selection of extracts from your data corpus and the written analysis of these. But it is much more than a list of extract-analysis-extract-analysis and so on; it should be a coherent and structured discussion of your main analytical points or issues. As you work through the analysis section, each new extract and written analysis should build incrementally on the last.

It should add something new, building up a more detailed understanding of the analytical issues. In this way, the analysis section is like a narrative, where you are explaining the key features, how these work together, and how they culminate in a new understanding or insight of a specific area. Do not expect the extracts to 'speak for themselves'. You need to persuade the reader of your interpretation of the data by showing how your analysis is based on the features of the discourse itself. If you cannot demonstrate that your analysis is based on the extract provided, then you need to check your interpretations or else select a different extract.

Each extract should be given a number (and sometimes also a note or code to indicate where it is from or who is involved in the data clip) to allow you to easily refer to it in your report. They should also have line numbers (see Chapter 5 on transcription) and again this helps to easily refer to specific aspects of the data. Introduce each extract before you present it: for instance, write a sentence or two before the extract to indicate how it relates to the main analytical points, and whether there are any specific features or line numbers of the extract that are particularly important that the reader should focus on. The choice of extracts should be based on the analytical points – your core arguments – that you want to present. The extracts should exemplify and illustrate these points clearly. If the extract does not add anything different, then it probably does not need to be included. The extracts should also be in some way representative of the data corpus; they should not be 'cherry-picked' or chosen because they are unusual in some way (if they are, they might be a possible deviant case, and so should be highlighted as such). Be clear about the process used to select the extracts so that the reader can be reassured that this was done in a systematic and logical manner.

Box 8.4: Example analysis write-up

The following is taken from one of my own publications to provide an example of how the analysis can be written to focus the reader's attention on specific parts of an extract – noting line numbers, for example – as well as attending to broader analytical claims and other relevant literature. In this article, the focus was on how parents and children attend to claims of taste preferences (such as when people say 'I like' or 'I don't like' about a food or drink) and how these are managed alongside epistemic rights (people's rights to have knowledge or claim to have knowledge of something).

Extract 3: McMaster/Moore family

```
1. Grandma:   I'll have blue. (0.2) >I'll have ↓blue<
2.            (0.2) >no I don't like< skimmed milk (in)
```

```
3.                    (1.4)
4. Grandma:    <it tastes like> nothing.
5. Poppy:      ↑bl[ue::
6. Mum:           [that's why I like it (0.2) 'cause I
7.                don't actually like milk
8. Grandma:    no that's: true you don't li:ke milk
```

In this example, both adults provide SCAs [subjective category assessments] accompanied by a justification, such as 'it tastes like nothing' (line 4) and not liking the taste of milk (lines 6–7). When Grandma confirms Mum's assessment, this is produced as a confirmation ('that's true', line 8) and as such also claims equal epistemic rights to be able to know – and use this knowledge – about Mum's food preference despite being in second position, as a response rather than an initial claim to knowledge (Heritage & Raymond, 2005). As Mum's own mother (rather than mother-in-law), her position as being qualified to claim the food preferences of Mum then goes unchallenged in the interaction following this extract. (Wiggins, 2014: 11)

Discussion/conclusion

This section should be relatively concise, typically containing a brief summary of the main analytical points, a discussion of the implication of these in relation to existing literature, limitations with the research and possible areas for future research. Think of this section as being one in which you consider the 'so what?' question: So what was the point of doing this study? What have we learnt? What might we have done differently? What else is missing? This might seem a brutal question to consider – particularly if you have just spent months or years working in this area – but it is exactly the kind of question that readers might ask of the study themselves. So better that you ask it of yourself, first, and then have your answer ready.

References and appendices

The reference section should contain all and only those references cited in the report, and the formatting of this section will be dependent on the outlet of your report. Many students are often concerned with how many references are enough for a good report, and this is similar to asking 'how long is a piece of string?' The simple answer is that there should be enough to support your theoretical claims in the introduction, to evidence the type of analysis in the methods section, to validate your analyses and show your contribution to the literature in the discussion section. Make use of journal articles as much as if not more than textbooks and book chapters. These will demonstrate not only your reading of the literature in this area, but they will also alert you to new developments and analytical findings that are often missing from textbooks. Appendices might include transcripts (a full set would entail a rather lengthy appendix section, so this is not always required), a blank information sheet and consent form.

Box 8.5: The importance of length

At some point you will need to think about how long the report should be. In many cases, you will be provided with guidance about the word limit of your report or manuscript. For undergraduate dissertations, for example, these might be anywhere between 5,000 and 20,000 words, journal articles can vary from around 3,000 to 10,000 words, and doctoral theses can be anywhere around 80,000 to 100,000 words. You will need to check whether your word limit includes the reference list and/or appendices and if there is a specific word limit for the abstract. You will also need to consider how to divide this word limit up for each section of the report, and it can be easiest to do this in terms of proportions. For example, the analysis section is likely to be the longest, followed by the introduction, then the discussion, then methods, then the abstract. Do not get too caught up in exact word length, though; use these as guidelines and focus instead on making sure that your report is clear, detailed and focused.

Software to assist the writing and reporting processes

At the bare minimum, all you need to begin writing is word-processing software that will allow you to type words into a document on your computer or laptop. Microsoft Word or Pages for Mac are the two most common ones, and will see you through most eventualities. They also allow you to insert symbols, create numbered lists and indented sections that will become essential when you are creating and formatting your transcripts. Beyond this, the following are examples of software that can aid you at different points in the writing and reporting process of your research:

- Googledocs – for working collaboratively with other people on a written document online, avoiding the need for multiple versions of documents being emailed back and forth. Multiple people can work simultaneously on the document from different locations and use the 'chat' function or Skype to video conference at the same time.

- PowerPoint, Keynote, or Prezi – for oral presentations. PowerPoint is now almost ubiquitous in presentations but can be used in different ways, such as synchronising the audio or video file with the transcript as it appears, line by line, on the screen. Prezi offers a more fluid way of building a presentation. See also Box 8.6.
- Scrivener – for working on a substantial piece of writing (such as this book). Great for organisation of your notes, ideas and to keep all the writing in a structured space.
- Mendeley – for storing, organising and reading journal articles and book chapters. Like Endnote (another 'citation management system') it organises your references, though the advantage of Mendeley is that you can annotate and make comments on journal articles, and these can be saved or shared with others.
- Evernote – for making notes and storing different kinds of documents in a cloud storage system. Useful for keeping track of your analytical ideas on the go, and can be synchronised with files from other software (such as audio or video files).
- Toyviewer – for editing still images, such as from video recorded data. Useful to create a line-drawing effect or soften edges to help anonymise the data and use in publications or presentations. Other photo editing software (some free, some not) can do similar tricks.
- Comic Life – for creating a comic-strip style representation of interaction. Can import still images from video data to visually illustrate the moment-by-moment progression through the interaction. Snagit is another useful tool for editing images and adding speech bubbles and annotations.
- Camtasia – for screen capture and video editing. Can be used alongside other software (such as PowerPoint) to capture your presentations and upload onto the internet using YouTube or Vimeo to reach a wider audience.
- WordPress – for blogging about your research and to disseminate to a wider audience. Allows you to easily create your own website, though this will need maintaining. Also Twitter – for sharing news and comments, and gaining insights into other research work as well as disseminating your own.

Box 8.6: Tips for oral presentations

- Target the audience: who will be listening? What do they know already and what are they expecting from your presentation? Will your presentation be assessed?
- Use a short (no more than 15–30 seconds) video or audio clip of your data if you can: this can really bring your research to life and allow you to more clearly show

(Continued)

(Continued)

> the emphasis on discursive practices in everyday settings. Note that you will need to have consent from participants to use the data in this way.
>
> - Keep it simple: no more than three data clips and extracts and only a few key analytical points is a good guide for most presentations. It is more effective to give the audience a brief 'taste' of your research than to try to fit everything in. You can always discuss your research in full with people after your presentation.
> - Briefly explain the background context for the video clips, noting features such as the location, participants and purpose of the interaction.
> - Subtitles can be added to a video to show the discourse visually as well as audibly (i.e., to appear on the screen at the exact point at which they are spoken).
> - Limit your slides: if using presentation software like PowerPoint or Keynote, use the slides sparingly and avoid having lots of text.
> - Be enthusiastic and demonstrate your interest and understanding of your research: if you don't look interested, then your audience is not likely to be either.
> - Consider using other materials, such as photographs of the research setting or handouts with the transcripts from the extracts used in the presentation, to bring your presentation to life and to make it more engaging for the audience. I have been known to throw chocolate at audience members (well, I do study eating practices) if I think it is particularly relevant or appropriate.

Publication issues

Once you have gained confidence and competence in DP research and particularly in writing up your work, you may be ready to submit a manuscript to an academic journal. This requires a little further consideration of how we present our work. At the very least, each journal will have their own requirements (usually 'instructions for authors') regarding the type of manuscript that they accept, the disciplines, approaches or methodologies they consider, and the audience to whom they are appealing. This often hits hardest at the point of specifying word limits. Many journals have a restriction of around 7,000 to 8,000 words (and this is quite generous depending on the discipline with which you are familiar; it is not uncommon to have manuscripts of 3,000 or 4,000 words, for instance). Before you write your manuscript, therefore, you will need to be clear about where you would like to send it and what their requirements are. It is much easier to write the manuscript once you know the potential outlet. For those of you working with data in a language that is not English, see Nikander (2008) for a discussion and examples of how to deal with the overlapping issues of translation/transcription and how to prepare this for publication.

The first thing to consider when preparing a manuscript for publication, therefore, is who you want your audience to be. Do you see your research contributing to other discursive, linguistic or interactional research in a particular topic area? Or are you more concerned to speak to those working in a particular topic area? You might also want to consider the type of audience who is likely to read your research: academics, professionals, policy makers? Why are you conducting the research – what did you aim to achieve? In some cases, you might decide to write two manuscripts for different journals (one for academics, one for policy makers, or one for discursive/interaction researchers and one for research into your chosen topic area). So plan ahead, according to how much time you have to write and what you aim to achieve with these (potential) publications.

Aside from the word limit, many journals also have certain requirements for the formatting of your manuscript. This might require you to label or structure sections in a particular way (possibly 'findings' or 'results' rather than 'analysis'). They may also have limitations on how many extracts you can use, whether you can include tables or figures, and how these should be formatted. The formatting of extracts is one to pay particular attention to, as some journals are published with two narrow columns of text on each page. This means that your transcript may be mis-aligned during the printing preparation stage and the line numbers no longer match the lines of talk. Figure 8.1 provides an example of this from my first publication. So be sure to check this at the proof-reading stage and adjust your transcripts if at all possible.

Extract 1: SKWIA1aIM1

1	Sue:	>Come on< there was only a ↑tiny bit of (.)of
2		↓salmon just ↑ea:t salmon
3	Chole:	↑N:o its fo:ul
4		(2.0)
5	Emily:	I've eaten ↑mine
6	Sue:	Ye:ah ↑you've eaten ↓Yours
7		(1.0)
8	Chole:	I've been try:ing but (mine's inedible)

Figure 8.1 Example of mis-aligned transcript (from Wiggins et al., 2001)

This all means that there can be huge variation in the styles of DP analyses that we see in print, not only because of different authors and studies, but also because of different journal requirements and styles.

Technological developments – both in terms of the software we can use to present our data as well as the increase in the number of journals available online – mean that, for those of you who have video-recorded data, there are opportunities to include still images from your data. This is all dependent on consent from participants, of course, so you must first ensure that you have the consent of participants to publish their images (as a still screen-shot) before you go down this route. You might also consider the possibility of including a hyperlink to another website where readers could access the video or audio data extracts used in the publication. Although this is a new area of development and requires extended consideration of consent from participants, it offers an exciting way in which readers can get closer to the data for themselves.

Finally, having submitted a manuscript to a journal, you will need to go through the peer-reviewing process. This can vary depending on the journal, but typically takes the following structure:

- Manuscript is considered by the journal editor if it is appropriate for the journal. If it is, it is then sent out to reviewers. If not, it will be sent directly back to you. Do not despair if this happens to you (it has happened to me at least twice). Just reconsider your audience and the most appropriate outlet for your work. Sometimes it can result in finding a much more suitable and better place to publish your work (this also happened to me, twice).

- Manuscript is sent out to at least two reviewers (typically two or three, though sometimes more). These should be 'experts' or credible researchers in an appropriate area; they should know something about either the topic area or the analytical approach. They usually have between one and three months to read and provide a written review of the manuscript.

- Journal editor collects in the reviews once these are completed and adds their own comments. They will then make a decision as to whether the manuscript will be accepted (as it is, or requiring minor changes), needs revision (sometimes quite substantial changes are needed) or be rejected.

- Unless it is rejected completely – in which case try again somewhere else, taking into account any feedback you received – you will usually have a few months to make the revisions and resubmit it.

- Resubmitted manuscript will often go back out to review again, to the same reviewers if possible (but not always) or the editor will make a decision for themselves. You should then get a decision as to whether it is accepted or needs further changes.

The reviewing process can be lengthy and disheartening at times. For many academics, it is one of the challenging parts of our job – we receive feedback that can be encouraging, critical or just plain brutal. You may need to compromise either the content or structure of your report, and you will have to make a decision as to whether the compromise is appropriate or not. Some journals and reviewers will request, for example, that you remove all transcription symbols from data extracts, avoid repeating comments in the analysis section or – the horror – remove all data extracts from the analysis section because they 'got in the way of the analysis' (this did actually happen to me once). Sometimes it will be obvious that the reviewers take a very different theoretical or analytical approach from your own, and not everybody is professional and supportive in their comments.

This is not to put you off or to dissuade you from publishing. Far from it. The more DP research is published, the more that research can build on new analyses and develop theory and practical applications in different areas. Just be prepared for the rigours of the reviewing process. Seek support and help from your supervisor, peers or colleagues. Many will have been through the process themselves (often many times) and can help to guide you in terms of what to expect and how to deal with the process. I find that when I first get reviews back from a manuscript revision, I read them through two or three times, then put them aside for about a week. This gives me time to reflect on the comments, and also gives me some distance from the writing so that I am then ready to edit the work without being too sentimental about it. At the end of the day, what is important is that the research is disseminated and has some value and contribution to the literature.

KEY POINTS

- Start writing as soon as you can and do not worry about whether your writing is 'academic enough'.
- Drafting, re-drafting and editing is a normal part of the writing process.
- Reports should be well structured and coherent: focus on one or two main issues and stick to these throughout.
- Explain everything: be clear about the rationale for each stage of the research process.

(Continued)

(Continued)

- Make use of different kinds of software to help enrich the writing and dissemination of your research.
- Familiarise yourself with the publication process and consider how you might best disseminate your work to the most appropriate audience.

Recommended reading

Braun, V. & Clarke, V. (2013). *Successful qualitative research: A practical guide for beginners*. London: Sage. Particularly Chapter 13.

Heath, C., Hindmarsh, J. & Luff, P. (2010). *Video in qualitative research: Analysing social interaction in everyday life*. London: Sage. Particularly Chapter 6.

PART THREE

Applications

9

DP TOPICS, CASE STUDIES AND PROJECT IDEAS

Chapter contents

Themes in DP research	197
DP research by topic area	199
DP research by data type	205
Case studies	208
Developing a DP project	215

The aim of this chapter is to inspire and encourage you to develop your own DP research projects. It will provide a route-map of the range of DP work that has already been developed, including 'classic' and contemporary examples of empirical research. It is thus a chapter to dip into at any time, regardless of how familiar you are with the theory and methods of DP. Like the glossy photos of cookery books, it should discursively illustrate the kinds of things that are possible with DP research, and to encourage you to go out and begin your own projects. The chapter begins by outlining the overarching themes that have characterised DP research over the past 25 years; these provide a way of gaining some perspective on the sorts of theoretical (and analytical) issues that DP has tackled. This is followed by specific examples of empirical research by topic area or data type, so you can be guided according to your own interests and the availability of potential data. The messiness of DP research is then illustrated through three case studies, providing rare insights into the behind-the-scenes challenges that can occur during the research process. The chapter concludes with suggestions for DP projects and learning activities within a classroom or university framework.

Themes in DP research

When starting out with your own DP research, it can be helpful to know what areas of research have already been investigated and what sorts of questions have already been asked. This can help you to become more familiar with both the theory and practice of DP, and background reading is essential before you embark on your own research adventure. There are two edited books that provide a selection of DP research: Hepburn and Wiggins' (2007) *Discursive research in practice: New approaches to psychology and interaction* and Tileagă and Stokoe's (2015) *Discursive psychology: Classic and contemporary issues*. These books will be useful to dip into for ideas and inspiration as well as for detailed discussion of both theoretical and empirical issues. The former provides empirical examples of DP research with a particular focus on work that draws on naturalistic data – recorded interaction from everyday or institutional settings – and which illustrates the alternative ways in which psychological states can be understood in social settings. The latter is a compendium of theoretical chapters, each of which reflects on the contributions of a 'key' DP paper on theory and analysis in different areas of research. So that book will be particularly helpful in terms of bringing you 'up to speed' on core issues in DP research over the past 25 years or so, as well as highlighting areas that are yet to be fully explored.

In terms of familiarising yourself with the broad range of DP research, however, it can be helpful to consider empirical research as falling into different strands or themes. There have been a few ways of doing this, each of which attempts to categorise DP research. Edwards (2005b), for example, provides a classification of three interconnected core strands of DP research in terms of the theoretical stance of the research:

1. **Re-specification and critique**: where psychological concepts (such as attitudes, emotions, memory, scripts) are theorised not as cognitive states but as discursive practices. Rather than starting with a psychological topic (e.g., attitudes) and then critiquing this, such research would begin from a different point. For example, how scripting can be used to manage responsibility for one's actions (and thus have a social function) rather than being interpreted as evidence of a particular cognitive schema. Research in this strand often directly challenges cognitive interpretations of psychological concepts.

2. **The 'psychological thesaurus'**: where psychological terminology and categories (such as words for enacting attitudes, emotions, or memories, e.g., love, anger, remember) are examined for the interactional business that they perform. This work is clearly closely linked with the re-specification focus; research that examines the psychological thesaurus (such as my own work on food assessments, e.g., 'I like cheese') has implications for the re-specification of psychological concepts (such as food preferences).

3. **Managing psychological business**: where psychological themes (such as prejudice, emotional investment or doubt) are examined for how they are managed in interaction and how different categories of person are produced as a result. For example, how a person's sensitivity to particular food tastes might be characterised as a way of undermining their judgement of a meal.

Potter (2005) and Hepburn and Wiggins (2007) then add in a fourth strand that similarly focuses on a theoretical stance underpinning the research:

4. **Discursive psychology of institutions**: where psychological concepts are examined in terms of how they constitute institutions and perform institutional business. This builds on the 'managing psychological business' strand of research, with a particular emphasis on institutions such as education, healthcare and the law. For example, how emotional terms such as anger could be used to evidence a particular mental health issue or to assign responsibility for a criminal act. The management of psychological 'business' can therefore be examined for how it enables the institution to work *as an institution*.

By contrast, and using a chronological approach, Potter (2012; and Kent & Potter, 2014) makes a distinction between strands of DP research during the 1980s (focused on interviews and interpretative repertoires), the 1990s (focused on constructionism) and the 2000s onwards (focused on sequential analysis). This classification can help to demarcate the progression of DP research over time, and can also be used in combination with the four strands noted above. Since the initial development of DP was focused to some extent on providing a counter-argument to cognitive-based accounts of psychology, much of early DP research was often focused on issues that started where cognitive work began: with issues such as attitudes, attributions and memory. As DP developed, however, research was increasingly guided by questions that began from a different starting point: one that was grounded in a social constructionist approach and an interest in discursive practices.

The relevance of this for your own DP research is that it can be difficult, at first, to have a clear understanding of what issues or topics DP research has tackled. This is because it begins from the starting point of social practices, and of talk and text in everyday life, rather than the compartmentalisation of psychological concepts. As you become more confident and competent with DP, it will become easier to know which questions to ask and how to find DP research that relates to your own interests. Until then, it can be helpful to have an overview of DP research in terms of familiar psychological topics – just as you would in the contents page of a psychology textbook, for example – to get you started. McKinlay and McVittie (2008) do the same with their textbook covering different kinds of discursive research (including DP) on social psychology. So on that note, the following section provides a guide to DP research according to broad topic areas.

DP research by topic area

Since the emergence of discursive psychology in the 1980s, DP research has covered a range of topic areas from attitudes to identities to racism. What follows is thus a brief commentary of some of the topic areas that have been the focus of DP research so far, to give you a sense of the breadth of research as well as a flavour of some of the issues discussed. Specific references to empirical research – and the odd edited book or collection of papers – are scattered abundantly throughout so there are plenty of names and dates to get you started on your reading and to provide ideas and inspiration for your own research.

Attitudes and assessments

Some of the earliest work in DP began with a challenge to cognitive approaches to attitudes in social psychology, and the classic paper to read in this area is Potter (1998; see also Wiggins, 2015 for a review). Research in this area tends to use the terms *assessments* or *evaluations* (rather than 'attitudes'), to place the emphasis on the verbal production of a stance on an issue, rather than treating what was said as representative of a cognitive state. Work in this area has demonstrated the range of functions of assessments: that they can be used to manage first impressions (Humă, 2015), persuade others to eat (Wiggins & Potter, 2003), formulate opinions in focus groups (Puchta & Potter, 2002, 2004), and justify racist practices (Durrheim & Dixon, 2004; Wetherell & Potter 1992). The very nature of evaluations means that they provide a unique insight into what might be termed mundane morality, the subtle ways in which judgements about the 'goodness' or 'badness' of something becomes part of everyday social practices. For example, the process of receiving a gift can be a delicate occasion in which an appropriate assessment is required (Robles, 2012). Assessments can also come in many forms. They do not have to be terms such as 'good' or 'nice'. My own work in this area has begun to examine the ways in which assessments can be performed through prosody as much as lexical choice with terms such as 'mmm' and 'eugh' (Wiggins, 2002, 2013). Since the action of producing an assessment also implies that one has the knowledge of, or rights to be able to assess, something (Pomerantz, 1984), then this topic area also overlaps with other issues, such as identities or seeking advice.

Emotions

In a similar trajectory to DP work on attitudes, discursive research on the issue of emotions has argued that the emotion concept itself is a historical, social construction rather than a physiological or cognitive 'fact' (see Childs & Hepburn, 2015, for a review). That we 'have' emotions and that these are primarily internal, individual states is just one (albeit currently dominant) perspective; in effect, psychological research has done a very good job of convincing us that this is fact rather than an artefact of research procedures and assumptions. Your starting point for work in this area should be Edwards (1999), which explicates the core principles of the DP approach to emotion, using examples from marriage guidance counselling interaction and newspaper reports of the death of the

UK's Princess Diana. Here you will meet the now infamous – in DP research – 'Connie and Jimmie' extracts. Instead of treating emotion terms (such as 'angry' or 'jealous') as indicative of an internal state, DP research examines how emotions – as categories or assumed psychological states – are constructed *as individual* states in social interaction, and the functions to which they serve. Emotions can then be understood as situated social actions, within relationship counselling (Edwards, 1995), family mealtime interaction (Childs, 2014), helpline interaction (Hepburn & Potter, 2007; Weatherall & Stubbe, 2015 or even Bill Clinton's courtroom testimony (Locke & Edwards, 2003). Some of this work on emotions has begun to focus on features of 'affect' and delivery, such as the prosodic features of crying (Hepburn, 2004) and how being sensitive to the preliminary features of crying can have important institutional consequences for child protection officers (Hepburn & Potter, 2007). For a similar issue in relation to distress in animals during veterinary examinations, see work by MacMartin et al. (2014). For a collection of work on emotions in everyday interaction, including DP work, see Peräkylä and Sorjonen (2012); see also the topic of subjectivities below. In other strands of DP research, there has been an engagement with the recent 'turn to affect' (Wetherell, 2013, 2015) – the increasing attention on emotions in social research more broadly. The possible implications of this – theoretically as well as practically – signal interesting developments for discursive research.

Gender

Gender is another area of research in which DP has found a good home, given that gender can be understood in terms of one's identity, health or embodied status, or in relation to behaviours associated with one or more genders. Just as with other topics, DP research begins with gender in terms of social actions and how it is constructed and made relevant in discourse, rather than claiming that there is a fixed biological reality to gender or that there are gendered ways of talking (Stokoe, 1998). Much of the research in this area has examined how gender is *made relevant* by participants in different contexts and what purposes that serves, rather than using gender as an explanatory tool (as in 'he said that because he's a man'). For example, research has examined the use of gender as a resource in a classroom context with teenagers (Eriksson Barajas, 2010), in an online discussion forum about sick leave and housework duties (Flinkfeldt, 2011, or in newspaper accounts of Attention Deficit Hyperactivity Disorder (Horton-Salway, 2013). Gender category formulations (such as 'guy' or 'girl') might also be used to negotiate relationships with other people, such as in speed-dating interactions (Korobov, 2011; Stokoe, 2010) or in gay or lesbian families (Clarke & Kitzinger, 2004; Malmquist, 2015). Gender and sexualities can then be understood in terms of 'performance' or the accomplishment of gender in social interactions (Butler, 1990). We can then consider not only how different identities are negotiated, such as transsexual identities in a gender identity clinic (Speer & Parsons, 2006) or gender and morality in neighbour disputes (Stokoe, 2003), but also how claims of sexism or heterosexism are managed (Clarke et al., 2004; Korobov, 2004; Peel 2001; Speer & Potter, 2000). For theoretical, as well as analytical, discussions on gender in relation to DP research and related approaches, see Speer (2001, 2005), Stokoe (2006) and Weatherall (2002). For collections on gender and discourse, see McIlvenny (2002), Speer and Stokoe (2011), and Stokoe and Weatherall (2002).

Identities

Discursive research into identities is a vast area in itself, and there are three books on this topic alone (Antaki & Widdicombe, 1998; Benwell & Stokoe, 2006; McKinlay & McVittie, 2011). Identity, in DP terms, is understood as the way in which a person is characterised in a particular way, in a particular context, and for a particular purpose, in speech or writing. Identities are therefore bound up with social actions, and it is argued that there is no 'neutral' or 'true' identity lurking beneath the discourse. A distinction can also be made between oneself and others through the use of contrasts in talk, and this can be used to deprecate oneself or others (Dickerson, 2000). Since identity is understood as an accomplishment, situated within particular contexts, then authenticity becomes important; one must be able to effectively 'pass' as that identity or else risk being treated as false or unbelievable. This can be the case whether in face-to-face interaction (and punk culture, Widdicombe & Wooffitt, 1990; or intellectual disability, Rapley et al., 1998) or in online interaction (discussions on veganism: Sneijder & te Molder, 2009). Identities are also frequently intertwined with other issues – see other topic areas on gender, health and nationality, for example – and in many ways they are a core feature of DP research because they focus so much on who we are (a psychological concept) and how this characterisation is used within different social interactions (and thus social actions). The literature thus spans a wide-ranging set of issues. For example, there is an interesting strand of research on what might be broadly defined as 'academic identities': how people construct their identity as an avid or struggling reader in children's book talk (Eriksson & Aronsson, 2005, resist student identities in university settings (Attenborough & Stokoe, 2012; Benwell & Stokoe, 2002) or demonstrate learning in an online student task (Paulus & Lester, 2013). Research has also examined identities in relation to age (Nikander, 2009), autism (Lester & Paulus, 2012), and the interviewer stance (Widdicombe, 2015).

Health

DP research has much to offer our understanding of health concerns, from how everyday practices are orientated to as 'healthy' or not, to how health advice is sought or treatment adhered to and how health and illness are interwoven within mundane and institutional interactions. Health is not a neutral state of being and there is a rich seam of research examining how people manage their accountability for being healthy (or for dealing with illness appropriately), in relation to topics such as chronic fatigue syndrome (Guise et al., 2007; Horton-Salway, 2001), coeliac disease (Veen et al., 2010), infertility (de Kok & Widdicombe, 2008), physical activity or sports (Cosh et al., 2013; Lamont-Mills & Christensen, 2008; Locke, 2004; McGannon & Mauws, 2000; Miller, 2012), weight management (Cranwell & Seymour-Smith, 2012; Mycroft, 2008; Webb, 2009; Wiggins, 2009) and veganism (Sneijder & te Molder, 2004). At the heart of much of this work is the psychologising (and individualising) of healthcare issues and the way in which health is constructed as a personal choice and thus one for which you can be held to account. In some cases – and this is becoming noticeable in online discussion forum interaction – people may be held to account as to whether they are genuinely ill. This has been examined in forums where authentic membership is important for ensuring a supportive and safe environment, such as for self-harming (Smithson et al., 2011), eating disorders (Stommel & Koole, 2010), grieving (Varga & Paulus, 2014), depression (Lamerichs, 2003; Williams & Donaghue, 2010) and suicide (Horne & Wiggins, 2009; Wiggins et al., 2016). Seeking healthcare can also suggest a need for advice or expert knowledge and DP research has begun to consider how people manage these issues, particularly when the care required is not for ill-health but relates to social expectations or cultural norms such as regarding infertility (de Kok & Widdicombe, 2010), childbirth (Locke & Horton-Salway, 2010) and breastfeeding (Locke, 2009).

Nationality, ethnicities, geographies, spaces and places

Negotiating who we are, where we are from and where we belong are powerful psychological issues and the source of much dispute and tension. As such, the interwoven issues of nationalities, ethnicities, geographies, spaces and places are ideal for DP research. This is before we even consider the prejudice that might accompany such issues (see topic below). Some of the earliest DP work on national identity is Billig's (1995) 'banal nationalism' (see also Condor, 2001; and Gibson, 2015, for a review), which focused attention on the mundane but consequential ways in which national identities are invoked in everyday discourse and social settings. Perhaps more crucially, this work argued that nations are themselves social constructions: a way of dividing up the world, whether culturally, historically, economically or otherwise. Work by Condor and her colleagues has been particularly important in demonstrating this within the specific context of English and Scottish national identity and nationalism (e.g., Abell & Stevenson, 2011; Condor, 2000; Condor & Abell, 2006), football (e.g., Abell et al., 2007), the welfare state (Gibson, 2009) or military service (Gibson, 2011; Gibson & Condor, 2009). National identities also overlap considerably with ethnic identities, and DP research in this area has begun to examine the flexible nature of these identities and of how they can perform different functions (Merino & Tileagă, 2011; Varjonen et al., 2013;

Xenitidou & Morasso, 2014). The division of the world into nation states then introduces the issue of asylum-seeking and refugees, where people may be fleeing their country due to persecution, war or disaster. DP research in this area has begun to illustrate the delicate tensions in not only positioning oneself as being unable to return to one's home country due to concerns for one's safety (Goodman et al., 2015), but also not being able to criticise the host country due to risks of appearing 'ungrateful' (Goodman et al., 2014; Kirkwood, 2012). Some of this work brings together issues of place-identity and refugees (Kirkwood et al., 2015; Kirkwood et al., 2013), where place-identity (in DP terms) refers to how one is situated as belonging, or not belonging, to a particular place. DP research on place identity has considered the rights of citizenship for travellers (Barnes et al., 2004), the desegregation of South Africa's beaches (Dixon & Durrheim, 2000), the identity constructions of English incomers to a small Scottish island (McKinlay & McVittie, 2007), and preserving the 'rural way of life' in the English countryside (Wallwork & Dixon, 2004). Place-identity can also be understood within a much narrower context, such as the distinction between house and neighbour boundaries (Stokoe & Hepburn, 2005; Stokoe & Wallwork, 2003) and within online spaces (Goodings et al., 2007).

Prejudice

The topic of prejudice in DP research is broadly the topic of how people are categorised in discourse, and how these categories are used to blame, condone, accuse or otherwise legitimate the unfair treatment of people or individuals. Underlying much of this work in DP is an examination of prejudice as primarily a social and discursive act, and Billig (1985), Condor (1988) and Wetherell and Potter (1992) are the classic texts to immerse yourself in first. With DP, we can examine how categories of people (as being a particular 'kind' of person, for example) are produced within discourse, and how such categories are used flexibly to perform different interactional business. Being prejudiced (racist, sexist, etc.) is thus treated as a social and discursive act, not an individual or psychological trait or uniquely cognitive function (Whitehead & Stokoe, 2015). One of the characteristics of this is that people can often deny being prejudiced, while still making prejudicial arguments (and often through the use of disclaimers such as 'I'm not sexist, but…'). This is what has been termed the 'norm against prejudice' (Billig, 1988; see Augoustinos & Every, 2007, for a review) and there is a growing literature on the denial of prejudice as a discursive act in itself (Condor, 2000; Condor et al., 2006; Goodman & Burke, 2010; Goodman & Rowe, 2013; Kirkwood et al., 2013; Korobov, 2004; Rapley, 1998; Speer & Potter, 2000). There is also increasing evidence for 'deracialised' discursive practices, where racial explanations are downplayed or substituted in favour of other accounts (Augoustinos & Every, 2007). DP research into the tension between identities that rest on the construction of nations, ethnicities and cultures has been particularly revealing in the context of Australia (Augoustinos et al., 1999; Hanson-Easey et al., 2014; Rapley, 1998; Sala et al., 2010; Simmons & LeCouteur, 2008) and South Africa (Durrheim & Dixon, 2004, 2005; Durrheim et al., 2015). Some of this work has also focused on the delicate issue of apologising for prejudicial acts (Augoustinos et al., 2011; Hastie & Augoustinos, 2012; LeCouteur, 2001).

Seeking help, advice or support: Counselling, therapy and helplines

The centrality of talking and interaction in many approaches to counselling and therapy make this topic ideal for discursive approaches. Work in this area has drawn heavily on conversation analysis, such as dealing with delicate issues in AIDS counselling (Silverman & Peräkylä, 1990; see also Silverman, 1997). In a similar way to the accountability of health issues, DP research can demonstrate the ways in which issues of knowledge (in support for children who have been exposed to domestic violence: Iversen, 2014), remembering (in couples therapy: Muntigl & Choi, 2010) and morality (in domestic violence counselling: Kurri & Wahlström, 2001) are managed and consequential in therapy or helpline settings. Research in this area can also be broadly characterised by a concern with asking for help, advice or support in whatever form that takes. While counselling and therapy might often be face to face, there is increasing research into telephone helpline interaction (Baker et al., 2005), particularly regarding the protection of children (Butler et al., 2010; Potter & Hepburn, 2003). Online support is also an area in which DP research can examine the discursive management of psychological issues involved in bullying (Osvaldsson, 2011), self-harming (Smithson et al., 2011) and suicide (Wiggins et al., 2016), for example. This topic area potentially overlaps with what might be broadly termed forensic or criminal issues, where violence has occurred or an offence has been committed. DP research in this area has examined the accounts of perpetrators (Auburn, 2010; Auburn & Lea, 2003; LeCouteur & Oxlad, 2011; MacMartin & LeBaron, 2006) as well as those of the victims (MacMartin, 1999).

DP research by data type

In addition to having examples of DP research that relate to specific topic areas, it can also be useful to have examples of research according to the type of data used for guidance when planning your own data collection. Table 9.1 provides details of three pieces of empirical research from across a range of different forms of data. In itself this illustrates the diversity of forms of discursive practices that can be analysed using DP and the variety of projects that can be undertaken.

Table 9.1

Type of data analysed	Example of empirical research	Analytic focus of the paper
Face-to-face interaction (everyday)	Humă (2015)	First impressions and assessments in different examples of everyday talk and text between friends
	Stokoe (2010)	Accounting for past relationships in speed-dating interaction
	Veen, te Molder, Gremmen and van Woerkum (2013)	Family mealtime interaction involving children with coeliac disease
Face-to-face interaction (institutional)	Auburn (2010)	Cognitive distortions as social practices in sex offender treatment programmes
	Edwards (1999)	Emotion discourse in relationship counselling interaction
	Stokoe (1998)	Gender categories in student tutorial interaction
Interviews (researcher-led)	de Kok & Widdicombe (2010)	Interviews with women in Malawi about fertility problems
	Kirkwood, McKinlay & McVittie (2013)	Interviews with asylum seekers in the UK
	Merino & Tileagă (2011)	Constructions of a minority ethnic identity in Chile
Interviews (institution-led)	Iversen (2014)	Interviews taken from intervention to support children exposed to parental violence
	Locke & Edwards (2003)	Emotion talk in Bill Clinton's Grand Jury testimony about Monica Lewinsky
	Tileagă (2010)	Published interview with the director of a Romanian newspaper
Focus groups	Goodman & Burke (2010)	Student focus groups about asylum seeking
	Korobov (2004)	Homophobia and sexism in adolescent male talk in focus groups
	Puchta & Potter (2002)	Focus group talk analysed for how 'attitudes' are produced
Experiments	Gibson (2013)	A discursive analysis of the audio recordings of the Milgram 'obedience' experiments
	Gilbert & Mulkay (1984)	Analysis of scientists' discourses
	Wooffitt & Allistone (2005)	The organisation of 'consciousness' in parapsychology experiments
Telephone interaction (everyday)	Edwards (2005a)	Managing complaints in everyday phone calls between friends
	Edwards & Fasulo (2006)	Honesty phrases and assessments in phone calls between friends

Type of data analysed	Example of empirical research	Analytic focus of the paper
Telephone helplines	Patterson & Potter (2009)	Calls between a young adult with a learning disability and her family members
	Butler et al. (2010)	Calls to an Australian children's helpline
	Cromdal et al. (2012)	Calls to the Swedish emergency services
	Potter & Hepburn (2003)	Constructing concern in a UK child protection helpline
Internet discussion forums	Rowe & Goodman (2014)	Discussions about Gypsies in the UK following news reports on this topic
	Sneijder & te Molder (2009)	Identity management in a Dutch online forum for veganism
	Stommel & Koole (2010)	Managing identity as a new member to a German eating disorder discussion forum
Radio discussion programmes	Brooks (2009)	UK radio phone-in programmes discussing eating disorders
	Hanson-Easey, Augoustinos & Moloney (2014)	Calls to an Australian radio show on the topic of immigration
	McMullen (2005)	Doing modesty on Canadian radio chat shows
Television programmes (typically chat shows or live discussion programmes)	Childs (2012)	Fly-on-the wall documentary programmes of family interaction
	Clarke & Kitzinger (2004)	Lesbian and gay parental discourse on televised talk shows
	Gibson (2011)	Discussion of the Iraq war on UK's *Question Time* TV programme
News reports (newspapers or online news media)	Gibson (2009)	Online discussions of the welfare state on a UK (the BBC) news website
	Horton-Salway (2013)	UK newspaper reports of gender and attention deficit hyperactivity disorder (ADHD)
	Simmons & Lecouteur (2008)	News reports of 'race riots' in Australia
Other texts	Barnes, Auburn & Lea (2004)	Letters of complaint to a local council about travellers
	Humä (2015)	First impressions and assessments in mobile phone text messages and other data
	Lester & Gabriel (2014)	The construction of intelligence in introductory educational psychology textbooks

Case studies

In this section, I will discuss three examples from my own DP research in more detail to illustrate the messiness of research and to demonstrate how order can emerge from chaos (as well as how the chaos can begin in the first place). Doing so also illustrates how DP research can be used with different types of data: everyday video-recorded interaction, online discussion forum interaction and interviews (and focus groups). Each case study highlights issues that were addressed and lessons to be learnt.

Case study (1)
Food disgust in family mealtimes: video recordings of everyday interaction

The first case study relates to a piece of my own research on disgust markers – specifically, the utterances 'eugh/urgh', 'yuck' or 'disgusting' – as spoken by parents or children in family mealtime interaction. This can be seen in a journal article (Wiggins, 2013) and book chapter (Wiggins, 2014). The process of getting from initial idea to a published piece of work, however, is far messier than it ever appears in print. The finished publications focus on how the enactment of disgust is as much a social event as it might be a personal experience; they identify patterns in the use of disgust markers, in relation to people's rights to be able to claim that something is disgusting or not, and to how the *urgh* or *yuck* is organised within the conversational structure. The issues raised by this case study are: (a) the organisation of archived data, (b) secondary data analysis, and (c) identifying the analytical concept.

The first issue relates to the way in which this disgust research began, with the slow and sporadic building of a corpus of audio and video recordings of family mealtime interaction over around 15 years, since my PhD research in this area. Aside from my doctoral research, none of this data collection had been funded – I had undertaken it with the help of students or whenever I could fit it into my work schedules – and so I did not begin with a systematic approach to organising the corpus. Some, but not all, of the corpus had been transcribed, and at the time of the disgust studies, there was around 90 hours over 222 recorded mealtimes. Searching this corpus – both manually by watching through the videos, listening to the audio, or searching the transcripts where available – was thus an incredibly time-consuming labour of love. While the outcome was worth the effort, it did highlight the importance of organising and creating an easily accessibly archive. Sometimes you set out on research knowing that you will collect a large amount of data, and you can plan for this at the start. But sometimes your data corpus might grow slowly and organically as you develop in your own research career, so it is still important to organise and ensure appropriate long-term storage of original recordings as well as signed consent forms, transcripts, analytical notes and draft manuscripts (and I highly recommend Corti et al., 2014, to assist with this process).

The second issue relates to the first in that I would not have been able to conduct the analysis of disgust in mealtimes if I had not had this existing corpus. This is because the analysis required what is sometimes referred to as 'secondary data analysis': where you return to an existing data set and conduct a different analysis from that which was originally planned. If I had set up a new study to examine disgust in mealtime talk, then I could potentially pre-empt or encourage people to refer to disgust when they might not typically have done so (i.e., if it is a focus for the study, then participants might be attuned to this and thus produce responses that are designed for the study). It would also have taken many months (or even years) to collect sufficient data to find enough examples to be able to analyse these. Instead, the data had been collected with the broad aim of gathering examples of everyday family mealtimes, with no specific agenda or analytical focus. I had already been working on food assessments (such as 'I like the bread'), and previously had analysed what might be termed 'gustatory mmms': the *mmm* that people might make when apparently enjoying their food. The time had come, it seemed, to turn to the darker side of food assessments, to examine those moments when people are apparently claiming to be disgusted by the food. These moments were much less frequent in the data corpus, but all the more interesting because of that.

This brings me onto the final issue raised by this case study: how to identify the analytical concept (disgust) without first defining it and claiming it exists before you have analysed it. By defining disgust in a particular way (as something expressed through the utterances *urgh* or *yuck*, for instance), I was already suggesting that this 'thing' (disgust) had occurred in the participants, that they were 'expressing disgust' and all I was doing was then observing it. So I had to be clear in the use of what I referred to as 'disgust markers' (*urgh* or *eugh* or *yuck* or *disgusting*) – that these terms were recognisable, culturally available terms for disgust – but that this did not mean I was assuming that some physiological or experiential process had occurred prior to or during the utterance. In short, taking a DP approach, I could not claim that because people said *urgh*, that they were experiencing disgust. These disgust markers allowed me to focus on possible moments *where* disgust was being made relevant. My next task – the analysis – was then to show *how* disgust was made relevant, and what 'disgust' looked like as a social practice in those settings. So the process of searching the corpus for disgust examples, and analysing these, was much more iterative and messy than might be expected. It is not a case of defining a concept, then searching for it, then analysing it. Sometimes you have to first work with some extracts from your data, analyse those, then return to the full corpus to search again. The analytical process itself also follows a very twisty path: many of my initial notes were never used or were not relevant (or were just plain wrong),

I often had to simplify and reduce the scope of the research, and the analysis had to be fitted into the many other tasks and commitments that filled my days.

In summary, then, this case study is a good example of how research can emerge gradually and without a clear plan from the start. It took a long time to get to those publications, and presenting my initial analyses at data sessions and conference presentations helped to refine my ideas and gain feedback from colleagues in different disciplines. Doing DP research requires us to reflect theoretically as well as analytically about the 'thing' that we are researching: how will we define it? Can we define it before we have analysed it? Where will we find instances of the thing that we are trying to examine?

Case study (2)
Suicide and accountable identities: online discussion forum interaction

The second case study involves the use of online data in the form of textual discussion forums. This case study spans two different projects – one reported in Horne and Wiggins (2009) and the other in Wiggins, McQuade and Rasmussen (2016) – which shared a similar topic area and analytical approach. The specific focus for these publications was the management of identity in suicide discussion forums: how do people introduce themselves to a suicide forum and present themselves as being genuinely suicidal, and how is support provided by other forum members? This case study provides an illustration of DP research which uses online textual data (rather than online video or audio data, for example), and it raises three issues: (a) the potential for student projects, (b) working with texts and online data, and (c) ethical issues and consent with online data.

The research into suicide discussion forums began as a Master's study. One of my students at the time (Judith Horne) was interested in this area and could see the potential of using a DP approach to analysing online forum interaction. The topic area of suicide was particularly relevant for the management of psychological 'business', such as how people describe themselves as having mental health concerns, situating themselves as needing help or support (and thus why they were on the forum in the first place), and potentially being held accountable for mental states and possible future behaviours. Judith's Master's research involved the selecting of an online discussion forum, the copying and pasting of all discussion 'threads' (an opening message and all the replies to that message) into a word file, and the subsequent coding and analysis of that data. Similarly, another student (Robert McQuade), working on his undergraduate dissertation with my supervision, was inspired by the Horne and Wiggins (2009) paper and wanted to follow up other analytical issues in that area. Although both published papers look very different from the original student submissions – one at undergraduate level, one at Master's level – they demonstrate the potential that can be gained from student projects.

This leads me onto the second issue raised by this case study: the use of texts and online data for DP research. You might be forgiven for thinking that 'cutting and pasting' is a quick and easy way to conduct research, and preferable to spending months finding participants and setting up video cameras. While it does involve less effort initially, and thus provides a plausible option for projects where time is short, there are some caveats. Just as with any form of data collection, when we prepare a transcript – in this case, the copied words from the discussion forum – we are producing a different representation of the social context. Do we include the emoticons, avatars or layout from the original discussion forum? What do we need to include to ensure that our data is both ethically sensitive to the forum users (see below) and faithful to the original text? We need to preserve the interactional context: the turn-taking between forum posts and the time- and date-stamps for each message. We also need to consider how the discussion forum is just one space within which people interact, and that there are other spaces, both online and offline, that may be more appropriate for our topic area. But as mobile technology develops and the distinction between online/offline interaction becomes increasingly blurred, then there is the potential to use DP to examine the ways in which social actions and psychological issues are managed in these spaces.

The final issue relates to ethics and consent. As noted above, collecting data from online sources may be quicker than recording 'live' interaction, and it also avoids having to directly face your participants (handy if you are socially awkward or living in a different place from the participants). It can also mean, however, that the issue of consent can be overlooked, even if you have obtained ethical approval from your institution to conduct the study. It is debatable as to whether researchers should tell forum members that their interaction is going to be analysed: in many cases, while this might help to gain 'informed consent' for those participants who agree, it may also lead to distress for the forum members. What is common practice, however, is that research should use only those forums that are publicly accessible (with no password required). Dealing with a sensitive or highly personal issue, such as suicide, also demands more care. In my own research in this area, my concern was to ensure at all times that the discourse was treated respectfully – and focusing on the discursive patterns and online interaction, rather than making assumptions about the individuals who posted the messages – and with a focus on ensuring the research added some insight into the topic area. One could argue that it is even more important that we research and provide understanding of such issues *because* they are sensitive and life-threatening, that we should not shy away from researching them just because they are challenging. There is no simple solution to how to deal ethically with a topic or piece of research, the main thing is that you consider each issue carefully as it arises, and can justify any decisions that you make.

To summarise, this case study tackles a potentially delicate topic area (suicide) with a form of data collection that is likely to be used increasingly often as our online interactions merge with face-to-face interactions. This kind of data is particularly amenable to student projects, when time may be particularly short or when you do not have access to a specific participant group. For a topic such as suicide, for example, it would be hard to access the situations where face-to-face discussion of suicide took place; these might be more likely to occur in counselling or therapy settings, for example.

Case study (3)
Using wigs for alopecia: interview and focus group interaction

The final case study is taken from a project about the experiences of people with alopecia – a medical condition that causes partial or full hair-loss – and specifically about their use of wigs or hair prostheses (see Wiggins, Moore-Millar & Thomson, 2014, for more details; and yes, my name is very appropriate for this topic). This project was conducted in collaboration with colleagues in design and engineering, and my involvement was based on my background in psychology and qualitative research methods. The project was funded internally by the university, as part of an incentive to increase cross-departmental collaborations. The aim of the project was to identify the experiences and needs of people who used wigs as a consequence of having alopecia in order to potentially improve wig design. This case study raised three main issues: (a) seeking adequate funding, (b) analysing interviews as situated accounts, and (c) managing expectations and aims of collaborators.

Although this is an example of a project that was funded, it quickly became apparent that we had not sought sufficient funding to achive all of our objectives in the timescales that we had planned and with our limited availability to work on the project. It involved the recruitment of participants for two focus groups, 14 individual interviews and six video diaries. This then required the transcription of over 40 hours of video or audio data, and the subsequent coding and analysis stages. All this had to be undertaken in 18 months, and although we had acquired funding for assistance with the transcription tasks, we were scheduled to work on everything else. This was a substantial amount of work, much more than the small percentage of our time that we had originally calculated. While we managed to achieve our main aim, this was at the expense of other work or meant that we did not have the time to follow through with all of our project ideas and expectations. Ensuring that you have sufficient funds to adequately conduct your research is therefore really important, both for the researchers and the funding bodies, who also want to see you achieve the project aims.

The second issue arose with the potential clash between the project aims (to understand experiences of wig use) and a constructionist approach to discourse. The use of different types of data (focus groups, interviews and video diaries) was decided in part due to the exploratory nature of the study: there was very little existing research in this area and we wanted to try different ways of investigating the issue. The focus groups were conducted with people who all had alopecia, which helped to encourage a supportive and friendly setting where people could talk in confidence about their experiences. The interviews allowed people to go into more detail about their use of wigs, and we had lots of examples of wigs for people to touch and handle as a 'prop' to encourage discussion. It worked: the interviews typically lasted around two hours each, and we provided hot drinks and biscuits for the participants, who seemed to appreciate the chance to talk about their alopecia. The video diaries then provided 'behind the scenes' data of people using wigs in their homes, providing examples of how they washed and cared for their wigs, had them fitted at a hair salon, or as a way to record their own reflections on using wigs.

This is where we faced a theoretical challenge: how to analyse the data. While the main aim of the project was to understand the experiences of wig users, we could also see the potential in examining the specific discursive practices about talking about wigs, and how people accounted for how they made changes in their use of wigs depending on the social setting. But taking a social constructionist approach to the data would mean treating the discourse *as a situated account* rather than a route to someone's experience or cognitions. So the data analysis was separated into different stages, with the same data being used for different analytical approaches (with one focusing on the discourse as representing individual cognitions, and one focusing on the discourse as social practice). The interview and focus group data, in particular, were therefore treated as accounts of people's social practices rather than the practices themselves. Being clear about the alignment of the project aims, the data collected, and the analytical approach was essential for ensuring a coherent and valid research framework. In this case study, this meant that the same data were used for different kinds of analysis, in a similar manner to the use of secondary data analysis, as noted in case study 1 above.

The final issue that arose with this case study was the management of the aims and expectations of each of the collaborators on the project. In this example, I was working with people from different disciplines, and who therefore had expertise in different theories, approaches and research methods. This provided a great opportunity to consider a project from a new perspective, as well as learning to work together as a team. It also highlighted the assumptions that we each had about research and the topic area: how would we collect data? What was the purpose of the project? What were the main outcomes? At various points in the project it became apparent that we had different expectations about issues such as: who was responsible for different project tasks, how we would share the data and analytical notes, and who would write up any reports. While these were resolved along the way, it was often after a period of confusion or misinterpretation. Ultimately, we learnt to be much more explicit in terms of discussing project issues, tasks and timescales. When working in a team, being super-organised and discussing issues clearly at every step can be the best way to ensure effective working practice.

In summary, this case study highlights issues that might arise in projects if these have not been adequately funded. When a project is funded, then there is usually a commitment to producing specific outcomes (e.g., publications, open-access data archives, reports) within a restricted timeframe. So while they can really help to develop your research, if not planned carefully they can lead to considerable pressure on your time and resources. Working collaboratively with other people – whether from your own field of expertise or a different discipline – can lead to unique insights and is a great way to develop your research as well as broaden your knowledge and skills. It is important, however, to keep discussions open at all times and to set out your expectations from the start.

Box 9.1: Lessons learnt from the case studies

1. Organise your data as soon as you collect it, and create a searchable archive that is both secure (confidential and protected) and robust (can be stored for many years without loss of quality).

2. Consider how you might use your own or other data corpuses for secondary data analysis. Some funders now require that researchers create 'open data' sources that can be used by other researchers. Find out if there are any relevant to your own project interests (see Chapter 4 for more details).

3. Think critically about what it is that you are analysing. Don't assume that you can 'spot it' in the data without first having done some analysis. Be prepared to move between the transcription, coding and analytical stages of research (see Chapters 5 and 6).

4. Student projects can turn into publications, even if you need to collect a little more data or re-analyse or re-write your dissertation.

5. Online discussion forum interaction is one example of textual data that are relatively quick and easy to access, but still require careful handling to ensure the interactional context is not lost.

6. Ethics are central to any research project, and some topic areas or forms of data collection require additional consideration.

7. Be realistic in what can be achieved given your timescales and funding. Don't underestimate the time needed to conduct your research appropriately.

8. Be clear and specific about how your data collection method will correspond with your analytical approach. Does the theory match the methods?

9. Be open and discuss specific aims and approaches with any collaborators from the start. This can save time later on and help you all to work towards a positive outcome.

Developing a DP project

In this section, you will find ideas for the scope of different DP projects that vary according to how much time you have available or what level of competence you have reached. Some of these could be used as classroom activities, whether you have only an hour or two for an undergraduate class or a few weeks for a Master's module in DP. Note that the topic area here is left blank. It is up to your own research interests (and see the previous sections of this chapter, as well as Chapter 3) to design the content of the project. See Box 9.2 if you are tutoring DP, or if you only have time to practise DP rather than conducting your own research project. The point is that there is always some DP research or practice analysis that you can do, no matter how small. Everyone has to start somewhere.

Small projects

Suitable for: short undergraduate projects, up to a few weeks' long.

With small projects, your main concerns are likely to be: how much time do you have and what is your level of competence with DP? Assuming that the answer to both is 'not much', then here are some tips to plan accordingly. You may or may not need to write up your analysis as a report, and this will also impact on what you can achieve in a short space of time.

- Ethical approval may have been gained by your class tutor, since you probably do not have time to obtain approval for individual projects, so first find out the guidelines, restrictions or criteria for your coursework.

- Focus on getting the data fairly quickly, to give you more time for transcription, coding and analysis. While ideally it is always nice to have 'great data', it is better to have a great analysis of poor data than a poor analysis of great data.

- The kinds of data that work well for very short projects are: video, audio or text data from the internet (see Box 4.1) or radio or television chat shows. These can be accessed fairly quickly and easily, have fewer ethical concerns, and provide a wealth of topic areas.

- Follow any guidelines you are given for quantity of data, but as a rule-of-thumb you should aim to collect 1–2 hours' worth of audio or video data, or 15–20 pages of text data. You may not need to analyse all of this, but that should give you enough data to code a smaller corpus for analysis.

- Try to find some DP research on a topic (or using a type of data) that you are interested in, and use this as your focal point. This can be particularly useful if you do not feel competent yet in using DP. Empirical research articles sometimes have suggestions for future research.

- When analysing your data, focus on just one or two 'issues' or features (i.e., one main research question) and aim to do these well. Depth is always better than breadth when it comes to DP analysis.

Medium projects

Suitable for: longer undergraduate projects, up to an undergraduate dissertation level (circa 6–9 months) or Master's level coursework (circa 1–3 months).

With medium projects, you can go into a little more detail and will probably have time to gain ethical approval, so make sure that you plan in sufficient time for that, as well as for writing up any report or presentation.

- As with the small projects, you might find it useful to identify a piece of existing research and consider how you could develop or build on that work. For example, you could use a similar research question with a different type of data or social context.

- Don't rush the data collection stage for this type of project, and ensure that you have good quality audio/video recordings if using conversational (rather than textual) data.

- Most forms of data that are suitable for DP (see Chapter 4) should work for a medium-sized project, though avoid data that involve a hard-to-reach population or a sensitive issue that you are tackling with face-to-face interaction. This can considerably slow down the ethics and recruitment stages, and leave you less time for analysis and writing up.

- Aim for around 5–10 hours of audio/video data or 40–80 pages of text for an undergraduate dissertation, or 3–5 hours and 30–40 pages of text for a Master's coursework, though always check the guidelines provided by your tutor. As before, these are suggested amounts to enable you to collect sufficient data to find enough instances of your research focus. So they could vary considerably, depending on what you are looking for (e.g., less frequently occurring issues will need a larger data set to begin with).

- The analysis can still focus on a small number of issues (up to three should be enough); what the medium-sized projects add is the quality of the analysis (again, go for depth) and how you situate this within the research literature. So you will be demonstrating not only your analytical skills, but also your theoretical ones. You should focus on reading widely across the topic area (and specifically relevant DP research).

- Think of an undergraduate project as being a pilot study for a larger piece of research. That way, you don't have to try to do everything, and can focus on how your work is a small but vital piece of a bigger jigsaw puzzle.

Large projects

Suitable for: Master's projects (circa 6–9 months), doctoral research (circa 3–5 years) or established researchers.

These are projects that might appear very wide-ranging and 'big' when you start, but by the time you have finished, they will suddenly seem to have only just scratched the surface of the issue or topic area you focused upon. These are also projects in which you can develop research that you might have begun at Master's or undergraduate level.

- With large projects, you can be more ambitious with the type of data you use – here you can try out something innovative or blend a mix of data sources – as well as the topic area or participant group. Don't shy away from challenging or sensitive issues, but be prepared to have an alternative plan (or plans) for when it comes to data collection if your first plan doesn't work out. Even a long piece of research can suddenly seem short if you can't find anyone to take part.

- It is typical to collect one large data corpus and then analyse different issues or topics within this, rather than trying to conduct separate small studies within the larger project. These different areas can then become different chapters of your thesis or publications for your research outputs.

- Good quality data – with good sound and visual quality, collected in an appropriate setting and well aligned to your research question – is essential for large projects, so take the time to plan, collect and organise your data carefully.

- The volume of data can vary considerably, but anywhere between 20–40 hours' worth of audio/video or 50–150 pages of textual data should be sufficient for a DP doctoral thesis, assuming it is all good quality.

- Don't assume that a large project has to examine lots of different aspects of the data. As with the medium-sized project, what you should be aiming for is an increased depth or complexity of the analysis, and a more thorough understanding of theoretical issues. So quality is more important than quantity.

Box 9.2: DP in the classroom

The following can be used as suggestions for tutoring DP theory and/or practice, according to how much time you have in class in total (e.g., four hours over two weeks).

With 1–2 hours

- Short lecture on DP theory – focus on (a) social constructionism (see Box 1.3 for example activity or see below) and assumptions, (b) brief examples of DP in practice (choose some of the research referenced earlier in this chapter).

- An activity that can be used to help students to 'get their heads around' the idea that discourse as socially constructed is to use news media. Find two or three short news articles from different sources (e.g., national versus local newspapers) reporting on the same issue. I have used UK weather reports (e.g., reports of storm damage or 'extreme' weather) quite effectively for this task. Then ask students to read these and try to identify how they differ: how the same event ('reality') is described in different ways ('constructed'), and the potential implications of these different versions of events.

- Select one or two discursive devices (see Chapter 7), reading through the worked examples and applying these to another data extract. With just a short amount of time, this is likely to be a sample of data that the tutor provides. Work in pairs or small groups if possible to discuss ideas together.

With 3–6 hours

- As above, but add on:
- Use a 1–2 page transcript – either data that you have access to yourself, or use data found from the internet (see Box 4.1), ideally playing the video/audio in class alongside the transcript. Use an activity to familiarise students with the transcription symbols: play the recording a few times and let the students read the transcript while having a copy of the transcription key alongside.

- Work through two or three more discursive devices with the longer transcript, or let students decide on a research question in small groups.

With a few weeks (e.g., as part of a class/module)

- Depending on your class sizes and room layouts, you might either have a large (>100) class with fixed seating in a tiered lecture theatre, or a small (<50) class with flexible seating in a level teaching space. This will have an impact on what you can do, but wherever possible try to integrate short activities (to be done in pairs or small groups) to allow students to discuss different aspects of DP.

- Focus on theory (what is DP?) and analysis (how do you conduct a DP analysis?), so use exercises that encourage students' understanding of these aspects (e.g., the newspaper task above, and using various discursive devices).

- Provide sample data or, better still, ask students to collect some of their own (see Box 4.1) guided by their own interests. This will pay dividends later on as they are more likely to be interested in doing the analysis on data they have chosen themselves.

- Use the data to illustrate both the theory and analysis of DP: ask the students to identify research questions *after* they have collected their data (so showing that the research question does not need to be fixed or clear in advance of data collection), then use their practice analysis exercises on their own data.

- If using an assignment, consider focusing this on just one part (e.g., only write up the analysis section) to encourage depth over breadth.

With a full term or semester (e.g., as a whole module)

- With a whole module you can cover each stage of the research – from research question, data collection, transcription, coding and analysis. As far as possible, allow students to collect their own data. Working collaboratively in groups can help to make this task more manageable.

- Build on the tasks suggested for shorter time periods, but spend longer on each task, and include time for discussion and critical reflection.

KEY POINTS

- DP has covered a range of different topic areas and issues, and often resists being compartmentalised into separate areas of research.
- Think about what 'issues' or topic areas you are interested in, but be flexible and consider how your research might change its focus, depending on the data that you collect.
- There are many different types of data that you can use for a DP project.
- Research is *always* more complicated and messy than you can ever plan for.
- There is always some DP theory or analysis you can practise, whether you have only a few hours or a few months.

Recommended reading

McKinlay, A. & McVittie, C. (2008). *Social psychology and discourse.* Chichester: Wiley-Blackwell.

Tileagă, C. & Stokoe, E. (Eds.) (2015). *Discursive psychology: Classic and contemporary issues.* New York: Routledge.

10

APPLICATIONS AND FUTURE DEVELOPMENTS

Chapter contents

Applications of DP research: encouraging change	222
Future developments of DP research	227
Epilogue	230

In this final chapter, we will consider the possibilities of applying discursive psychological (DP) research and how it might develop in the future. As such, it will build on Chapter 9, where we explored the range of existing areas of DP research to provide inspiration for your own projects. In considering applications of DP, it is important to situate this within the wider academic environment. The current climate of higher education, while varying considerably across institutions and cultures, is marked by staff accountability, consumerism and the demand for a high volume of research outputs. Academics and researchers are required not only to produce sufficient high-quality research, but also to demonstrate the impact of this on some aspect of the world. We are accountable not only to our students, our institutions and funding organisations, but also to society at large – to the public whose money is spent on education and research. It is therefore all the more important to consider different ways in which our research can be applied – and how we might (re)define application – without feeling pressured into producing research worthy of a Nobel prize. All research which is carefully and appropriately conducted, and which engages with theories and methods, is worthwhile. Sometimes you just have to think about different ways in which your research can encourage change.

I would also argue that the full potential of DP research has yet to be realised. There is so much more we can contribute to different realms of research and social life. With the magical combination of discourse, social actions and psychological notions, DP is perfectly placed to examine the social world. With our data for the most part being taken from everyday life, one could argue that our research is already applied, since it does not need to translate research findings from a laboratory or questionnaire to the 'real world'. It both begins and ends with people's practices. It is an approach that thrives on the apparent chaos and messiness of everyday social interaction. What is needed, therefore, is not for DP to be more applied, but to be more vocal and visible about the different ways in which we are already applied, to be more open to the ways in which research might develop and evolve, and to embrace the exciting possibilities of research that lie ahead.

Applications of DP research: encouraging change

Before we can consider the applications of DP, we first need to be clear about what we mean by 'applied'. The term is often used as a contrast to what might be described as pure, theoretical or basic research. Doing so constructs a dichotomy between research that does, or does not, serve a practical purpose. It is much more complicated than that, of course, and it can become embroiled in political or moral discussions about what research *should* be doing and for whose purpose it serves (see, for example, Hepburn (2006) for a discussion on such issues in relation to NSPCC helpline research; see also Antaki (2011) and Richards and Seedhouse (2005) for applications in CA research). Similarly, one may hear arguments that we should make research relevant for the 'real world'. Another assumption of this 'ideology of application' (Potter, 1982) is that the exchange of knowledge is thought to be uni-directional: that research can be applied to real-world practice, but not the other way around. A number of questions therefore arise when we consider applied research:

- What is being applied?
- For what purpose is the research being applied?
- Who benefits from the application?
- What are the actual benefits of application?
- At what stage should the research be applied?

These questions also raise the issue of knowledge: what knowledge is being produced by the research and whose knowledge counts as being more valid than another? In other words, can we claim that our research 'findings' (or results, analyses) are more important or more valid than anyone else's understanding of the issue? Who are we to say that our research should change other people's practices? These are challenging issues for a relativist, social constructionist approach such as DP. We cannot take lightly the assumption that our research has the answers that will solve others' problems. This does not mean that our research cannot be applied, only that we should be critical and reflexive throughout the process. Being relativist does not mean that we cannot take a stance on an issue. Quite the opposite: it means that we are acutely aware of the political implications of taking a stance and of the consequences of different versions of reality. Our choices are thus all the more carefully made.

In summary, then, the issue of application is not a straightforward one. We need to be cautious about making a distinction between various components – e.g., researcher/researched, theory/practice, pure/applied research – otherwise we risk perpetuating the very dichotomies that we are aiming to deconstruct. Instead, it may be helpful to consider the application of DP in terms of *encouraging change*. It is 'encouraging' because it does not assume that change can or will occur. There are many other agents involved in the world, and our research is only one small piece of the picture. Possible changes could be anything from changing ideas or theories on a specific topic, changing everyday practices (such as the words we use to describe something) or change at a wider policy or societal level. In that sense, application can be understood as a means through which the research is relevant beyond the confines of the study itself. We do not have to make big changes to make a difference; sometimes the smallest research paper can set in motion other ideas or practices. See also Box 10.1 for a comment on how dissemination can be application in itself.

With this in mind, the rest of this section discusses three ways in which DP research can encourage change. These collect together a range of different ideas that can used to stimulate ways of engaging with the world.

1. Application through challenging research

One of the core ways in which DP research can be applied is through challenging research, whether that be the broad approaches (e.g., cognitivist perspectives on emotion), theories and models (e.g., tripartite model of emotion) or methods (e.g., using questionnaires to measure emotional states) that underpin research practice. We might use DP research to challenge how we theorise 'attributions' or 'thinking', for example, or how we interpret people's talk as part of social practices rather than a direct reflection of internal states. In this way, the application is developed through a direct engagement with other research, and specifically, offering an alternative perspective on one or more stages in the research process. Some of the earliest DP research could be understood as applied in that sense, in that it challenged cognitivist or experimental approaches to attributions, memory and attitudes. This is encouraging change among researchers about the ways in which we conduct our research or theorise our concepts.

While this understanding of application engages first with academic research, this does not preclude much wider consequences. Changing research practices can have a knock-on effect in other spheres, such as the content of university courses (and thus what students learn and take with them into their future careers), trends in funding patterns, dissemination to the public, and so on. We therefore do not have to directly change people's practices to have an influence on those areas. What is happening is that we are encouraging change at a different, and earlier, stage. It is application at the heart of an issue, where ideas and concepts emerge and take shape in the academic sphere. To encourage change by challenging research, your work (written reports, presentations and so on) should engage directly with a specific aspect of research. It will need to demonstrate a balanced and critical understanding of other research, to clearly explicate how your work contributes to this and builds an argument towards the need for change. This may not necessarily be achieved in one report or journal article; for some of the bigger issues, it will need to be built up gradually with a body of literature in support of a particular argument. It can happen in the conversations you have with colleagues or fellow students, in the text of your written publications and in the ways in which you might disseminate your research in social media. Each piece of evidence, each report, is important in itself; we need all the pieces of the jigsaw to make the bigger picture.

Box 10.1: Dissemination as application?

The development of the internet, and its various online spaces, has opened up new ways of disseminating research beyond academic journals and conferences. While the increasing use of 'open access' journals is beginning to break down the financial barrier to research findings, there are other ways of engaging with people outside your university. For instance, you can create a website or blog to discuss research issues or report on projects, use Twitter or social media to garner interest in your research and share ideas with other people, or use YouTube videos to show a presentation or analytical skill. We could therefore consider this kind of dissemination as a form of application, of encouraging change in some way. This new era of greater access to research is an exciting time, though it also brings new issues that have yet to be fully realised. The internet not only allows you to share your research, it also means that other people have greater access to you and your research. This can be a very positive thing, and certainly there are examples of researchers being invited to talk about their research on local or national radio or television, or being reported in news media. It also means, however, that we need to be prepared to discuss (and defend) our research with a much wider range of people than our academic peers or fellow students. Maintaining a professional approach is vital.

2. Application through showing the DP lens (critical reflection)

Another way in which DP research can be applied is through showing people the materials of our research, showing the world through the DP lens. The process of collecting audio, video or text-based materials, transcribing these into word documents, and collating instances of patterns or specific interactional practices can provide, in itself, an insight into everyday social life in a way that people are typically not familiar with. This means that DP research can be applied at a very early stage in analysis, following a coding stage to collect together instances of an issue, but before a polished analysis of the transcripts has been completed. Just seeing the transcripts and/or being shown clips from the videos can be enough to highlight something that people had not previously noted. It is easy to forget that the skills we gain as DP researchers – in examining social interaction and psychological notions in detail, in taking apart discourse to see how it 'works' – are valuable in themselves. While people may be familiar with seeing videos (of themselves and others) in daily life and on the internet, they may be much less familiar with approaching these videos with a focus on the detail of discourse and interaction. By showing others a glimpse into life under the DP lens, therefore, we can illuminate aspects of social interaction that were previously unnoticed and illustrate the psychological actions performed therein.

This form of application might also be understood as a way of providing people with the resources (the videos, the transcripts, the coded clips) in which they can reflect on or examine their own practices: critical reflection. In the first instance, this can be done with the participants who were involved in the research. This must be carried out sensitively, however; it is not simply a case of sharing your data files. A workshop or meeting should be arranged to enable you to feed back to your participants as well as providing them with the opportunity to ask questions, discuss issues or request further resources. Assuming you have ethical approval to share the data, you could then also invite other interested individuals or organisations to the workshop. A resource pack – in the form of video/audio files, selected transcripts, and guidance notes – should then be provided for the long-term use of individuals or institutions. This will need to be planned into the project at the early stages when seeking ethical approval (or even when seeking funding).

3. Application through turning practices into strategies

The third way in which DP research might be applied develops from the second, and can be considered the next stage in the process. Examples of research in this area are therefore closely aligned with the previous ones. This is application through turning discursive practices into strategies for action – through the identification of a specific discursive practice and making a recommendation as to how this can be adopted, modified or (removed) in order to change people's practices. There is an important aspect to this: it focuses on participants' practices as being the key to the (new) strategies, rather than a researcher-imposed authority as to what is 'correct' or appropriate behaviour. Researchers must work closely with participants in what might be referred to as the 'dissemination' stages. This might first involve the identification of a problem or issue that needs to be resolved, and in that sense this form of application is particularly relevant for institutional practices where there are more likely to be routine patterns of interaction that recur frequently.

One of the ways in which this might happen is first to hold a workshop – as described in the second application example above – in which participants can see the materials and begin to reflect on their existing practices. The process of turning these into strategies would then require a second stage, such as further workshops in which participants could collaboratively examine the data and decide on alternative strategies for changing their practices. There might be outputs produced by the participants, to help make the changes more concrete. In Lamerichs and te Molder's (2011) work, for example, their participants (14–17 year olds) presented their conclusions in a play. This kind of application is therefore more likely to be a long-term project, where adequate time can be planned to ensure that the research is used to its full potential.

Box 10.2: Top tips when 'applying' DP

- **Start small**: Be focused and specific. Discursive practices and social interaction are diverse and context-dependent, so try to identify a small, situated practice to focus on. Your research is more likely to have an application if it is clearly defined and limited to a small aspect of social life.

- **Take your time**: Creating an intervention or applying research usually happens gradually, so be patient and think about the long-term process of application.

- **Involve others**: If applying DP in a setting that involves changing people's practices, it is important to involve those people at all times in the process. Do they actually want to change their practices? Whose responsibility is it to make the change? Applied research works better as a collaborative process.

- **Think creatively**: There are many ways in which research can be applied, and not all involve directly changing people's practices or theory. Working collaboratively with researchers in other disciplines or with people in different organisations (e.g., industry, commerce, charitable work) can be a way of developing an applied strand to your work.

- **Find a pattern**: Institutional practices are more likely to be regular than everyday, mundane settings (i.e., counselling or therapy talk versus chatting with friends), and finding a regular pattern might be the first step in identifying how that pattern has consequences for social practices or psychological issues.

- **Focus on your passions**: Research can be an exciting though also effortful and time-consuming process, so only do research that you are really passionate about. Consider ways of encouraging change that work within your time and resource levels; as noted above, there is more than one way to be 'applied'.

Future developments of DP research

Writing a section on the future developments of any area of research is, of course, a tricky business. We cannot predict the future, but we can reflect on current developments and speculate as to how these might be taken forward. This section will highlight three areas of DP research that are beginning to emerge in recent years to provide further inspiration for your own research. These developments are important both for the theoretical and the analytical progress of DP: we need to move forward and adapt to changing circumstances.

1. DP and technology

The ever-increasing integration of mobile technology with people's practices provides a rich source of ideas for DP research. In our everyday lives, we are likely to interact with screens, devices and equipment in some form on a regular basis. We use technology to work, to connect with people, to plan our schedules, entertain ourselves and find out about the world. Some forms of technology become extensions of our physical bodies: not only can we wear technology, but it shapes the way in which we move in the spaces around us. Other areas of research, such as ethnomethodology, human–computer interaction and conversation analysis, have already begun to explore the way in which interaction is shaped in, and through, technologies. DP research has the potential to play a very important part in research in this area, given its interest in discursive practices and psychological and social actions, for these, too, are often at the core of technological developments.

There are different ways in which we can approach this area. Research into online interaction is still in the early stages and at the moment is mainly focused on message board interaction where forum members discuss a particular topic, seek advice or support. As online spaces morph into new objects – such as email, Twitter, Facebook, blogs, vlogs and Instagram – these provide different ways of examining how people live their lives in 'virtual space'. These are spaces in which identities are negotiated, accountabilities are managed and relationships are made or broken. They are exciting areas, where there are psychological implications of talk and text, and where psychological terms and issues are used to manage delicate social practices. So we need to develop new ways of capturing these kinds of data (see Meredith & Stokoe, 2014, for example) and analysing that data in a way that is sensitive to the original social context within which they were produced.

We can also examine the ways in which technology is integrated within 'offline' interaction: what happens as people use technology in social settings rather than what happens in the online spaces themselves. This can be illustrated with the example of the phone. There is now an established body of work on telephone helpline interaction, with what happens when people phone a helpline, and how these calls are managed. There is much less, however, on how people use and interact with phones while they are also involved in other social settings. With smartphones, for example, people can be much more mobile and be involved in multiple tasks while using phones. So DP research could examine how these interactions are managed and how they are used to accomplish particular psychological and social business. This may require not only new methods of data capture but also new ways of analysing the embodied interaction (how the physical as well as the psychological spaces are managed).

2. DP and subject/object relations

While the origins of DP where immersed in a time when cognitive psychology was particularly popular, the current academic climate in the social sciences has seen a shift towards emotional states and embodied practices. This includes the 'turn to affect': the renewed consideration of emotions and 'experiences' from physiological, psychological and phenomenological perspectives. Researchers from a range of approaches and epistemological stances are (re)engaging with this aspect of embodiment, and of how this alters the way in which we interact with others and the world around us. There has been a subtle shift, then, from a focus on cognitivist explanations to experiential ones. From a DP perspective, this shift still assumes a dualist stance, in which there is an inner/outer body and a separation of mind/body. This develops an area that Edwards (2005a) has already noted as warranting further DP interest – subject/object relations – or how discursive practices construct, enact or reify the distinction between the subject (people) and objects (the world).

One way in which DP research might engage with this is to explore embodiment as a central issue: how the practices or processes of the physical body are invoked in discourse and used to accomplish social actions. At what point does crying or laughing become a social act, for example, and how does this implicate other people in terms of accountability or identities? What about bodily pain or pleasure, or emotional states – supposedly individual and 'internal' sensations? How are these produced in interaction and made relevant for social actions? We can also consider the issue of subject/object relations in terms of how distinctions are made between mind and body, how mental versus physical states are invoked in interaction to achieve specific goals. These might be in the service of institutional concerns (such as for medical care, educational achievements or legal cases) or in more mundane – but still highly consequential – settings, such as chatting with friends or family.

Engaging with the issue of subject/object relations will therefore require a thorough engagement with theoretical issues and to dig much deeper into some of the psychological concepts that have already been considered by DP (and other) research. It will remain resistant to dualist and cognitivist accounts – which separate out mind/body or assume an underlying cognitive explanation for human behaviour – and focus instead on everyday social practices. It will involve engaging with researchers from a range of approaches and assumptions, with those who seek to get 'inside' the individual. DP provides a way of re-specifying the concepts of psychology, but this involves a radical change in both our theories and methods.

3. DP and other approaches

It was noted in Chapters 1 and 2 that there are a number of different approaches that might be broadly glossed as 'discourse analysis'. Beyond these, there is a further array of approaches – both theoretical and methodological – which analyse talking and interaction in some form. Some of these are concerned with individuals rather than interaction, or with culture rather than communication. Beyond research that deals primarily with words (which we might group together as 'qualitative'), there is research that aims to examine cause and effect and to identify the rules of human behaviour. These approaches vary in terms of their ontological (what exists in the world) and epistemological (how we know about what exists in the world) stances, and there is considerable antagonism and tension between the political and ideological aims of each approach. There is, in short, something for everyone.

As different approaches develop, however, there is a tendency for each to become ever more insular and isolated from the others. Sometimes this is due to the need to be distinctive, to be clear about what makes one research project 'discursive psychology' rather than 'critical discursive psychology', for example. This in itself is not a bad thing; it is helpful to be able to distinguish approaches to ensure that each is theoretically and methodologically coherent, and it can help in terms of training new researchers and ensuring quality control in research. It can, however, lead to what has been termed 'methodolatry': the privileging of methodology over other research considerations. We are at risk of becoming increasingly divided, looking only at our own micro-areas of research in order to keep up with the latest developments while missing the bigger picture. Add to this the challenges of diversifying one's skills in different methodologies and the lure of being a 'specialist' in one's preferred area of research, and one can easily lose sight of the really important research questions.

The third potential area for the development of DP research, therefore, is to engage more fully with different approaches both within and across single disciplines. This will be challenging work: to find ways of maintaining the integrity of each approach while also truly collaborating on research. The possibilities, however, are immense, whether we engage with researchers who study the same topic (but from a different approach), or those from different cultural perspectives, different disciplines, methodologies and ideologies. While DP might have emerged from within psychology, it is almost interdisciplinary (or multidisciplinary) by definition in its concern with various components of social interaction and of how psychological concepts are made relevant in and for interaction.

Box 10.3: Activity: the future of DP

The future of DP has yet to be written, and your own research may play a part in how it develops. Consider for a moment how you think DP should evolve: What issues might it consider? How should we develop our means of 'collecting' data? How might it be used more effectively alongside other research? You might also consider what practical considerations need to be put into place to help facilitate this development. Do we need journals or conferences that are 'just' for DP research or would this be too insular? What sorts of technological developments might help to change the landscape of DP research? What DP research would you do if money and time were not an issue?

Epilogue

Since the beginnings of DP, much has been achieved in terms of challenging theory and research practice. It has considered a broad range of psychological issues and social settings, developed alongside critical debates and technological advances, and flourished alongside the growing range of methodologies and approaches across the social sciences. Not bad for an approach that has had to fight against much resistance and conflict along the way. I did say that this was a feisty area of research. And yet these debates have been important in the development of DP. They have encouraged a healthy and active reflection on just what it is we are studying, and why it is important to do so. Without discussion – without discursive practices, social action and the management of psychological issues – DP would not exist. But we are in the early days of this approach. There is still so much more to be done.

KEY POINTS

- Applying DP research can be understood in terms of encouraging change, whether that is change to theory, methods or practices.
- Start small and don't rush into trying to be 'applied'. Even the smallest piece of research can have lasting impact.
- As a research process that is grounded in the wonderful chaos of people living their lives, DP research should adapt in as many ways as life changes.
- Possible future areas for DP research are: (1) examining psychological actions in and through technology, (2) explicating subject/object relations, and (3) closer engagement with other approaches and disciplines

Recommended reading

Abell, J. & Walton, C. (2010). Imagine: Towards an integrated and applied social psychology. *British Journal of Social Psychology*, 49(4), 685–690.

The special issue of the *British Journal of Social Psychology* (2012, vol. 51) provides a reflection on 25 years of DP by some of the key researchers in this area.

FREQUENTLY ASKED QUESTIONS (FAQS) ABOUT DISCURSIVE PSYCHOLOGY

In this section, you will find some common or potential criticisms and concerns of DP that may be faced at any time in one's research career in DP. Whether you are a student with your own questions, a tutor facing quizzical looks from your students, or an established professor pre-empting critical comments on a grant application, it can be helpful to know what questions you may be asked and some strategies on how to respond. They have been grouped according to whether the FAQs relate to theory, transcription or analysis (the three core areas where questions are often asked). The FAQs are written in **bold** with responses immediately underneath.

FAQs about DP theory

What is the point of DP?... or Why should I use it?

Discursive psychology offers a rigorous and systematic way in which we can examine how psychological business is involved in, and used for, the purposes of social actions. It can illuminate the detail of discursive practices – how people talk and interact in different settings – and the consequences of these practices. It is ideally suited to answering questions such as how we are held accountable for our actions, how our identities are invoked in different contexts and how psychological matters are used to perform social actions.

Isn't DP the same as discourse analysis?

No, since discourse analysis is a broad set of approaches to analysing discourse, each of which has different theoretical assumptions and analytic tools. DP is one form of discourse analysis and so shares the argument that discourse constructs (rather than reflects) reality, but has its own range of principles (see Chapter 1) and ways of doing research (see Chapters 3–8). See Chapter 2 for a comparison of DP to other forms of discourse analysis.

Isn't DP just like conversation analysis?

No, though it was inspired by and continues to be influenced by developments in conversation analysis (CA). The similarities between CA and DP are the focus on the detail of talk and interaction (and using these to drive research questions), a focus on participants' orientations and a preference for naturalistic data. The differences are primarily in terms of DP's constructionist focus (on how categories are invoked in talk and how particular versions of reality are constructed) and its anti-cognitivist stance (arguing against the reduction of language to cognitive processes).

Doesn't DP ignore subjectivity?

DP does consider subjectivity, but theorises this in terms of how people make relevant and manage subjectivity in the unfolding sequence of social interaction. For instance, this is tackled in the form of subject/object relations, with how people invoke subject-side constructions (e.g., experiences, thoughts, emotions) as a contrast to object-side constructions (e.g., objects in the world, facts, events) and how these are involved in social actions. So it takes a different theoretical and analytical stance on what subjectivity is: placing this in the social and discursive world, rather than the intra-individual world of cognitions, perceptions and bodily states.

Isn't DP more like linguistics or English language studies rather than psychology?

Like linguistics or English language studies, DP is interested in discourse, but it differs in that it is about discursive practices: with how people talk and interact in social settings. Linguistics and related disciplines, by contrast, are typically interested in individual understandings of language and language production. DP also places psychology at the heart of social interaction, with how psychological concepts are managed and made consequential in the way in which we talk and interact with each other. It is about people and their practices, and the dynamic interplay between discourse, psychology and social life. How much more psychological does it need to be?

Isn't DP a bit like behaviourism?

No, in that DP does not bracket off psychological concerns and treat these as analytically unavailable. Nor does it reduce discourse and interaction to an individual level. Instead, DP examines how people's categories and understandings are produced in interaction, and how minds, emotions, perceptions, and so on, are made 'real' in particular ways and the consequences of these in social settings.

Do we have to know about psychology to use DP?

No, psychology as a discipline doesn't have exclusive rights to knowledge about psychological issues (just as we do not have to be a medical doctor to have a right to know about our bodies and health). While it may be helpful to have a background in psychology studies, DP research does not assume that you know psychological theory or research.

Why does DP seem to reject the idea that there are cognitive (and other 'internal') processes? Surely it is obvious that we all think and feel things?

DP does not deny that there are cognitive processes or that people have emotions or ways of experiencing the world. But it does challenge the assumption that these concepts should be used as a way of making sense of people's *discursive practices* (talking, writing, interacting with other people). In other words, it argues against the referential view of language, which assumes that the words we speak are used to refer directly to 'internal' states or processes. So DP challenges cognitivism, not cognition. Discourse is theorised primarily as action, not as representation: as performing social business rather than representing an apparent intra-individual state.

Why don't we learn about why people use language?

This is an interesting and important research question to ask, but DP research does not seek to determine causal relationships (it works with a different set of theoretical assumptions about discourse; see Chapter 1). However, it does provide a powerful analytical tool to examine *how* people use language and the consequences this has in different social settings. In some ways, we could argue that this is even more important than why people use language in the first place, since it focuses us on the ways in which discourse, social practices and people are woven together. It allows us to examine not why people use language, but what happens when they do.

FAQ questions about DP transcription

How do you know which bits to transcribe? Are we simply picking sections at random (I don't have time to transcribe it all)?

If you have a lot of data, it can be more time-efficient to first watch or listen to all of your data and make detailed notes (see Chapter 5) before you begin any transcription. As you do so, identify any possible sections of the data that are relevant to your research question; these are the sections that you can then transcribe first. If you have a small amount of data, you can follow the same procedure or else start from the beginning and transcribe the whole corpus. When you first transcribe, however, it is usually more efficient to just transcribe words-only. Once you are more familiar with the data, then you can transcribe sections in detail.

How do you know what to transcribe in detail?

Once you have produced some words-only transcripts, and coded these for different instances or occasions in which a psychological category is being invoked, then you can identify those sections to transcribe in more detail. Start with just a few first, and transcribe more as you do more analysis; sometimes the analysis will point to sections of transcript that require more detail. So work slowly at first, and intersperse transcription with coding and analysis.

When creating a coded corpus, how much of the transcript should I copy across for each 'instance' that I find?

When identifying particular instances or psychological categories in the data corpus, you will need to copy-and-paste these into a separate coded document. You should include a few lines of talk before and after the 'thing' in the transcript that you are focused on so that you capture some of the surrounding interactional context. It is always better to include a little more transcript than you think you will need, than to risk missing out on some piece of interaction that you later have to search for again.

When do you start a new line?

There are no hard-and-fast rules for when to begin a new line when transcribing, and ultimately it will not damage your analysis if you have too many or too few words on each line. In principle, though, you should start a new line when: (a) there is a pause of around (1.0) or more, as this typically indicates a noticeable pause in the interaction, (b) a change of speaker or when some other feature needs to be noted (such as a door closing or movement of people), and (c) before you get to the end of the page. Create a reasonably wide margin in your transcript, as this not only helps ease of reading, but it can also provide space for analytical notes or for the formatting of many academic journals.

When using Jefferson symbols, do you place the symbol before or after the word?

In most cases, the symbol is placed *before* the letter or word to which it applies; for example, when noting ↑rising or ↓falling pitch sounds. With symbols such as CAPITALS for louder talk, or underlining for emphasis, then the symbol features at the same time as the letter or word. Sometimes, as in the case of interpolated laughter (laughing while talking), the symbol features within the w(h)ord, just at the point at which it is audible. Finally, some symbols, such as those indicating °quieter°, >speeded-up< or <slowed down> talk, should be placed before and after the words to which they apply.

Do I need to include all the symbols if I won't be referring to these in my analysis?

Yes. You cannot know from the start which features of the discourse will be relevant for your analysis, and the analysis itself relies on having a detailed transcript to work from (alongside the audio/video file where this is available). So always include as much detail as you can. Conversely, however, you won't need to refer to all the transcription symbols when you are analysing or interpreting the data; they are there to provide a written representation of the video/audio data.

Should I transcribe things as they are said, or how they should be spelt?

It is usually preferable to transcribe things as they are said, to capture the particular intonation or inflection of the talk. Never 'tidy' up the talk or improve the grammar. You need to transcribe the talk as it was said, not how you think it should have been said. There are occasions, however, when it can be helpful to have standard spellings being used if you are searching for particular words or phrases across a data corpus. In such cases you may just need to be sensitive to alternative forms of the word when searching or else begin with standard spelling when transcribing to words-only level, then refine it once you include the Jefferson transcription symbols.

How do I transcribe regional accents?

There is no prescribed way of transcribing regional accents, though the characteristic nature of certain accents (such as frequent rising/falling pitch, raised pitch towards the end of turns at talk, different vowel sounds, and so on) can usually be indicated through careful use of the Jefferson transcription symbols and spelling words as they sound phonetically rather than orthographically. The steak example used in this book, for instance, features a strong Scottish accent saying the words 'does not'; this was transcribed as 'disnae' to represent this in a way that was more faithful to the spoken dialect. If regional accents are particularly important to your study, then you can also note the accents that are used when describing the participants in your report.

When and how do you transcribe visual information?

This is typically done as a third (or later) stage in transcription. When first starting to transcribe, code and analyse your data, it may not be apparent as to which visual features are going to be important for the analysis. For example, are eye gaze, pointing at something, holding of objects or movements of the body going to be relevant? To include *all* visual information in a transcript would not only be an incredibly lengthy process; it would also make the transcript almost impossible to read. Better to use the video recording as your first point of contact, and add in one or two visual features as and when you begin to consider these in your analysis. For suggestions on how to transcribe these, see Chapter 5.

My data are in a language other than English. Do I need to translate this and, if so, do I analyse it *before* or *after* I have translated it?

It is more usual to transcribe the data in its original language, analyse it as such, then provide a translation into English if presenting this for an English-language publication (which is the majority of academic journals). See Nikander (2008) for a very helpful discussion on such issues.

FAQ questions about DP analysis

Why are there no fixed guidelines about how I should analyse the data using DP?

Like many approaches, DP analysis requires a sensitivity to different aspects of discursive and social practices that cannot be reduced to something akin to a mathematical formula or a controlled experiment. It is a skill as much as a process, but there are broad stages that can be followed (see Chapter 6) to ensure that DP research is coherent and rigorous. Because social interaction and discursive practices vary so considerably there can never really be fixed guidelines – the analytical context will always vary. This is what makes DP research exciting; we have a set of procedures to follow, but each piece of DP research will provide unique insights and new ideas.

How do I get started on analysis with DP?

DP analysis begins when you start considering your research area; it starts with your research question and how you approach the world in a particular way. But when you have a piece of transcript, and you want to know how to start analysing this, see Chapter 6, stage 1. Your first stage is to read the data and familiarise yourself with what is there.

Why don't I just count the words? Wouldn't a statistical analysis be more effective (and less hassle)?

You can count the words, but it wouldn't tell you anything about how they work to perform social actions. It would just tell you how many words there are, and the frequency of some over others. This can be helpful in some cases as a starting point – for instance,

I have used this approach to gain an overview of the different types of words used to make food assessments (e.g., Wiggins, 2014) – but it needs to be followed up by a more detailed analysis of the interaction. A statistical analysis would require large data sets and could be possible, but that typically draws on assumptions about the referential status of language (that words refer directly to intra-individual concepts, such as attitudes, desires, beliefs, etc.).

Does 'action orientation' mean that people are deliberately motivated or consciously using their language in a particular way?

No, it means the way in which the discourse makes available certain social actions, without needing to explicitly state these. For example, in Extract 1 in Chapter 1, Lucy's 'I prefer red' works as a request for red wine, without her needing to state this specifically. Even if people were deliberated motivated or consciously using their language in a particular way, we wouldn't be able to access that particular cognitive process or structure. We can, however, examine how people *treat each other* as being motivated, biased and so on, and that in itself is often more important for social practices.

What is a 'device' in DP and how would I know if I found a new one?

The DP devices are broadly analytical tools; they are features of talk that are identifiable in some way, so in that sense they need to be prevalent enough in discourse and interaction to be recognisable. The list in Table 6.1 are those which are most often used in DP research, though there are others that are just emerging and which yet may be added. You may find a new one in your own research, though it might not be apparent that you have found one until it can be used or applied in other research; that is, to be regular enough to work across different contexts. What is important is that the devices allow us to investigate the psychological and social actions being performed in the talk, and to focus our attention on these rather than with other aspects of discourse.

If discourse is seen to vary so much all the time, does this mean that we are unpredictable in the way that we talk or act?

No, and quite the opposite. One of the things that conversation analysis (and DP) has shown is that social interaction is actually highly ordered, even to the level of pauses, interruptions and turn-taking. So we are not as unpredictable as might be expected.

Why can't I just summarise the gist of what was said? Why do I need to include extracts in the results section?

How would you know what the 'gist' was, anyway? If you try to pick out the things that you think are important, then you would be missing all the detail of what is actually going on, and how the social actions are being performed. By providing extracts in the results section, we not only stay grounded in the data, and ensure that our interpretation is close to the evidence (reducing the 'interpretative gap', see Edwards, 2012), but also make this analytical process clear and transparent to anyone reading our analyses. In that way, we are opening ourselves up to the scrutiny and allowing readers to make their own decisions about our interpretations.

How do I link my analyses to other research? Does this have to be other DP research or can it be any other study?

One of the key ways in which you can ensure that your analysis is valid and coherent is to show how your study is situated within a broader research context. This might be other DP research or from any discipline or analytical approach. Drawing on DP research in your analyses can help to show how the devices you are using, the categories or psychological business you are analysing, have been considered by other research. So it can show whether your analysis adds something new, for example, or builds on the scope of previous studies. When referring to other (non-DP) research in your analysis section, just be sure that you are consistent with the theoretical approach taken in your study. Another piece of research might make very different claims, for example, about a topic area or psychological concept, so what they 'find' and what you are 'finding' might be very different things.

What if other people come to a different interpretation or conclusion from mine? Does this mean that DP isn't scientific? Should I use inter-rater reliability?

Other people are entitled to have different interpretations and conclusions, and these may well add some new insights. This is very different from saying that DP isn't scientific. Science is about debate, ideas and interpretations as much as it is about rigour, evidence and systematic observation (again, see Edwards, 2012). DP is a social constructionist approach. If we argued that there was only one interpretation, then we would be arguing against our own epistemological stance. It would also sound pretty dogmatic. Inter-rater reliability also suggests that there is some fixed truth or version of reality that we are trying to observe, and that with enough independent observers, we will be able to identify it. We can, however, incorporate other interpretations and ideas in the analytical process through data sessions and feedback at presentations of our work. These help us to check out the credibility of our interpretations and how well they stand up against critique.

So we are not aiming to find 'the truth' about the data. We are aiming to provide an interpretation that is grounded in the data and which says something interesting and useful (whether that usefulness is about theory or practice; see Chapter 10).

How do I know if my analysis is correct? Surely it is all subjective? (aka... how do I know that I am not just making this up?)

First, there are epistemological issues to be considered here. DP doesn't claim to have the 'correct answers' because it argues that there are many different versions of reality and no single version has precedence over another. Similarly, it would take issue with the claim that some things are 'objective' (and 'true') and others are 'subjective' (and, by corollary, supposedly 'less true'). At the same time, there is a very practical concern here, and that is that we need to know when we are doing 'DP analysis' and when we are doing something very different. What is important, then, is that we focus on the three core principles of DP (see Chapter 1) and apply these to the analysis: working with participants' orientations, grounding our research questions in the data, and using the DP devices to orientate us to the psychological business and social actions that are being performed. See Chapter 6 on validating the analysis for further discussion on this.

How can a DP study be representative of the wider population when it uses small samples of talk from just a few people?

DP doesn't claim to be representative of a wider population any more than a statistical analysis of data from 100 people claims to be. The aim of DP is to examine discursive practices and how these work in different social contexts, and it argues that each interaction is unique. The 'wider population', and its many social interactions, is too diverse anyway to try to capture something that might represent it all (or even part of it). Instead, DP research can illuminate ways of talking about different psychological concepts and how these are involved in different social actions. And it does so in real, applied, settings; in the places where people live their lives and in which ways of talking have direct consequences. Rather than trying to 'apply' or translate our findings onto another section of the population, we can instead show how our research has direct relevance in actual social settings.

GLOSSARY

Account A particular version of events, a description or explanation provided for a specific purpose.

Accountability The activity of being held to account for something, or managing one's responsibility (or lack of it) for an event or behaviour. This can also include one's responsibility to provide an account. It is similar to the issue of blaming, but being accountable for something does not necessarily mean that the person is to blame for it.

Action-orientation The feature of discourse (talk and text) that focuses it towards a particular social action (i.e., 'orientates it'). For example, the action-orientation of the statement, 'it's cold' might be as a request to close a window or turn up the heating.

Agency The property or ability of something to be the cause of an action, e.g., being able to take control of something, make choices or be able to act independently.

Approach A set of principles and assumptions for undertaking research, including everything from theory to data collection to analysis. The term 'approach' is thus much broader than theory, methodology or model.

Assessment The judgement or evaluation of something; making a claim about the quality of an object, event or person, for example.

Attitude A psychological concept that is typically associated with a cognitivist approach, where it refers to an evaluative belief or perception about something in the world. In DP research, an attitude is understood as a discursive accomplishment, an assessment or evaluation that is situated within a specific discursive context.

Attribution Inferring or ascribing a cause for an event; whether or not the attribution is understood to be cognitive or discursive is dependent on the theoretical approach taken.

Bottom-up analysis (or approach) An analysis (or approach) where the data are the starting point for developing an analysis, rather than ideology or theory.

Categorisation The process through which objects, people or places are assigned to categories. In DP research this is achieved through discursive practices (through talking and writing) rather than being ascribed to cognitive processes.

Category entitlements The rights and responsibilities associated with a particular category.

GLOSSARY

Coding The process of sorting through a data set and separating out those parts of the data – both the transcript and the associated recording – that relate to the research question.

Cognitivism An approach which interprets people's talk and behaviours primarily in terms of underlying cognitive causes.

Cognitive agnosticism Taking a neutral stance on whether or not (particular) cognitive states exist.

Construction The process through which different concepts (such as identity or attitudes) are produced in particular ways in discursive practices.

Context The setting in which something takes place, the limits of which are taken as relevant for the research, specifically in terms of data collection and analysis.

Conversation analysis An approach to analysing everyday and institutional discourse that examines the sequential organisation and action-orientation of talk-in-interaction.

Critical discourse analysis A set of approaches that analyses how discourses are both productive of and produced by ideologies and power relations.

Critical discursive psychology An approach to analysing discourse that combines both macro and micro features of discourse analysis.

Critical realism A theoretical position which argues that we cannot directly access reality as it will always be represented or mediated in some way. For example, the words we use to describe something are a way of representing that thing, but they are not that 'thing' in itself.

Data All the materials – in DP, this is talk or text in social interaction – collected (e.g., in online discussion forum interaction) or generated (e.g., in a focus group) for research. In DP research, data are therefore the original texts or audio/video recordings as well as any representations of this (e.g., transcripts). **Data corpus** refers to the whole set or collection of data for a research project.

Deconstruction The process through which discourse is 'taken apart', i.e., the unpacking or exposing of the assumptions which underlie concepts or ways or talking.

Deviant cases Those instances (cases) or sections of the data that do not appear to fit into the interpretation or explanation provided in the analysis.

Disclaimer A phrase that makes a direct claim against the speaker being accused of something (e.g., racism) even if the subsequent talk might perform that action. For example, one might say, 'I'm not racist…' before stating something that could be interpreted as racist.

Discourse Any form of spoken or written language – talk or text. In some forms of discourse analysis, this can also be extended to other ways in which meaning is produced in interaction, such as gestures, symbols and objects.

Discourse analysis A broad collection of approaches that analyse discourse in all its forms. They share in common the assumption that discourse produces and creates reality rather than reflects it.

Discursive action How things are accomplished in talk and text (e.g., asking questions, blaming someone, teasing, flirting, excusing).

Discursive devices The analytical tools used by discursive psychology (and other forms of discourse analysis) to examine the constituent parts or structure of discursive practices.

Dispreferred A turn in interaction that is potentially problematic for the other speaker or which does not fit the normative pattern of a particular sequence. Preference here is understood in the sense of what is preferred for smooth, untroubled social interaction.

Emic analysis Analysis that privileges the interpretations, orientations or terminology used by the participants in the research.

Epistemology The study of, or theory of, knowledge, of 'how we know what we know'. It can cover everything from what counts as knowledge, how we obtain or produce knowledge to what are the consequences of this knowledge.

Essentialism The argument that there are fixed qualities or 'essences' inside people – such as personality or intelligence – that are relatively enduring and not changed by the social context.

Ethnography An approach that studies groups of people and their practices.

Ethnomethodology An approach that aims to understand the methods through which people make sense of each other's practices in everyday settings: how people *make sense* of what they are doing. It often examines the processes through which the social world is made orderly and coherent.

Etic analysis   Analysis that privileges the interpretations, orientations or terminology used by the researchers, rather than those of the participants in the research.

Extreme case formulation (ECF)   An ECF is a semantically extreme word or phrase that works rhetorically to build an end-of-the-line description while also accomplishing other social actions.

Focus group   A method of data collection whereby a person (called the moderator) asks a series of questions or instigates discussion in a group of people who have been organised for that purpose. The discussion is typically focused on a particular topic.

Footing   The stance that people take on an issue; the 'participant role' that is produced in the interaction at a particular moment.

Formulation   A summary or gist of a previous discussion or statement.

Foucauldian discourse analysis   An approach to discourse analysis that draws on the work of Michel Foucault, and which examines the socio-historical aspects of discourse and the impact of these on social and psychological life.

Hedging   The marking of a turn in interaction as being in some way tentative, conditional or provisional. It can also mark talk as potentially problematic.

Ideology   A coherent and organised set of ideas, which often underpins social structures or political arguments.

Indexicality   How the meaning of an utterance or turn in interaction is understood to be situated both within the turn-by-turn sequential context as well as the broader interactional and rhetorical context. To identify what is 'meant', therefore, analysis should be based on what comes before and what comes after the turn.

Interpretative repertoire   A collection of words or ways of talking about objects or events in the world which provide a relatively coherent and culturally recognisable characterisation of that object or event.

Linguistic determinism (see also **Sapir-Whorf hypothesis**)   A theory that states that our language shapes (or determines) our thought processes. There are weaker versions of this (sometimes called linguistic relativity or the Sapir-Whorf hypothesis) that argue that language influences, rather than determines, our perceptions and experiences of the world.

Macro analyses Analyses that draw on broader contextual issues, such as socio-historical aspects, culture, ideology and power, to analyse data.

Membership Categorisation Analysis (MCA) A sub-set of conversation analysis that analyses the categories used to make inferences about people and events in the social world.

Meta-theory A theory of theory, i.e., a way of understanding and analysing what makes a theory.

Method The tool or technique used to collect data or carry out the research.

Methodology The set of theoretical assumptions that underpin research, from the research questions, to the data and how they are collected, to the analytical procedure.

Micro-analyses Analyses that focus on the specifics of the interaction, such as turn-taking organisation and the words and gestures used within an interaction.

Multimodality Broadly defined, this refers to research or analysis that considers different 'modes' of communication or interaction. In conversation analysis, this might refer to talk, gesture, facial movement and use of objects. Multimodal critical discourse analysis, on the other hand, refers to visual imagery (photographs, diagrams, pictures) as well as language in the analysis of texts.

Naturally occurring data (or naturalistic data) Data collected from settings that would have occurred regardless of the research taking place, such as family mealtimes, online discussion forums or doctor–patient interaction. Such data are often contrasted with researcher-generated data, where the setting is specifically designed for the research (such as interviews or focus groups).

Next-turn proof procedure The process of checking the interpretation of a turn in talk by examining the next turn in the sequence, and focusing on how the speakers themselves understand or orientate to a turn in talk, rather than the analyst's assumptions.

Norm A pattern or regular feature of human behaviour or interaction; something that is treated as expected or for which someone might be held accountable if they do not adhere to the norm.

Ontology The study of things in the world: what exists, what form this takes, and the relationship between things in the world and our understandings of these.

Orientating/orientation The way in which a section of talk (or speaker) attends to, or makes relevant, a particular action or interpretation.

Orthographic transcript A written version of an audio or video recording that includes only the words spoken but not the way in which they are spoken.

Paralinguistic The features of speech that detail how words are delivered, such as emphasis, volume of speech, rising or falling pitch. It can also include non-lexical sounds such as coughs, laughter or crying.

Participant The term used to refer to the people who take part in our research, or whose discursive practices we are analysing.

Post-structuralism A set of theoretical approaches that developed as a response to structuralist approaches to language. They argue that meaning is produced through discourse, and that there are not fixed (structured) links between meaning and language.

Prosody The features of speech that relate to its production and sound, such as pitch, volume, timing and voice quality. These are sometimes referred to as the rhythmic or musical aspects of speech.

Pseudonym The fake name that you give to participants or places to protect their anonymity.

Realism (see also **critical realism**) An ontological and epistemological position that assumes that there is a single reality that we can access or know in some way, that a real world exists independently of our representations or interpretations of it.

Reflexivity The acknowledgement of the researcher's involvement in the production of knowledge.

Relativism An epistemological position that assumes that there are multiple realities (rather than a single one). It argues that there is no basis on which we can claim that one version of reality is more 'real' than another. Thus all versions are, in theory, equally valid. This is not the same as saying that all versions of reality have equal status. A relativist can still argue for one version over another, but they should be transparent in stating that this is not an absolute truth.

Reliability According to a realist position, this is the extent to which a study might be replicated and the same results observed. According to a relativist position, this is the extent to which other researchers (or readers) might interpret the data and analysis in a similar way to our interpretations.

Reported speech/thought A section of talk or text in which the speaker (or writer) appears to provide a literal representation of something that had been previously said. It is sometimes known as 'active voicing'.

GLOSSARY

Research question   The question used to guide the research in a specific and structured way. It is not as prescriptive as a hypothesis, but should still narrow the focus of the research.

Rhetoric   The design features of talk that favour one interpretation over others; the persuasiveness or argumentative features of talk.

Script/ed   Where discourse appears to present a set of events or behaviours as if these were recurrent, normative or frequent.

Semiotics   The study of signs, and use of signs in meaning-making in social practices.

Sequencing   The turn-by-turn organisation of conversation and social interaction.

Social constructionist/m   An approach that examines how social phenomena are primarily the product of discursive practices and social interaction. The emphasis is on the social concepts that are produced, rather than an individual's learning or understanding of them (cf. social constructivism).

Social constructivist/m   A theoretical approach that examines how knowledge and human development is produced in social interaction, though with the emphasis on individual processes of understanding (including cognitive processes).

Sociolinguistics   An area of study that examines language in society, with a focus on linguistic features rather than social or psychological issues.

Synthesised discourse analysis (also known **as multi-level DA**)   A blended version of discourse analysis that draws across different forms (such as blending discursive psychology and critical discursive psychology).

Talk-in-interaction   A term used to emphasise the way in which talk is produced within, and should therefore be analysed as part of, conversation and interaction.

Texts   Discourse in a written format (also includes text messages on a smartphone).

Theory   An explanatory framework for an area of research.

Top-down analysis   An analysis that draws on theoretical or ideological concepts to make sense of data and uses these as the starting point for analysis.

Transcription The process through which audio or video data are transferred into a written document and presented as a sequential series of turns, with each turn at talk written on a new line. Transcripts that are described as 'words-only', 'basic' or 'first-pass' are those which include line numbers, speaker names and the words spoken by speakers. Those described as 'Jefferson transcripts' also include paralinguistic features (e.g., rising or falling pitch, emphasis, volume of speech).

Validity In realist terms, this is the extent to which a study reflects the reality that it seeks to observe (i.e., how 'true' it is). In relativist terms, this is the extent to which a study is consistent with the social context in which it was produced (i.e., how true to the context it is).

REFERENCES

Abell, J., Condor, S., Lowe, R. D., Gibson, S. & Stevenson, C. (2007). Who ate all the pride? Patriotic sentiment and English national football support. *Nations and Nationalism*, *13*(1), 97–116.

Abell, J. & Stevenson, C. (2011). Defending the faith(s)? Democracy and hereditary right in England. *Political Psychology*, *32*(3), 485–504.

Abell, J. & Walton, C. (2010). Imagine: Towards an integrated and applied social psychology. *British Journal of Social Psychology*, *49*(4), 685–690.

Antaki, C. (2006). Producing a 'cognition'. *Discourse Studies*, *8*(1), 9–15.

Antaki, C. (Ed.) (2011). *Applied conversation analysis: Intervention and change in institutional talk*. Basingstoke: Palgrave Macmillan.

Antaki, C., Billig, M., Edwards, D. & Potter, J. (2003). Discourse analysis means doing analysis: A critique of six analytic shortcomings. *Discourse Analysis Online (DAOL)*, *1*(1).

Antaki, C. & Widdicombe, S. (Eds.) (1998). *Identities in talk*. London: Sage.

Attenborough, F. & Stokoe, E. (2012). Student life; student identity; student experience: Ethnomethodological methods for pedagogical matters. *Psychology Learning & Teaching*, *11*(1), 6–21.

Auburn, T. (2005). Narrative reflexivity as a repair device for discounting 'cognitive distortions' in sex offender treatment. *Discourse & Society*, *16*(5), 697–718.

Auburn, T. (2010). Cognitive distortions as social practices: An examination of cognitive distortions in sex offender treatment from a discursive psychology perspective. *Psychology, Crime & Law*, *16*(1–2), 103–123.

Auburn, T. & Lea, S. (2003). Doing cognitive distortions: A discursive psychology analysis of sex offender treatment talk. *British Journal of Social Psychology*, *42*(2), 281–298.

Augoustinos, M. & Every, D. (2007). The language of 'race' and prejudice: A discourse of denial, reason, and liberal-practical politics. *Journal of Language and Social Psychology*, *26*(2), 123–141.

Augoustinos, M., Hastie, B. & Wright, M. (2011). Apologizing for historical injustice: Emotion, truth and identity in political discourse. *Discourse & Society*, *22*(5), 507–531.

Augoustinos, M., Tuffin, K. & Rapley, M. (1999). Genocide or a failure to gel? Racism, history and nationalism in Australian talk. *Discourse & Society*, *10*(3), 351–378.

Austin, J. (1962). *How to do things with words*. Cambridge, MA: Harvard University Press.

Baker, C., Emmison, M. & Firth, A. (Eds.) (2005). *Calling for help: Language and social interaction in telephone helplines* (Vol. 143). Amsterdam: John Benjamins.

Banda, F. & Mawadza, A. (2015). 'Foreigners are stealing our birth right': Moral panics and the discursive construction of Zimbabwean immigrants in South African media. *Discourse & Communication*, *9*(1), 47–64.

Barcelos, C. A. (2014). Producing (potentially) pregnant teen bodies: Biopower and adolescent pregnancy in the USA. *Critical Public Health*, *24*(4), 476–488.

Barnes, R., Auburn, T. & Lea, S. (2004). Citizenship in practice. *British Journal of Social Psychology*, *43*(2), 187–206.

REFERENCES

Barthes, R. (1964). *Elements of sociology*. New York: Hill & Wang.

Benwell, B. & Stokoe, E. H. (2002). Constructing discussion tasks in university tutorials: Shifting dynamics and identities. *Discourse Studies*, *4*(4), 429–453.

Benwell, B. & Stokoe, E. H. (2006). *Discourse and identity*. Edinburgh: Edinburgh University Press.

Bernasconi, O. (2010). Being decent, being authentic: The moral self in shifting discourses of sexuality across three generations of Chilean women. *Sociology*, *44*(5), 860–875.

Bhatia, A. (2006). Critical discourse analysis of political press conferences. *Discourse & Society*, *17*(2), 173–203.

Billig, M. (1985). Prejudice, categorization and particularization: From a perceptual to a rhetorical approach. *European Journal of Social Psychology*, *15*(1), 79–103.

Billig, M. (1987). *Arguing & thinking: A rhetorical approach to social psychology*. Cambridge: Cambridge University Press.

Billig, M. (1988). The notion of 'prejudice': Some rhetorical and ideological aspects. *Text: Interdisciplinary journal for the study of discourse*. *8*(1–2): 91–110.

Billig, M. (1995). *Banal nationalism*. London: Sage.

Billig, M. (1999). Whose terms? Whose ordinariness? Rhetoric and ideology in conversation analysis. *Discourse & Society*, *10*(4), 543–558.

Billig, M., Condor, S., Edwards, D., Gane, M., Middleton, D. & Radley, A. (1988). *Ideological dilemmas: A social psychology of everyday thinking*. London: Sage.

Braun, V. & Clarke, V. (2013). *Successful qualitative research: A practical guide for beginners*. London: Sage

Brooks, S. (2009). Radio food disorder: The conversational constitution of eating disorders in radio phone-ins. *Journal of Community & Applied Social Psychology, 19*(5): 360–373.

Burke, S. & Goodman, S. (2012). 'Bring back Hitler's gas chambers': Asylum seeking, Nazis and Facebook: A discursive analysis. *Discourse & Society*, *23*(1), 19–33.

Burr, V. (2015). *Social constructionism*. London: Routledge.

Butler, J. (1990). *Gender trouble and the subversion of identity*. New York: Routledge.

Butler, J. (1993). *Bodies that matter: On the discursive limits of 'sex'*. New York: Routledge.

Butler, C. W. & Fitzgerald, R. (2010). Membership-in-action: Operative identities in a family meal. *Journal of Pragmatics*, *42*(9), 2462–2474.

Butler, C. W., Potter, J., Danby, S., Emmison, M. & Hepburn, A. (2010). Advice-implicative interrogatives building 'client-centered' support in a children's helpline. *Social Psychology Quarterly*, *73*(3), 265–287.

Caldas-Coulthard, C. R. (1994). On reporting reporting: The representation of speech in factual and factional narratives. In M. Coulthard (Ed.), *Advances in written text analysis*, London: Routledge, pp. 295–308.

Carabine, J. (2001). Unmarried motherhood 1830–1990: A genealogical analysis. In M. Wetherell, S. Taylor & S. J. Yates (Eds.), *Discourse as data: A guide for analysis*. London: Sage, pp. 267–310.

Childs, C. (2012). 'I'm not X, I just want Y': Formulating 'wants' in interaction. *Discourse Studies, 14*(2): 181–196.

REFERENCES

Childs, C. (2014). From reading minds to social interaction: Respecifying theory of mind. *Human Studies*, *37*(1), 103–122.

Childs, C. & Hepburn, A. (2015). Discursive psychology and emotion. In C. Tileagă & E. Stokoe (Eds.), *Discursive psychology: Classic and contemporary issues*. New York: Routledge, pp. 114–128.

Childs, C. & Murray, C. D. (2010). 'We all had an experience in there together': A discursive psychological analysis of collaborative paranormal accounts by paranormal investigation team members. *Qualitative Research in Psychology*, *7*(1), 21–33.

Chomsky, N. (1965). *Aspects of the theory of syntax*. Cambridge, MA: MIT Press.

Clarke, V. & Kitzinger, C. (2004). Lesbian and gay parents on talk shows: Resistance or collusion in heterosexism? *Qualitative Research in Psychology*, *1*(3), 195–217.

Clarke, V., Kitzinger, C. & Potter, J. (2004). 'Kids are just cruel anyway': Lesbian and gay parents' talk about homophobic bullying. *British Journal of Social Psychology*, *43*(4), 531–550.

Condor, S. (1988). 'Race stereotypes' and racist discourse. *Text: Interdisciplinary Journal for the Study of Discourse*, *8*(1–2), 69–90.

Condor, S. (2000). Pride and prejudice: Identity management in English people's talk about this country. *Discourse & Society*, *11*(2), 175–205.

Condor, S. (2001). Nations and nationalisms: Particular cases and impossible myths. *British Journal of Social Psychology*, *40*(2), 177–181.

Condor, S. & Abell, J. (2006). Vernacular constructions of 'national identity' in post-devolution Scotland and England. In J. Wilson & K. Stapleton (Eds.), *Devolution and Identity*. Aldershot: Ashgate, pp. 51–75.

Condor, S., Figgou, L., Abell, J., Gibson, S. & Stevenson, C. (2006). 'They're not racist…' Prejudice denial, mitigation and suppression in dialogue. *British Journal of Social Psychology*, *45*(3), 441–462.

Corcoran, T. (2009). Second nature. *British Journal of Social Psychology*, *48*(2), 375–388.

Corti, L., Van den Eynden, V., Bishop, L. & Woollard, M. (2014). *Managing and sharing research data: A guide to good practice*. London: Sage.

Cosh, S., Crabb, S. & LeCouteur, A. (2013). Elite athletes and retirement: Identity, choice, and agency. *Australian Journal of Psychology*, *65*(2), 89–97.

Cranwell, J. & Seymour-Smith, S. (2012). Monitoring and normalising a lack of appetite and weight loss: A discursive analysis of an online support group for bariatric surgery. *Appetite*, *58*(3), 873–881.

Cromdal, J., Landqvist, H., Persson-Thunqvist, D. & Osvaldsson, K. (2012). Finding out what's happened: Two procedures for opening emergency calls. *Discourse Studies*, *14*(4): 371–397.

Davies, B. & Harré, R. (1990). Positioning: The discursive production of selves. *Journal for the Theory of Social Behaviour*, *20*(1), 43–63.

de Kok, B. & Widdicombe, S. (2008). 'I really tried': Management of normative issues in accounts of responses to infertility. *Social Science & Medicine*, *67*(7), 1083–1093.

de Kok, B. & Widdicombe, S. (2010). Interpersonal issues in expressing lay knowledge: A discursive psychology approach. *Journal of Health Psychology*, *15*(8), 1190–1200.

REFERENCES

Derrida, J. (1976). *Of grammatology* (G. C. Spivak, trans.). Baltimore, MD, and London: Johns Hopkins University Press.

Dickerson, P. (2000). 'But I'm different to them': Constructing contrasts between self and others in talk-in-interaction. *British Journal of Social Psychology*, *39*(3), 381–398.

Dixon, J. & Durrheim, K. (2000). Displacing place-identity: A discursive approach to locating self and other. *British Journal of Social Psychology*, *39*(1), 27–44.

Drew, P. & Heritage, J. (1992). *Talk at work: Interaction in institutional settings*. Cambridge: Cambridge University Press.

Durrheim, K. & Dixon, J. (2004). Attitudes in the fiber of everyday life: The discourse of racial evaluation and the lived experience of desegregation. *American Psychologist*, *59*(7), 626–636.

Durrheim, K. & Dixon, J. (2005). Studying talk and embodied practices: Toward a psychology of materiality of 'race relations'. *Journal of Community & Applied Social Psychology*, *15*(6), 446–460.

Durrheim, K., Greener, R. & Whitehead, K. A. (2015). Race trouble: Attending to race and racism in online interaction. *British Journal of Social Psychology*, *54*(1), 84–99.

Edley, N. (2001). Analysing masculinity: Interpretative repertoires, ideological dilemmas and subject positions. In M. Wetherell, S. Taylor & S. J. Yates (Eds.), *Discourse as data: A guide for analysis*. London: Sage, pp. 189–228.

Edley, N. & Wetherell, M. (1995). *Men in perspective*. Harlow: Pearson Education.

Edley, N. & Wetherell, M. (1997). Jockeying for position: The construction of masculine identities. *Discourse & Society*, *8*(2), 203–217.

Edley, N. & Wetherell, M. (1999). Imagined futures: Young men's talk about fatherhood and domestic life. *British Journal of Social Psychology*, *38*(2), 181–194.

Edley, N. & Wetherell, M. (2001). Jekyll and Hyde: Men's constructions of feminism and feminists. *Feminism & Psychology*, *11*(4), 439–457.

Edwards, D. (1991). Categories are for talking: On the cognitive and discursive bases of categorization. *Theory & Psychology*, *1*(4), 515–542.

Edwards, D. (1994). Script formulations: An analysis of event descriptions in conversation. *Journal of Language and Social Psychology*, *13*(3), 211–247.

Edwards, D. (1995). Two to tango: Script formulations, dispositions, and rhetorical symmetry in relationship troubles talk. *Research on Language and Social Interaction*, *28*(4), 319–350.

Edwards, D. (1997). *Discourse and cognition*. London: Sage.

Edwards, D. (1999). Emotion discourse. *Culture & Psychology*, *5*(3), 271–291.

Edwards, D. (2000). Extreme case formulations: Softeners, investment, and doing nonliteral. *Research on Language and Social Interaction*, *33*(4), 347–373.

Edwards, D. (2005a). Moaning, whinging and laughing: The subjective side of complaints. *Discourse Studies*, *7*(1), 5–29.

Edwards, D. (2005b). Discursive psychology. In K. L. Fitch & R. E. Sanders (Eds.), *Handbook of language and social interaction*. Mahwah, NJ: Lawrence Erlbaum Associates, pp. 257–273.

Edwards, D. (2012). Discursive and scientific psychology. *British Journal of Social Psychology*, *51*(3), 425–435.

Edwards, D., Ashmore, M. & Potter, J. (1995). Death and furniture: The rhetoric, politics and theology of bottom line arguments against relativism. *History of the Human Sciences*, *8*(2), 25–49.

REFERENCES

Edwards, D. & Fasulo, A. (2006). 'To be honest': Sequential uses of honesty phrases in talk-in-interaction. *Research on Language and Social Interaction, 39*(4): 343–376.

Edwards, D. & Mercer, N. (1987). *Common knowledge: The development of understanding in the classroom*. London: Methuen/Routledge.

Edwards, D. & Potter, J. (1992). *Discursive psychology*. London: Sage.

Edwards, D. & Stokoe, E. H. (2004). Discursive psychology, focus group interviews and participants' categories. *British Journal of Developmental Psychology, 22*(4), 499–507.

Eriksson, K. & Aronsson, K. (2005). 'We're really lucky': Co-creating 'us' and the 'Other' in school booktalk. *Discourse & Society, 16*(5), 719–738.

Eriksson Barajas, K. (2010). The pimp and the happy whore: 'Doing gender' in film talk in a school setting. *Scandinavian Journal of Educational Research, 54*(6), 581–596.

Fairclough, N. (1989). *Language and power*. London and New York: Longman.

Fairclough, N. (1993). Critical discourse analysis and the marketization of public discourse: The universities. *Discourse & Society, 4*(2), 133–168.

Fairclough, N. (1995). *Media discourse*. London: Bloomsbury.

Fairclough, N. (2001). The discourse of new labour: Critical discourse analysis. In M. Wetherell, S. Taylor & S. J. Yates (Eds.), *Discourse as data: A guide for analysis*. London: Sage, pp. 229–266.

Finlay, W. M., Walton, C. & Antaki, C. (2008). Promoting choice and control in residential services for people with learning disabilities. *Disability & Society, 23*(4), 349–360.

Fitzgerald, R. & Housley, W. (Eds.) (2015). *Advances in membership categorisation analysis*. London: Sage.

Flinkfeldt, M. (2011). 'Filling one's days': Managing sick leave legitimacy in an online forum. *Sociology of Health & Illness, 33*(5), 761–776.

Foucault, M. (1970). *The order of things*. New York: Vintage.

Foucault, M. (1972). *The archaeology of knowledge*. London: Routledge.

Foucault, M. (1979). *The history of sexuality*. London: Allen Lane.

Fowler, R. (1991). *Language in the news: Language and ideology in the press*. London: Routledge.

Garfinkel, H. (1967). *Studies in ethnomethodology*. Englewood Cliffs, NJ: Prentice-Hall.

Gergen, K. J. (1973). Social psychology as history. *Journal of Personality and Social Psychology, 26*(2), 309.

Gibson, K. E. & Dempsey, S. E. (2015). Make good choices, kid: Biopolitics of children's bodies and school lunch reform in Jamie Oliver's Food Revolution. *Children's Geographies, 13*(1), 44–58.

Gibson, S. (2009). The effortful citizen: Discursive social psychology and welfare reform. *Journal of Community & Applied Social Psychology, 19*(6), 393–410.

Gibson, S. (2011). Social psychology, war and peace: Towards a critical discursive peace psychology. *Social and Personality Psychology Compass, 5*(5), 239–250.

Gibson, S. (2013). 'The last possible resort': A forgotten prod and the in situ standardization of Stanley Milgram's voice-feedback condition. *History of Psychology, 16*(3): 177–194.

Gibson, S. (2015). Banal nationalism, postmodernism and capitalism: Revisiting Billig's critique of Rorty. In C. Tileagă & E. Stokoe (Eds.), *Discursive psychology: Classic and contemporary issues*. New York: Routledge, pp. 289–302.

REFERENCES

Gibson, S. & Condor, S. (2009). State institutions and social identity: National representation in soldiers' and civilians' interview talk concerning military service. *British Journal of Social Psychology*, *48*(2), 313–336.

Gilbert, G. N. & Mulkay, M. (1984). *Opening Pandora's box: A sociological analysis of scientists' discourse*. Cambridge: Cambridge University Press.

Goffman, E. (1959). *The presentation of everyday life*. New York: Anchor Books.

Goffman, E. (1961). *Asylums: Essays on the social situation of mental patients and other inmates*. New York and Oxford: Doubleday.

Goffman, E. (1979). Footing. *Semiotica*, *25*(1–2), 1–30.

Goodings, L., Locke, A. & Brown, S. D. (2007). Social networking technology: Place and identity in mediated communities. *Journal of Community & Applied Social Psychology*, *17*(6), 463–476.

Goodman, S. & Burke, S. (2010). 'Oh you don't want asylum seekers, oh you're just racist': A discursive analysis of discussions about whether it's racist to oppose asylum seeking. *Discourse & Society*, *21*(3), 325–340.

Goodman, S. & Burke, S. (2011). Discursive deracialization in talk about asylum seeking. *Journal of Community & Applied Social Psychology*, *21*(2), 111–123.

Goodman, S., Burke, S., Liebling, H. & Zasada, D. (2014). 'I'm not happy but I'm ok': How asylum seekers manage talk about difficulties in their host country. *Critical Discourse Studies*, *11*(1), 19–34.

Goodman, S., Burke, S., Liebling, H. & Zasada, D. (2015). 'I can't go back because if I go back I would die': How asylum seekers manage talk about returning home by highlighting the importance of safety. *Journal of Community & Applied Social Psychology*, *25*(4), 327–339.

Goodman, S. & Rowe, L. (2013). 'Maybe it is prejudice… but it is NOT racism': Negotiating racism in discussion forums about Gypsies. *Discourse & Society*, *25*(1), 32–46.

Goodwin, C. (1995). Co-constructing meaning in conversations with an aphasie man. *Research on Language and Social Interaction*, *28*(3), 233–260.

Goodwin, C. (2000). Action and embodiment within situated human interaction. *Journal of Pragmatics*, *32*(10), 1489–1522.

Griffin, C. (2007). Being dead and being there: Research interviews, sharing hand cream and the preference for analysing 'naturally occurring data'. *Discourse Studies*, *9*(2), 246–269.

Guise, J., Widdicombe, S. & McKinlay, A. (2007). 'What is it like to have ME?': The discursive construction of ME in computer-mediated communication and face-to-face interaction. *Health*, *11*(1), 87–108.

Haddington, P., Keisanen, T., Mondada, L. & Nevile, M. (Eds.) (2014). *Multiactivity in social interaction: Beyond multitasking*. Amsterdam: John Benjamins.

Hamlyn, D. W. (1990). *In and out of the black box: On the philosophy of cognition*. Oxford: Basil Blackwell.

Hammersley, M. (2003). Conversation analysis and discourse analysis: Methods or paradigms? *Discourse & Society*, *14*(6), 751–781.

Hanson-Easey, S., Augoustinos, M. & Moloney, G. (2014). 'They're all tribals': Essentialism, context and the discursive representation of Sudanese refugees. *Discourse & Society*, *25*(3), 362–382.

REFERENCES

Harré, R. & Gillett, G. (1994). *The discursive mind*. London: Sage.

Harré, R. & Secord, P. F. (1972). *The explanation of social behaviour*. London: Sage.

Hastie, B. & Augoustinos, M. (2012). Rudd's apology to the stolen generations: Challenging self-sufficient arguments in 'race' discourse. *Australian Psychologist*, 47(2), 118–126.

Heath, C., Hindmarsh, J. & Luff, P. (2010). *Video in qualitative research: Analysing social interaction in everyday life*. London: Sage.

Henriques, J., Hollway, W., Urwin, C., Venn, C. & Walkerdine, V. (1984). *Changing the subject: Psychology, social regulation, and subjectivity*. Hove, UK: Psychology Press.

Hepburn, A. (2004). Crying: Notes on description, transcription, and interaction. *Research on Language and Social Interaction*, 37(3), 251–290.

Hepburn, A. (2006). Getting closer at a distance theory and the contingencies of practice. *Theory & Psychology*, 16(3), 327–342.

Hepburn, A. & Bolden, G. B. (2013). The conversation analytic approach to transcription. In J. Sidnell & T. Stivers (Eds.), *The handbook of conversation analysis*. Chichester: John Wiley & Sons, pp. 57–76.

Hepburn, A. & Potter, J. (2003). Discourse analytic practice. In C. Seale, G. Gobo, J. F. Gubrium & D. Silverman (Eds.), *Qualitative research practice*. London: Sage, pp. 168–184.

Hepburn, A. & Potter, J. (2007). Crying receipts: Time, empathy, and institutional practice. *Research on Language and Social Interaction*, 40(1), 89–116.

Hepburn, A. & Wiggins, S. (Eds.) (2007). *Discursive research in practice: New approaches to psychology and interaction*. Cambridge: Cambridge University Press.

Heritage, J. & Greatbatch, D. (1986). Generating applause: A study of rhetoric and response at party political conferences. *American Journal of Sociology*, 92(1), 110–157.

Heritage, J. & Maynard, D. W. (Eds.) (2006). *Communication in medical care: Interaction between primary care physicians and patients* (Vol. 20). Cambridge: Cambridge University Press.

Hollway, W. (1989). *Subjectivity and method in psychology: Gender, meaning and science*. London: Sage.

Hook, D. (2001). The 'disorders of discourse'. *Theoria: A Journal of Social and Political Theory*, 97, 41–68.

Horne, J. & Wiggins, S. (2009). Doing being 'on the edge': Managing the dilemma of being authentically suicidal in an online forum. *Sociology of Health & Illness*, 31(2), 170–184.

Horton-Salway, M. (2001). Narrative identities and the management of personal accountability in talk about ME: A discursive psychology approach to illness narrative. *Journal of Health Psychology*, 6(2), 247–259.

Horton-Salway, M. (2013). Gendering attention deficit hyperactivity disorder: A discursive analysis of UK newspaper stories. *Journal of Health Psychology*, 18(8), 1085–1099.

Humă, B. (2015). Enhancing the authenticity of assessments through grounding in first impressions. *British Journal of Social Psychology*, 54(3), 405–424.

Iversen, C. (2014). 'I don't know if I should believe him': Knowledge and believability in interviews with children. *British Journal of Social Psychology*, 53(2), 367–386.

Jackson, S., Vares, T. & Gill, R. (2012). 'The whole playboy mansion image': Girls' fashioning and fashioned selves within a postfeminist culture. *Feminism & Psychology*, 23(2), 143–162.

REFERENCES

Jaworski, A. & Coupland, N. (Eds.) (1999). *The discourse reader*. London: Routledge.

Jefferson, G. (1984). On the organization of laughter in talk about troubles. In J. M. Atkinson & J. Heritage (Eds.), *Structures of social action: Studies in conversation analysis*. Cambridge: Cambridge University Press, pp. 346–369.

Jefferson, G. (1989). Notes on a possible metric which provides for a 'standard maximum' silence of approximately one second in conversation. In D. Roger and P. Bull (Eds.), *Conversation: An interdisciplinary perspective*. Clevedon, UK: Multilingual Matters, pp. 166–196.

Jefferson, G. (1990). List construction as a task and resource. In G. Psathas (Ed.), *Interaction competence: Studies in ethnomethodology and conversation analysis*. Lanham, MD: University Press of America, pp. 63–92.

Jefferson, G. (2004a). Glossary of transcript symbols with an introduction. In G. H. Lerner (Ed.), *Conversation analysis: Studies from the first generation*. Philadelphia, PA: John Benjamins, pp. 13–23.

Jefferson, G. (2004b). 'At first I thought': A normalizing device for extraordinary events. In G. H. Lerner (Ed.), *Conversation analysis: Studies from the first generation*. Philadelphia, PA: John Benjamins, pp. 131–167.

Jenkins, L. (2015). Negotiating pain: The joint construction of a child's bodily sensation. *Sociology of Health & Illness*, *37*(2), 298–311.

Keller, R. (2007). Analysing discourses and dispositifs: Profiling discourse research in the tradition of sociology of knowledge. *Forum Qualitative Sozialforschung/Forum: Qualitative Social Research*, *8*(2).

Kent, A. (2011). Directing dinnertime: Practices and resources used by parents and children to deliver and respond to directive actions. PhD dissertation, Loughborough University.

Kent, A. & Potter, J. (2014). Discursive social psychology. In T. Hargreaves (Ed.), *The Oxford handbook of language and social psychology*. Oxford: Oxford University Press, pp. 295–316.

Kirkwood, S. (2012). 'Refugee' is only a word: A discursive analysis of refugees' and asylum seekers' experiences in Scotland. PhD dissertation, University of Edinburgh.

Kirkwood, S., Goodman, S., McVittie, C. & McKinlay, A. (2015). *The language of asylum: Refugees and discourse*. Basingstoke: Palgrave Macmillan.

Kirkwood, S., McKinlay, A. & McVittie, C. (2013). 'They're more than animals': Refugees' accounts of racially motivated violence. *British Journal of Social Psychology*, *52*(4), 747–762.

Korobov, N. (2001). Reconciling theory with method: From conversation analysis and critical discourse analysis to positioning analysis. *Forum Qualitative Sozialforschung/Forum: Qualitative Social Research*, *2*(3).

Korobov, N. (2004). Inoculating against prejudice: A discursive approach to homophobia and sexism in adolescent male talk. *Psychology of Men & Masculinity*, *5*(2), 178–189.

Korobov, N. (2011). Mate-preference talk in speed-dating conversations. *Research on Language and Social Interaction*, *44*(2), 186–209.

Kress, G. (2009). *Multimodality: A social semiotic approach to contemporary communication*. London: Routledge.

Kurri, K. & Wahlström, J. (2001). Dialogical management of morality in domestic violence counselling. *Feminism & Psychology*, *11*(2), 187–208.

REFERENCES

Laclau, E. & Mouffe, C. (1985). *Hegemony and socialist strategy: Towards a radical democratic politics*. London: Verso.

Lamerichs, J. (2003). Discourse of support: Exploring online discussions on depression. PhD dissertation, Wageningen University.

Lamerichs, J. & te Molder, H. F. (2003). Computer-mediated communication: From a cognitive to a discursive model. *New Media & Society, 5*(4), 451–473.

Lamerichs, J. & te Molder, H. F. (2011). Reflecting on your own talk: The discursive action method at work. In C. Antaki (Ed.), *Applied conversation analysis: Intervention and change in institutional talk*. Basingstoke: Palgrave Macmillan, pp. 184–206.

Lamont-Mills, A. & Christensen, S. (2008). 'I have never taken performance enhancing drugs and I never will': Drug discourse in the Shane Warne case. *Scandinavian Journal of Medicine & Science in Sports, 18*(2), 250–258.

Latour, B. & Woolgar, S. (1979). *Laboratory life: The social construction of scientific facts*. Beverly Hills, CA: Sage.

Lawes, R. (1999). Marriage: An analysis of discourse. *British Journal of Social Psychology, 38*(1), 1–20.

LeCouteur, A. (2001). On saying 'sorry': repertoires of apology to Australia's Stolen Generations. In A. McHoul & M. Rapley (Eds.), *How to analyse talk in institutional settings: A casebook of methods*. London: Continuum, pp. 146–158.

LeCouteur, A. & Oxlad, M. (2010). Managing accountability for domestic violence: Identities, membership categories and morality in perpetrators' talk. *Feminism & Psychology, 21*(1): 5–28.

Lester, J.N. & Gabriel, R. (2014). The discursive construction of intelligence in introductory educational psychology textbooks. *Discourse Studies, 16*(6): 776–791.

Lester, J. N. & Paulus, T. M. (2011). Accountability and public displays of knowing in an undergraduate computer-mediated communication context. *Discourse Studies, 13*(6), 671–686.

Lester, J. N. & Paulus, T. M. (2012). Performative acts of autism. *Discourse & Society, 23*(3), 259–273.

Levinson, S. C. (1983). *Pragmatics*. Cambridge: Cambridge University Press.

Locke, A. (2004). Accounting for success and failure: A discursive psychological approach to sport talk. *Quest, 56*(3), 302–320.

Locke, A. (2009). 'Natural versus taught': Competing discourses in antenatal breastfeeding workshops. *Journal of Health psychology, 14*(3), 435–446.

Locke, A. (2015). Agency, 'good motherhood' and 'a load of mush': Constructions of baby-led weaning in the press. *Women's Studies International Forum, 53*, 139–146.

Locke, A. & Edwards, D. (2003). Bill and Monica: Memory, emotion and normativity in Clinton's Grand Jury testimony. *British Journal of Social Psychology, 42*(2), 239–256.

Locke, A. & Horton-Salway, M. (2010). 'Golden age' versus 'bad old days': A discursive examination of advice giving in antenatal classes. *Journal of Health Psychology, 15*(8): 1214–1224.

Machin, D. & Mayr, A. (2012). *How to do critical discourse analysis: A multimodal introduction*. London: Sage.

MacMartin, C. (1999). Disclosure as discourse: Theorizing children's reports of sexual abuse. *Theory & Psychology, 9*(4), 503–532.

REFERENCES

MacMartin, C., Coe, J. B. & Adams, C. L. (2014). Treating distressed animals as participants: I know responses in veterinarians' pet-directed talk. *Research on Language and Social Interaction*, *47*(2), 151–174.

MacMartin, C. & LeBaron, C. D. (2006). Multiple involvements within group interaction: A video-based study of sex offender therapy. *Research on Language and Social Interaction*, *39*(1), 41–80.

MacMartin, C. & LeBaron, C. D. (2007). Arguing and thinking errors: Cognitive distortion as a member's category in sex offender group therapy talk. In A. Hepburn & S. Wiggins (Eds.), *Discursive research in practice: New approaches to psychology and interaction*. Cambridge: Cambridge University Press, pp. 147–165.

MacMillan, K. & Edwards, D. (1999). Who killed the princess? Description and blame in the British press. *Discourse Studies*, *1*(2), 151–174.

Malmquist, A. (2015). Pride and prejudice: Lesbian families in contemporary Sweden. PhD dissertation, Linköping University.

McGannon, K.R., Berry, T.R., Rodgers, W.M. & Spence, J.C. (2016). Breast cancer representations in Canadian news media: a critical discourse analysis of meanings and implications for identity. *Qualitative Research in Psychology*, *13*(2), 188–207.

McGannon, K. R. & Mauws, M. K. (2000). Discursive psychology: An alternative approach for studying adherence to exercise and physical activity. *Quest*, *52*(2), 148–165.

McIlvenny, P. (Ed.) (2002). *Talking gender and sexuality* (Vol. 94). Amsterdam: John Benjamins.

McKinlay, A. & McVittie, C. (2007). Locals, incomers and intra-national migration: Place-identities and a Scottish island. *British Journal of Social Psychology*, *46*(1), 171–190.

McKinlay, A. & McVittie, C. (2008). *Social psychology and discourse*. Chichester: Wiley-Blackwell.

McKinlay, A. & McVittie, C. (2011). *Identities in context: Individuals and discourse in action*. Chichester: Wiley-Blackwell.

McMullen, L.M. (2005). Talking about receiving, giving and taking in radio interviews: Doing modesty and making a virtue out of necessity. *British Journal of Social Psychology, 44*(4), 557–570.

Meredith, J. & Stokoe, E.H. (2014). Repair: comparing Facebook 'chat' with spoken interaction. *Discourse & Communication, 8*(2): 181–207.

Merino, M. E. & Tileagă, C. (2011). The construction of ethnic minority identity: A discursive psychological approach to ethnic self-definition in action. *Discourse & Society*, *22*(1), 86–101.

Miller, P. K. (2012). Arsene didn't see it: Coaching, research and the promise of a discursive psychology. *International Journal of Sports Science & Coaching*, *7*(4), 615–645.

Mondada, L. (2009). The methodical organization of talking and eating: Assessments in dinner conversations. *Food Quality and Preference*, *20*(8), 558–571.

Monk, R. (1990). *Wittgenstein: The duty of genius*. London: Jonathan Cape.

Muntigl, P. & Choi, K. T. (2010). Not remembering as a practical epistemic resource in couples therapy. *Discourse Studies*, *12*(3), 331–356.

Mycroft, H. (2008). Morality and accountability in a commercial weight management group. *Journal of Health Psychology*, *13*(8), 1040–1050.

REFERENCES

Nevile, M., Haddington, P., Heinemann, T. & Rauniomaa, M. (Eds.). (2014). *Interacting with objects: Language, materiality and social activity*. Amsterdam: John Benjamins.

Nikander, P. (2008). Working with transcripts and translated data. *Qualitative Research in Psychology*, 5(3), 225–231.

Nikander, P. (2009). Doing change and continuity: Age identity and the micro–macro divide. *Ageing and Society*, 29(6), 863–881.

Norrick, N. R. (2004). Hyperbole, extreme case formulation. *Journal of Pragmatics*, 36(9), 1727–1739.

Osvaldsson, K. (2011). Bullying in context: Stories of bullying on an internet discussion board. *Children & Society*, 25(4), 317–327.

Paltridge, T., Mayson, S. & Schapper, J. (2014). Welcome and exclusion: An analysis of *The Australian* newspaper's coverage of international students. *Higher Education*, 68(1), 103–116.

Parker, I. (1989). *The crisis in modern social psychology – and how to end it*. London: Routledge.

Parker, I. (1992). *Discourse dynamics*. London: Routledge.

Patterson, A. & Potter, J. (2009). Caring: Building a psychological disposition in pre-closing sequences in phone calls with a young adult with a learning disability. *British Journal of Social Psychology*, 48(3): 447–465.

Paulus, T. M. & Lester, J. N. (2013). Making learning ordinary: Ways undergraduates display learning in a CMC task. *Text & Talk*, 33(1), 53–70.

Paulus, T. M., Lester, J. N. & Dempster, P. G. (2014). *Digital tools for qualitative research*. London: Sage.

Peel, E. (2001). Mundane heterosexism: Understanding incidents of the everyday. *Women's Studies International Forum*, 24(5), 541–554.

Peräkylä, A. & Sorjonen, M. L. (2012). *Emotion in interaction*. Oxford: Oxford University Press.

Pomerantz, A. (1984). Agreeing and disagreeing with assessments: Some features of preferred/dispreferred turn shapes. In J. Atkinson & J. Heritage (Eds.), *Structures of social action*. Cambridge: Cambridge University Press, pp. 57–101.

Pomerantz, A. (1986). Extreme case formulations: A way of legitimizing claims. *Human Studies*, 9(2–3), 219–229.

Potter, J. (1982). ...Nothing so practical as a good theory: The problematic application of social psychology. In P. Stringer (Ed.), *Confronting social issues: Applications of social psychology*. London: Academic Press, pp. 23–49.

Potter, J. (1996). *Representing reality: Discourse, rhetoric and social construction*. London: Sage.

Potter, J. (1998). Discursive social psychology: From attitudes to evaluative practices. *European Review of Social Psychology*, 9(1), 233–266.

Potter, J. (2003). Discursive psychology: Between method and paradigm. *Discourse & Society*, 14(6), 783–794.

Potter, J. (2004). Discourse analysis. In M. Hardy & A. Bryman (Eds.), *Handbook of data analysis*. London: Sage, pp. 607–624.

Potter, J. (2005). A discursive psychology of institutions. *Social Psychology Review*, 7, 25–35.

Potter, J. (2010a). Contemporary discursive psychology: Issues, prospects, and Corcoran's awkward ontology. *British Journal of Social Psychology*, 49(4), 657–678.

REFERENCES

Potter, J. (2010b). Disciplinarity and the application of social research. *British Journal of Social Psychology*, *49*(4), 691–701.

Potter, J. (2012). Re-reading discourse and social psychology: Transforming social psychology. *British Journal of Social Psychology*, *51*(3), 436–455.

Potter, J. & Edwards, D. (2001). Discursive social psychology. In W. P. Robinson & H. Giles (Eds.) *The new handbook of language and social psychology*. Chichester: John Wiley & Sons, pp. 103–118.

Potter, J. & Hepburn, A. (2003). 'I'm a bit concerned': Early actions and psychological constructions in a child protection helpline. *Research on Language and Social Interaction, 36*(3): 197–240.

Potter, J. & Hepburn, A. (2005). Qualitative interviews in psychology: Problems and possibilities. *Qualitative Research in Psychology*, *2*(4), 281–307.

Potter, J. & Hepburn, A. (2007). Life is out there: A comment on Griffin. *Discourse Studies*, *9*(2), 276–282.

Potter, J. & Wetherell, M. (1987). *Discourse and social psychology: Beyond attitudes and behaviour*. London: Sage.

Puchta, C. & Potter, J. (2002). Manufacturing individual opinions: Market research focus groups and the discursive psychology of evaluation. *British Journal of Social Psychology*, *41*(3), 345–363.

Puchta, C. & Potter, J. (2004). *Focus group practice*. London: Sage.

Rapley, M. (1998). 'Just an ordinary Australian': Self-categorization and the discursive construction of facticity in 'new racist' political rhetoric. *British Journal of Social Psychology*, *37*(3), 325–344.

Rapley, M., Kiernan, P. & Antaki, C. (1998). Invisible to themselves or negotiating identity? The interactional management of 'being intellectually disabled'. *Disability & Society*, *13*(5), 807–827.

Rapley, T. (2007). *Doing conversation, discourse and document analysis*. London: Sage.

Rapley, T. (2015). Questions of context: Qualitative interviews as a source of knowledge. In C. Tileagă & E. Stokoe (Eds.), *Discursive psychology: Classic and contemporary issues*. New York: Routledge, pp. 70–84.

Raymond, G. & Heritage, J. (2006). The epistemics of social relations: Owning grandchildren. *Language in Society*, *35*(5), 677–705.

Reynolds, J. (2013). *The single woman: A discursive investigation*. London: Routledge.

Reynolds, J. & Wetherell, M. (2003). The discursive climate of singleness: The consequences for women's negotiation of a single identity. *Feminism & Psychology*, *13*(4), 489–510.

Richards, K. & Seedhouse, P. (2007). *Applying conversation analysis*. Basingstoke: Palgrave Macmillan.

Riley, S., Thompson, J. & Griffin, C. (2010). Turn on, tune in, but don't drop out: The impact of neo-liberalism on magic mushroom users' (in)ability to imagine collectivist social worlds. *International Journal of Drug Policy*, *21*(6), 445–451.

Robles, J. S. (2012). Troubles with assessments in gifting occasions. *Discourse Studies*, *14*(6), 753–777.

REFERENCES

Rowe, L. & Goodman, S. (2014). 'A stinking filthy race of people inbred with criminality' A discourse analysis of prejudicial talk about Gypsies in discussion forums. *Romani Studies*, *24*(1): 25–42.

Sacks, H. (1984). On doing 'being ordinary'. In J.M. Atkinson & J. Heritage (Eds.), *Structures of social action: Studies in conversation analysis*. Cambridge: Cambridge University Press, pp. 413–429.

Sacks, H. (1992). *Lectures on conversation* (Vols I & II). Oxford: Blackwell.

Sacks, H., Schegloff, E. A. & Jefferson, G. (1974). A simplest systematics for the organization of turn-taking for conversation. *Language*, *50*(4): 696–735.

Sala, E., Dandy, J. & Rapley, M. (2010). 'Real Italians and wogs': The discursive construction of Italian identity among first generation Italian immigrants in Western Australia. *Journal of Community & Applied Social Psychology*, *20*(2), 110–124.

Schegloff, E. A. (1997). Whose text? Whose context? *Discourse & Society*, *8*(2), 165–187.

Searle, J. R. (1969). *Speech acts: An essay in the philosophy of language* (Vol. 626). Cambridge: Cambridge University Press.

Seymour-Smith, S. & Wetherell, M. (2006). 'What he hasn't told you...': Investigating the micro-politics of gendered support in heterosexual couples' co-constructed accounts of illness. *Feminism & Psychology*, *16*(1), 105–127.

Seymour-Smith, S., Wetherell, M. & Phoenix, A. (2002). 'My wife ordered me to come!': A discursive analysis of doctors' and nurses' accounts of men's use of general practitioners. *Journal of Health Psychology*, *7*(3), 253–267.

Silverman, D. (1997). *Discourses of counselling: HIV counselling as social interaction*. London: Sage.

Silverman, D. (1998). *Harvey Sacks: Social science and conversation analysis*. Oxford: Oxford University Press.

Silverman, D. & Peräkylä, A. (1990). AIDS counselling: The interactional organisation of talk about 'delicate' issues. *Sociology of Health & Illness*, *12*(3), 293–318.

Simmons, K. & LeCouteur, A. (2008). Modern racism in the media: Constructions of the possibility of change 'in accounts of two Australian riots'. *Discourse & Society*, *19*(5), 667–687.

Smithson, J., Sharkey, S., Hewis, E., Jones, R. B., Emmens, T., Ford, T. & Owens, C. (2011). Membership and boundary maintenance on an online self-harm forum. *Qualitative Health Research*, *21*(11), 67–75.

Sneijder, P. (2014). The embedding of reported speech in a rhetorical structure by prosecutors and defense lawyers in Dutch trials. *Text & Talk*, *34*(4), 467–490.

Sneijder, P. & te Molder, H. F. (2004). 'Health should not have to be a problem': Talking health and accountability in an internet forum on veganism. *Journal of Health Psychology*, *9*(4), 599–616.

Sneijder, P. & te Molder, H. (2009). Normalizing ideological food choice and eating practices: Identity work in online discussions on veganism. *Appetite*, *52*(3), 621–630.

Speer, S. A. (2001). Reconsidering the concept of hegemonic masculinity: Discursive psychology, conversation analysis and participants' orientations. *Feminism & Psychology*, *11*(1), 107–135.

Speer, S. A. (2002). 'Natural' and 'contrived' data: A sustainable distinction? *Discourse Studies*, *4*(4), 511–525.

REFERENCES

Speer, S. A. (2005). *Gender talk: Feminism, discourse and conversation analysis*. Hove, UK: Psychology Press.

Speer, S. A. (2008). Natural and contrived data. In P. Alasuutari, L. Bickman & J. Brannen (Eds.), *The Sage handbook of social research methods*. London: Sage, pp. 290–312.

Speer, S. A. & Parsons, C. (2006). Gatekeeping gender: Some features of the use of hypothetical questions in the psychiatric assessment of transsexual patients. *Discourse & Society*, *17*(6), 785–812.

Speer, S. A. & Potter, J. (2000). The management of heterosexist talk: Conversational resources and prejudiced claims. *Discourse & Society*, *11*(4), 543–572.

Speer, S. A. & Stokoe, E. (Eds.) (2011). *Conversation and gender*. Cambridge: Cambridge University Press.

Stanley, S., Barker, M., Edwards, V. & McEwen, E. (2015). Swimming against the stream: Investigating psychosocial flows through mindful awareness. *Qualitative Research in Psychology*, *12*(1), 61–76.

Stokoe, E. H. (1998). Talking about gender: The conversational construction of gender categories in academic discourse. *Discourse & Society*, *9*(2), 217–240.

Stokoe, E. H. (2003). Mothers, single women and sluts: Gender, morality and membership categorization in neighbour disputes. *Feminism & Psychology*, *13*(3), 317–344.

Stokoe, E. H. (2006). On ethnomethodology, feminism, and the analysis of categorial reference to gender in talk-in-interaction. *The Sociological Review*, *54*(3), 467–494.

Stokoe, E. (2008). Dispreferred actions and other interactional breaches as devices for occasioning audience laughter in television 'sitcoms'. *Social Semiotics*, *18*(3), 289–307.

Stokoe, E. (2010). 'I'm not gonna hit a lady': Conversation analysis, membership categorization and men's denials of violence towards women. *Discourse & Society*, *21*(1), 59–82.

Stokoe, E. (2012). Moving forward with membership categorization analysis: Methods for systematic analysis. *Discourse Studies*, *14*(3), 277–303.

Stokoe, E. (2014). The Conversation Analytic Role-play Method (CARM): A method for training communication skills as an alternative to simulated role-play. *Research on Language and Social Interaction*, *47*(3), 255–265.

Stokoe, E. & Edwards, D. (2008). 'Did you have permission to smash your neighbour's door?' Silly questions and their answers in police–suspect interrogations. *Discourse Studies*, *10*(1), 89–111.

Stokoe, E. & Hepburn, A. (2005). 'You can hear a lot through the walls': Noise formulations in neighbour complaints. *Discourse & Society*, *16*(5), 647–673.

Stokoe, E. H. & Wallwork, J. (2003). Space invaders: The moral-spatial order in neighbour dispute discourse. *British Journal of Social Psychology*, *42*(4), 551–569.

Stokoe, E. H. & Weatherall, A. (2002). Guest editorial: Gender, language, conversation analysis and feminism. *Discourse & Society*, *13*(6), 707–713.

Stommel, W., & Koole, T. (2010). The online support group as a community: A micro-analysis of the interaction with a new member. *Discourse Studies*, *12*(3), 357–378.

Streeck, J., Goodwin, C. & LeBaron, C. (2014). *Embodied interaction: Language and body in the material world*. Cambridge: Cambridge University Press.

Szczepek Reed, B. (2010). *Analysing conversation: An introduction to prosody*. Basingstoke: Palgrave Macmillan.

REFERENCES

te Molder, H. & Potter, J. (2005). *Conversation and cognition*. Cambridge: Cambridge University Press.

Ten Have, P. (2007). *Doing conversation analysis: A practical guide*. London: Sage.

Tileagă, C. (2005). Accounting for extreme prejudice and legitimating blame in talk about the Romanies. *Discourse & Society*, *16*(5), 603–624.

Tileagă, C. (2010). Cautious morality: Public accountability, moral order and accounting for a conflict of interest. *Discourse Studies*, *12*(2): 223–239.

Tileagă, C. & Stokoe, E. (Eds.) (2015). *Discursive psychology: Classic and contemporary issues*. New York: Routledge.

Tucker, I. (2004). 'Stories' of chronic fatigue syndrome: An exploratory discursive psychological analysis. *Qualitative Research in Psychology*, *1*(2), 153–167.

Van Dijk, T. A. (1993). Principles of critical discourse analysis. *Discourse & Society*, *4*(2), 249–283.

Van Dijk, T. A. (1998). *Ideology: A multidisciplinary study*. London: Sage.

Van Dijk, T. A. (2000). New (s) racism: A discourse analytical approach. In S. Cottle (Ed.), *Ethnic minorities and the media*. Philadelphia, PA: Open University Press, pp. 33–49.

Van Dijk, T. A. (2001). Critical discourse analysis. In D. Schiffrin, D. Tannen & H. E. Hamilton (Eds.), *The handbook of discourse analysis*. Oxford: Blackwell, pp. 349–371.

Varga, M. A. & Paulus, T. M. (2014). Grieving online: Newcomers' constructions of grief in an online support group. *Death Studies*, *38*(7), 443–449.

Varjonen, S., Arnold, L. & Jasinskaja-Lahti, I. (2013). 'We're Finns here, and Russians there': A longitudinal study on ethnic identity construction in the context of ethnic migration. *Discourse & Society*, *24*(1), 110–134.

Veen, M., te Molder, H., Gremmen, B. & van Woerkum, C. (2010). Quitting is not an option: An analysis of online diet talk between celiac disease patients. *Health*, *14*(1), 23–40.

Veen, M., te Molder, H., Gremmen, B. & van Woerkum, C. (2013). If you can't eat what you like, like what you can: How coeliac disease patients and their families construct dietary restrictions as a matter of choice. *Sociology of Health and Illness*, *35*(4): 592–609.

Wallwork, J. & Dixon, J. A. (2004). Foxes, green fields and Britishness: On the rhetorical construction of place and national identity. *British Journal of Social Psychology*, *43*(1), 21–39.

Walters, S. R., Payne, D., Schluter, P. J. & Thomson, R. W. (2015). 'It just makes you feel invincible': A Foucauldian analysis of children's experiences of organised team sports. *Sport, Education and Society*, *20*(2), 241–257.

Walton, C., Coyle, A. & Lyons, E. (2004). Death and football: An analysis of men's talk about emotions. *British Journal of Social Psychology*, *43*(3), 401–416.

Weatherall, A. (2002). *Gender, language and discourse*. Hove, UK: Psychology Press.

Weatherall, A. & Stubbe, M. (2015). Emotions in action: Telephone-mediated dispute resolution. *British Journal of Social Psychology*, *54*(2), 273–290.

Webb, H. (2009). 'I've put weight on cos I've bin inactive, cos I've 'ad me knee done': Moral work in the obesity clinic. *Sociology of Health & Illness*, *31*(6), 854–871.

Wetherell, M. (1998). Positioning and interpretative repertoires: Conversation analysis and post-structuralism in dialogue. *Discourse & Society*, *9*(3), 387–412.

Wetherell, M. (2007). A step too far: Discursive psychology, linguistic ethnography and questions of identity. *Journal of Sociolinguistics*, *11*(5), 661–681.

REFERENCES

Wetherell, M. (2013). Affect and discourse –What's the problem&quest: From affect as excess to affective/discursive practice. *Subjectivity*, *6*(4), 349–368.

Wetherell, M. (2015). Tears, bubbles and disappointment – new approaches for the analysis of affective-discursive practices: A commentary on 'researching the psychosocial'. *Qualitative Research in Psychology*, *12*(1), 83–90.

Wetherell, M. & Edley, N. (1999). Negotiating hegemonic masculinity: Imaginary positions and psycho-discursive practices. *Feminism & Psychology*, *9*(3), 335–356.

Wetherell, M. & Edley, N. (2014). A discursive psychological framework for analyzing men and masculinities. *Psychology of Men & Masculinity*, *15*(4), 355.

Wetherell, M. & Potter, J. (1988). Discourse analysis and the identification of interpretative repertoires. In C. Antaki (Ed.), *Analysing everyday explanation: A casebook of methods*. London: Sage, pp. 168–183.

Wetherell, M. & Potter, J. (1992). *Mapping the language of racism: Discourse and the legitimation of exploitation*. Cambridge: Cambridge University Press.

Wetherell, M., Taylor, S. & Yates, S. J. (2001) *Discourse as data: A guide for analysis*. London: Sage.

Whitehead, K. A. (2015). Extreme-case formulations. In K. Tracy (Ed.), *The international encyclopedia of language and social interaction*. Chichester: John Wiley & Sons, pp. 1–5.

Whitehead, K. A. & Stokoe, E. (2015). Producing and responding to -isms in interaction. *Journal of Language and Social Psychology*, *34*(4), 368–373.

Widdicombe, S. (2015). 'Just like the fact that I'm Syrian like you are Scottish': Ascribing interviewer identities as a resource in cross-cultural interaction. *British Journal of Social Psychology*, *54*(2), 255–272.

Widdicombe, S. & Wooffitt, R. (1990). 'Being' versus 'doing' Punk: On achieving authenticity as a member. *Journal of Language and Social Psychology*, *9*(4), 257–277.

Wiggins, S. (2002). Talking with your mouth full: Gustatory mmms and the embodiment of pleasure. *Research on Language and Social Interaction*, *35*(3), 311–336.

Wiggins, S. (2009). Managing blame in NHS weight management treatment: Psychologizing weight and 'obesity'. *Journal of Community & Applied Social Psychology*, *19*(5), 374–387.

Wiggins, S. (2013). The social life of 'eugh': Disgust as assessment in family mealtimes. *British Journal of Social Psychology*, *52*(3), 489–509.

Wiggins, S. (2014). Adult and child use of love, like, don't like and hate during family mealtimes: Subjective category assessments as food preference talk. *Appetite*, *80*, 7–15.

Wiggins, S. (2015). From Loughborough with love: How discursive psychology rocked the heart of social psychology's love affair with attitudes. In C. Tileagă & E. Stokoe (Eds.), *Discursive psychology: Classic and contemporary issues*. New York: Routledge, pp. 101–113.

Wiggins, S., McQuade, R. & Rasmussen, S. (2016). Stepping back from crisis points: The provision and acknowledgment of support in an online suicide discussion forum. *Qualitative Health Research* (in press).

Wiggins, S., Moore-Millar, K. & Thomson, A. (2014). Can you pull it off? Appearance modifying behaviours adopted by wig users with alopecia in social interactions. *Body Image*, *11*(2), 156–166.

REFERENCES

Wiggins, S. & Potter, J. (2003). Attitudes and evaluative practices: Category vs item and subjective vs objective constructions in everyday food assessments. *British Journal of Social Psychology*, *42*(4), 513–531.

Wiggins, S., Potter, J. & Wildsmith, A. (2001). Eating your words: Discursive psychology and the reconstruction of eating practices. *Journal of Health Psychology*, *6*(1), 5–15.

Wilkinson, R. (2015). Conversation and aphasia: Advances in analysis and intervention. *Aphasiology*, *29*(3), 257–268.

Williams, A. & Donaghue, N. (2010). 'Now that's a fair dinkum academic debate, but this affects people's lives': A discursive analysis of arguments for and against the provision of warnings about potential side effects of SSRIs in a public debate. *Critical Public Health*, *20*(1), 15–24.

Willig, C. (2013). *Introducing qualitative research in psychology: Adventures in theory and method*. Maidenhead: McGraw-Hill Education (UK).

Wittgenstein, L. (1953). *Philosophical investigations*. Oxford: Blackwell.

Wodak, R. (1996). *Disorders of discourse*. London: Longman.

Wodak, R. & Matouschek, B. (1993). 'We are dealing with people whose origins one can clearly tell just by looking': Critical discourse analysis and the study of neo-racism in contemporary Austria. *Discourse & Society*, *4*(2), 225–248.

Wood, L. & Kroger, R. (2000). *Doing discourse analysis: Methods for studying action in talk and text*. London: Sage.

Wooffitt, R. (1991). 'I was just doing X...when Y': Some inferential properties of a device in accounts of paranormal experiences. *Text*, *11*(2), 267–288.

Wooffitt, R. (2005). *Conversation analysis and discourse analysis: A comparative and critical introduction*. London: Sage.

Wooffitt, R. & Allistone, S. (2005). Towards a discursive parapsychology language and the laboratory study of anomalous communication. *Theory & Psychology, 15*(3): 325–355.

Wright, S. T. (2014). Accounting for taste: Conversation, categorisation and certification in the sensory assessment of craft brewing. PhD dissertation, Lancaster University.

Xenitidou, M. & Morasso, S. G. (2014). Parental discourse and identity management in the talk of indigenous and migrant speakers. *Discourse & Society*, *25*(1), 100–121.

INDEX

Page numbers in **bold** refer to the glossary

accounts, accounting for, 22, 41, 50, 72, 122–4, 128–9, 148, 152–5, 160–2, 165–6, 171–3, 203, 213, **241**
accountability, 14, 42, 66, 123–5, 147, 152, 155, 160, 166, 170, 170–2, 174, 203, 205, 228, **241**
action orientation, 14–5, 46, 66, 168, 238, **241**
agency/agentic, 24, 50–1, 55–7, 124–5, 169–71, **241**
Antaki, Charles, 27, 37, 42, 139, 202, 222
assessment, 36, 38, 40, 42, 44, 62, 66, 108, 123–31, 137–8, 141, 149–50, 187, 200, 206–7, 209, **241**
   dis/preferred, 123, 127, 150, **243**
   second assessment, 40, 123, 127, 149–50
attribution, 4, 133, 160, 199, 223, **241**

behaviourism, 7, 24, 233
Billig, Michael, 26, 45–6, 203–4
blame, 63–4, 66, 108, 122, 124, 204

categories, 7, 11, 20, 22, 24, 33, 37–8, 119, 125, 161, 164, 168–9, 171–3, 198, 201, 204, 233, 235, 239, **241**
   category entitlements, 33, 38, 125, 161, 163–4, 172, 175, **241**
coding, 89, 95, 99, 107–12, 131, 137, 142, 144, 185, 214–5, 219, 225, 235, **242**
cognitivism, 28, 41, 133–4, **242**
consensus and corroboration, 124, 160–2
consent, 68, 71, 79–82, 85, 87, 184, 188, 190, 192, 209, 211
constructionism *see* social constructionism
constructivism, **247**
context, 5, 9–10, 12–6, 18–20, 24, 29–30, 34, 45–6, 50, 54–5, 58, 64–7, 70, 91, 119, 122, 134, 184, 201–4, 211, 214, 226, **242**
conversation analysis (CA), 18, 20–1, 32–40, 58, 90, 102, 104, 134, 150, 205, 227, 232, 238, **242**
critical discursive psychology, 26, 32–3, 41, 44–9, 58, **242, 247**
critical realism, **242**

deviant case, 33, 131, 136–7, 139, 185–6, **242**
discourse analysis, 4, 6–7, 15, 22, 26, 31–5, 41, 46, 58, 77, 91, 229, 231, **243**
   critical discourse analysis, 31–5, 45–6, 54–8, **242, 245**
disclaimer, 33, 124, 162–4, 175, 204, **243**

Edwards, Derek, 4, 6, 10, 15, 26–7, 30, 33, 41–2, 44, 77, 125, 128–9, 145, 153–4, 164, 168, 170–1, 198, 200–1, 206, 228, 239
embodiment, embodied, 27, 37, 133–4, 158, 228
emotions, 29, 41–2, 46, 50, 119, 125, 133–4, 141, 158–9, 171–2, 198, 200–1, 206, 228–9, 233–4
epistemology, 27, **243**
ethics, 67–9, 75, 77, 79–81, 85, 184, 211, 215–6, 225
ethnomethodology, 19–21, 36, 41, 45, 227, **243**
evaluation *see* assessment
extreme case formulations, 33, 57, 123, 127–9, 153–6, 161, 164, **244**

focus groups, 33, 42, 46, 71, 74, 76–7, 152, 200, 206, 212–3, **244**
footing, 19, 33, 40, 122–4, 147–8, 164, 166, **244**
Foucauldian discourse analysis, 28, 32–5, 41, 45, 49–55, 58, **244**
Foucault, Michel, 23–5, 33, 49–50, **244**

Garfinkel, Harold, 19, 24, 36
gender, 11, 26, 45–7, 50, 97, 169, 172, 201–2, 206–7
gesture, 10, 20, 27, 29, 36–8, 43, 74, 82, 91, 103–7, 117, 134
Goffman, Erving, 7, 19–20, 24, 36, 147

health, 50, 72, 151, 174–5, 199, 202–3, 205, 210
Hepburn, Alexa, 27, 38, 44, 77, 79, 100, 158–9, 199–201, 204–5, 207, 222
Heritage, John, 37, 40, 71, 157, 187

identity, 19, 37, 42–3, 49, 55, 63, 71, 78, 122–4, 134, 154, 162–3, 166, 169, 171, 184, 201–4, 206, 207, 210
ideology, 54–5, 222, **244**
indexicality, 13, 119, 129, **244**
institutional, 19–21, 33, 37–8, 70–1, 76, 150–2, 157, 160, 167, 199, 201–2, 206, 226–7, 229
interpretative repertoire, 22, 26, 33, 45, 48, 199, **244**
interviews, 22, 26–7, 33, 42, 46, 51, 71, 74, 76–7, 140, 147, 154–5, 199, 202, 206, 212–3

Jefferson, Gail, 20, 33, 36, 150–1, 157–8, 172
Jefferson transcription system, 21, 92–3, 99–103, 109, 111–2, 137, 185, 235, 236, 248

INDEX

knowledge, construction of, 9–11, 15, 21–2, 30, 51, 55, 68, 222

language, theories of, 7–8, 16–9, 23–5, 29, 49, 54–5, 57, 233–4, 238
laughter, transcription of, 101–2, 158, 235

media, 33, 42, 56–7, 63, 64, 71, 83, 86, 207, 218, 224
membership categorisation analysis, 20, 37, **245**
metaphor, 16, 124, 164–5
methodology, 4, 7, 61, 183, 229, **245**
modal, 55, 57, 125, 169, 173–5
multimodality, 27, 37, 134, **245**

narrative, 124, 165–6
norms, 5, 7, 19, 36, 75, 150, 203

objectivity, 21–2, 135, 240
online data, 12, 33, 36, 42, 63, 65–8, 71–2, 76, 83–4, 134, 155–6, 162, 174, 201–5, 207, 210–11, 227–8, **242**
ontology, 17, **245**
orthographic transcription, 91–2, 95–9, 236, **246**
see also transcription

paralinguistic, 103, 114, 117, **246**
participants, 38, 42, 86–7, 97, 110, 135, 183–4, 209, 225–6, 246
 participants' orientations, 7, 12, 21, 46, 71, 122, 129, 136–7, 174, 201, 233, 240
 recruitment of, 66–9, 77, 79–81, 192, 211–3
poststructuralism, 23
Potter, Jonathan, 4, 6, 10, 15, 25–7, 29–30, 41–2, 45–6, 77, 79, 114, 125, 149, 159, 161, 172, 175–6, 191, 199–202, 204–7, 222

prejudice, 42, 153, 163, 198, 204–5
power, 49, 54–5, 57–8, 242, 245
prosody, 20, 27, 37, 119, 200, **246**
pseudonyms, 38, 42–3, 95, 97, **246**
psychology, 3–4, 6–7, 17, 23–7, 28–9, 40–1, 134, 199–200, 228–30, 233

realism, 9–10, **246**
 see also critical realism
reported speech, 96, 102, 124, 142, 166–7, **246**
rhetoric, 12–16, 26, 28, 41, 90, 119, 129, 137, 156–8, 164, 168, 171, 175

Sacks, Harvey, 20, 33, 36–7, 128, 172
script formulations, 125, 127, 168–9
social constructionism, 9–11, 218
software, 69, 87
 transcription and coding, 95, 96, 109–12
 writing up and presentation, 188–90
speech act theory, 16, 18–9, 20
stake and interest, 125–6, 154, 161, 167, 171–2, 175–6
Stokoe, Elizabeth, 11, 20, 27, 37, 44, 75, 77, 150, 170, 198, 201–2, 204, 206, 220, 228
subject positions, 33, 45–9, 51–3
subjectivity, 91, 164, 175, 240

turn-taking, 12, 20, 33, 40, 43, 211, 238
transcription *see* Jefferson transcription system; orthographic transcription
transparency, 136, 184

vagueness, 125, 161–3, 165

Wetherell, Margaret, 4, 25–8, 30, 33, 34, 45–6, 48–9, 58, 114, 200–1, 204
Wittgenstein, Ludwig, 16–19, 24–5, 28, 41

Printed in Great Britain
by Amazon